UNIVERSITY OF NORTH CAROLINA AT CHAPEL HILL
DEPARTMENT OF ROMANCE LANGUAGES

NORTH CAROLINA STUDIES
IN THE ROMANCE LANGUAGES AND LITERATURES

Founder: URBAN TIGNER HOLMES
Editor: STIRLING HAIG

Distributed by:

UNIVERSITY OF NORTH CAROLINA PRESS
CHAPEL HILL
North Carolina 27514
U.S.A.

NORTH CAROLINA STUDIES IN THE
ROMANCE LANGUAGES AND LITERATURES
Number 223

READING VOLTAIRE'S *CONTES*
A SEMIOTICS OF PHILOSOPHICAL NARRATION

READING VOLTAIRE'S
CONTES
A SEMIOTICS OF PHILOSOPHICAL NARRATION

BY

CAROL SHERMAN

CHAPEL HILL

NORTH CAROLINA STUDIES IN THE ROMANCE
LANGUAGES AND LITERATURES
U.N.C. DEPARTMENT OF ROMANCE LANGUAGES

1985

Library of Congress Cataloging in Publication Data

Sherman, Carol.
    Reading Voltaire's contes.

    (North Carolina studies in the Romance languages and literatures; no. 223)
    Chiefly English, some French.
    Bibliography: p.
    1. Voltaire, 1694-1778—Fictional works.   2. Philosophy   in   literature.
3. Narration (Rhetoric).   4. Semiotics and literature.   I. Title.   II. Series.

PQ2125.S52   1985   848'.509   84-20539
ISBN 0-8078-9227-0

I.S.B.N. 0-8078-9227-0

IMPRESO EN ESPAÑA

PRINTED IN SPAIN

DEPÓSITO LEGAL: V. 2.086 - 1984   I.S.B.N. 84-599-0231-5

ARTES GRÁFICAS SOLER, S. A. - LA OLIVERETA, 28 - 46018 VALENCIA - 1984

Comment pouvez-vous préférer, leur disait le sage Ouloug, des contes qui sont sans raison, et qui ne signifient rien?

"Epître dédicatoire," *Zadig*

CONTENTS

INTRODUCTION

> Le critique ne doit pas être un lecteur, mais
> le témoin d'un lecteur, celui qui le regarde lire et
> être mu. L'opération critique capitale est la déter-
> mination du lecteur.
>
> Paul Valéry, "Tel Quel"
> *Œuvres*, II, 557.

This book proposes to answer two questions: can the philosophical story be defined by the procedures of its reception? and can
recourse to a semiotic perspective help elucidate the ways in which
readers make sense of that literary sign? It performs a discourse-
analysis of four didactic fictions, Voltaire's *Micromégas* (1739?,
1752), *Zadig* (1747), *Candide* (1759), and *L'Ingénu* (1767). They
span about thirty years of the author's production and are the tales
about which the most has been written. [1] They thus offer the best
ground for the study of reception. I assume that their survival and
the frequency of comment upon them are signs of the richness they
provide. Some might say that they are still read because a tyrannical
bourgeoisie continues to impose its corpus. This would suppose that
most of us were not bourgeois and thus felt oppressed, that the
kinds of subversion operated by the tales are outdated, and that the
positive values they present have become clichés and have been
replaced by others. Tolerance may be a cliché, but it is not widely

---

[1] Haydn Mason, "Voltaire's 'Contes': an 'Etat présent,'" *Modern Language Review*, 65 (1970), 19-35. A check of the literature that has appeared
since 1970 continues to support Mason's generalization on this point. The term
conte philosophique was used by Voltaire only late in his career, and Angus
Martin finds only three works so named between 1740 and 1777: "Introduction"
to his *Anthologie du conte en France 1750-1799* (Paris: Union Générale d'Editions, 1981).

practiced, to say the least; and the dangers of religiosity's meddling in public affairs are still before us, to give only obvious examples. Voltaire's tales seem to me to be neither bourgeois instruments of oppression nor museum pieces dependent upon merely historical admiration.

For over two centuries the *contes* have been read with considerable agreement on most of their meanings. If interpretive communities change, and if we do not have much in common with the French aristocracy of the *ancien régime*, it is perhaps the text itself that constrains them and us to repeatedly similar actualizations. Many would not even pose this question, assuming that since it is a "classic," *Candide,* for example, *contains* a stable, eternal meaning. However, since I look upon texts as productive of sense and upon the classics not as containing meaning but as inciting re-created response, I wish to reflect upon the process of their reception.

The genre exhibits high determinacy; that is, readers tend to agree on its polemical import. The consensus surrounds criticism of the targets that are hit upon in passing and that are constants with Voltaire: corrupt priests and journalists, fanatics. All four of the stories treated below attack metaphysics and thus participate in one of the best known of the philosophe's campaigns; and they strike the common target of collusion between church and state that oppresses the just and the weak. The answers to the big questions remain under discussion: what does *Zadig* mean to say about Providence? does the final garden in *Candide* constitute advice against both metaphysics and all philosophical argument? There are differences in the readings of Eldorado's importance, and not all readers take at its tragic face-value the long final episode of *L'Ingénu*. *Micromégas* constantly offers lessons in relativism and prompts the least variety of readings. With the exception of the debated points just mentioned — and they have more than passing interest in an account of the potentials of reception — interpretation of the tales has not been the principal object of critical study. Except in introductions to editions prepared for students, writers rarely feel the need to interpret them for us, or not at least in any detailed way; and the occasion of much comment upon them is instead that of their sources, literary and biographical. The larger questions are less clear, and I think it is because they are issues that the stories refuse in the first place. They are the result both of the announced didacticism and of a particular tradition of reading that seeks a single meaning or solution, and this expectation is encouraged by satiric episodic narrative having arbitrary closure. In a curious way didactic fiction that is closed, in one sense, by its redundancy nevertheless ends by being an open work, not by permitting many articulations but by foregrounding so intensely its own process that it avoids its own formulaic reduction to meaning. Summarizing the lesson of a tale as being "against metaphysics" or "for relativism" condenses only one of the forms of its meaning by an abstract operation that points to the sign and gives some idea of part of its potential. Such phrases are far from exhausting its capacity to inspire complex actualizations of all the signifying qualities of the text.

Given the general broad agreement on a large portion of their meanings, I wish to ask how that consensus comes about, that is, how these texts make themselves clear; but I shall also show how certain of their significances deconstruct their premises, that is, how they are finally made unclear by the traces they bear both of past structures of experience and of ambient ideological changes. The enumeration of the sources of guidance and constraint occupies the first four sections of each chapter and supposes a cooperative reader, one who consents to be trained by the tale in interpreting the meanings repeatedly proffered. The fifth section of each chapter describes some ways in which each story's premises can be unraveled in a different moment of reading, that in which the reader exercises her capacity for resistance to the kind of tyranny that the philosophical tale proposes. In these two *possibles* of reception I account for both a hermeneutic project and a deconstructive one. Although in describing how a text guides our reception of it I cannot avoid interpretations, my goal is not to propose novel or eternal ones, but to account for the phenomenon of interpretation itself. It is true that the selection of elements to be explained and the choice of tools with which to do so are also already interpretations; but such considerations, while important for the critic's humility, cause infinite regress into epistemological relativism and paralyze both thinking and reading itself. I have thus chosen to use a certain number of tools, and the meta-interpretations that result describe the suggestions offered by the text for concretization and for meaning. They name some of the constraints imposed on the reader as she tries to make sense of it; they are not fundamentally exegetical.[2] In performing these exercises, I wished to become conscious of the specific powers of philosophical fiction. It is not pedagogical, for it does not offer primarily undiluted instruction. "Be tolerant" and "Do not listen to Jesuits" are very brief messages, direct statements of meaning, and raw injunctions to particular behavior. The sheer mass of the tales shows already that they are unlikely to be composed of similar pithy orders. Their lessons are conveyed by a story or in one; they are shown, not told. The *contes* are illustrative, illustrated messages; and they invite a double decoding, one of the literal dimension and one of their virtual or connotative scope.

The precise manner in which this union occurs has been a topic of speculation. Several years ago, Henri Coulet formulated the problem by evoking the paradox of fiction or untruths coupled with a lesson presenting itself as truth.[3] The specific techniques of the fusion have not yet been systematically described.[4] A speaker at the International Colloquium on Voltaire said that "il reste beaucoup à faire dans le domaine stylistique (ironie, comique, tempo). Narra-

---

[2] I shall use *he* for the narrators and *she* for the reader. This permits economical expression avoiding ambiguity, as well as showing that the feminine pronoun suits the audience most often represented, imagined, and addressed by Voltaire. His ideal reader is often female, and one such is figured in the dedication of *Zadig*. This is of both sociological and historical interest as well as being representative of eighteenth-century French literary custom. It recalls the remarks often repeated that novels are read by women and that they corrupt them. A seducer's tool, an uncontrolled genre, and the record of feelings, these traits tie it to the woman declared to be weak, disordered, and intuitive. These assumptions about literature and about its female readers are strictly opposed by the public Voltaire expects for his *contes*.

[3] He avoids, as I do, posing the genetic question of knowing which, fable or idea, comes first in the creating consciousness: "La Distanciation dans le roman et le conte philosophiques," *Roman et lumières au 18e siècle* (Paris: Editions Sociales, 1970), p. 439. Susan Suleiman declares the didactic text to be teleological, entirely determined by an end that surpasses it. This avoids genetic language but states the primacy of idea over fable: "Le Récit exemplaire," *Poétique,* 32 (1977), 486.

[4] Angus Martin briefly reviews studies of technique on pages 27-30 in the anthology cited in Note 1 above, the book by Dorothy McGhee being the earliest mentioned; but Martin finds that McGhee does not uncover the specific traits of the philosophical tale *(Voltairian Narrative Devices* [Menasha, Wisc.: Banta, 1933]).

tologie et sémiologie pourront fournir à cette étude une contribution non négligeable." [5] My purpose is to try to characterize by the methods he mentions a certain kind of philosophical narration and to study the *conte philosophique* by asking if it has a specificity as literary discourse. At present there is no synthetic theory available. It should be noticed that this search for a modest synthesis is not syncretism. The latter would simply be the marrying by force of fundamentally incompatible tendencies, whereas I believe that structural, narratological, intertextual, and modal considerations all contribute to a description of the text's semiotic potential. They must all inform any attempt to separate the compound and intricate processes of sense-making that the genre inspires.

How exactly is this to be done? The idea of making sense of literature has often supposed a model according to which an author puts a meaning into a work and the reader gets it out. This concept belongs to normative criticism where the text is seen as possessing ideal status, as reflecting a transcendental reality, as containing a meaning. In this view the reader's task is that of a coal miner: to dig until she finds It. Attacks on the work's ontological status followed the New Criticism's rejection of author-centered inquiries and are nearly as well-known today. My investigation situates itself in pragmatic or reader-centered criticism, and it views the tales as potential producers of meaning. I do not begin with their supposed referents nor with prescriptive principles such as unity and coherence, but with consideration of the ways in which the sign constructs itself in the perceiver's mind. This effort tries to define the nature and limits of the effects produced, and it includes recognizing the system of literary norms implied as well as the historical and social situation evoked by the work. Although they do not always figure in the signifier, both literary tradition and social conditions are cultural units that permit a more or less complex actualization of the text according to the particular competences of the reader. [6] Part

---

[5] J.-M. Moureaux, "Voltaire, l'écrivain," in *Résumé des communications* (Paris: Centre National des Recherches Scientifiques, 1978), pp. 19-20.

[6] The reader of this book will recognize my use of terms and of concepts shared by Umberto Eco, *The Role of the Reader* (Bloomington: Indiana University Press, 1979) — cultural units; Stanley Fish, *Is There a Text in This Class?* (Cambridge: Harvard University Press, 1980) — interpretive communi-

of the special nature of the philosophical story is its sustained reference to a group of cultural units. A certain, even complex, semiotic
functioning of the text can take place without the interpreter's
acquaintance with the material referents, however, since the tale
itself works to provide her with the ability to construct many of
them even if they are not part of her prior knowledge. The investigation of the tale as potential and dynamic producer of effects
therefore does not refuse to discuss referential questions nor even
prescriptive tendencies such as supposition of unity; instead of pos-
iting them, it helps to understand how they occur to readers in the
first place. [7] The so-called referential illusion is not one. When Voltaire says *France* and when he says *les Welches* for the French, we
do not actualize the work by refusing to acknowledge that reference.
Furthermore, we measure satire, parody, and ironic figures by some
relation to a norm, configuration, or reference outside the text. [8]
A recent article on irony states that

> ... l'ironie, comme métalogisme, n'est perçue que par con-
> frontation du message et du référent, elle est toujours 'cir-
> constantielle'...; elle oblige à scruter la fonction pragma-
> tique de l'énoncé et, d'une manière plus générale, le rapport
> de l'énoncé à ses contextes. [9]

For similar reasons, it seems unnecessary to avoid mention of the
author. The perception of irony makes it impossible to set aside the
creating subject. The figure supposes two subjects, one who creates
it and one who recreates it; and it also supposes that both have or
gain knowledge of a context.

At the same time as we grant reference to real places and to real
creators we nonetheless continue to observe the text's essential
opacity. Maurice Blanchot expresses such a view this way:

---

ties; and Wolfgang Iser, *The Act of Reading* (Baltimore: The Johns Hopkins
University Press, 1978) — determinacy, actualization, etc., to name only one
work by each of three of the many critics interested in the reader's activity.

[7] Jacques Derrida's well-known attack on the logocentric orientation of
Western language also helps to explain assumptions about unity and about the
ontological status of the text: *De la grammatologie* (Paris: Editions de Minuit,
1967).

[8] Lionel Duisit, *Satire, Parodie, Calembour*: *Esquisse d'une théorie des
modes dévalués* (Stanford: Anma Libri, 1978), pp. 5-7.

[9] Groupe μ, "Ironique et iconique," *Poétique*, 36 (1978), 428.

Le caractère du récit n'est nullement pressenti quand on voit en lui la relation vraie d'un événement exceptionnel, qui a lieu et qu'on essaierait de rapporter. Le récit n'est pas la relation de l'événement, mais cet événement même, le lieu où celui-ci est appelé à se produire, événement encore à venir et par la puissance attirante duquel le récit peut espérer lui aussi se réaliser. [10]

The story is not a reflection of anything even though some of its words and concepts refer to things we recognize in our lives. The didactic text benefits from these holes in the otherwise opaque tissue of narration, for it repeatedly invites assimilation or at least comparison of its structures and events with those of the reader's experience. Application is all, and so it uses certain kinds of reference in order to attach its lesson to the reader's life.

The results of the kinds of analysis reported here include those arising both from use of concepts of causality, sequence, and progression — such as folkloric schemes, mythic order, and other forms of narrative syntax — and from consideration of those that include a notion of the text as autonomous system, such as the discovery of paradigmatic structures. Both the metonymic and the metaphoric components of the text are thus respected. Viewing the textual space in this way gives rise to other terms that express the same distinction. In discussing the manner in which episodes succeed each other I shall call it the *sequential* aspect of the text. The structurations of the episodes themselves belong to the *analogical* component. This corresponds to Hjelmslev's distinction between process and system or between the *syntagmatic* and the *paradigmatic;* however, since I need the latter word for two other senses, I reserve it for naming the entire folkloric or heroic configuration in plot, which is a paradigmatic sequence in fact, and for naming the opposition of the synchronous relation that structures a particular episode or each in a series and thus constitutes its thematic paradigm.

Another set of words important to this study includes *sense, meaning,* and *significance.* I found I needed three concepts and learned that Victoria, Lady Welby, and Charles S. Peirce made a similar

---

[10] *Le Livre à venir* (Paris: Gallimard, 1971), p. 13.

distinction. [11] I arrange the definitions as follows, using the simpler
terms since they seem sufficiently refined for the analysis of an
entire work, as opposed to that of a single sentence: *sense,* the most
primitive, unanalyzed reference, response to environment (similar to
Iser's first code, information); *meaning,* direct effect actually produced by a sign on an interpreter of it (Iser: second code, aesthetic
object); *significance,* which includes sense and meaning but transcends them in range, covering far-reaching consequences (Welby),
implication "in any mind upon which circumstance should permit it
to work out its full effect" (Peirce). [12] Furthermore, my distinction
between a naïve or first reading of sense and a second critical one
of meaning does not assume that the two are necessarily rigidly successive; and depending upon previous and immediately acquired experience, in some actualizations the naïve reading may not even be
said to exist.

The concept of *deixis,* sign of the enunciative process, and the
use of *histoire, récit,* and *narration* will be explained in Chapter One.
The term *intertextuality* will cover any cultural system that is a
condition of signification; it will not only refer to literary sources
in the old sense. It includes both the conventions of certain kinds
of discourse and the presence of specific prior texts that participate
in some part of the discursive space encompassed by the new text.

Irony, a difficult term because it has become exceedingly banal,
will be studied naïvely and inductively both as a very important
element of response to Voltairian prose and as a generative strategy
producing a meaning that reverses the sense of a word, sentence, or
scene. In this restrained use of the concept, no single mass of discourse will be called *ironic;* the word will be applied only to specific
instances of reversal, to operations that go beyond univocal sense
by that method. It thus accounts for more than cases of antiphrasis,
commonly called *Voltairian irony* even though they are not more

---

[11] C. S. Peirce to Lady Welby, letter of 14 March 1909, *Semiotic and
Significs: The Correspondence between Charles S. Peirce and Victoria, Lady
Welby* (Bloomington: Indiana University Press, 1977).

[12] These are approximate equivalents of Peirce's immediate, dynamic, and
final interpretants, of Duisit's distinction among encoding, decoding, and impact
(*Satire, parodie, calembour,* passim), and of Hans Robert Jauss's *poiesis, aisthe-
sis,* and *catharsis:* "La Jouissance esthétique," *Poétique,* 39 (1979), pp. 261-74.

prevalent than other ironic procedures. In addition to the instances of verbal irony, we shall have occasion to consider three other types: that usually called *Socratic,* the use of an eiron, a character who is ignorant or pretends to be and who thus points out by his questions the ignorance and the inconsistencies of those around him; the *dramatic,* named after the common theatrical device of letting the audience and often certain characters know something of which the protagonist or another is ignorant; and *circumstantial* or *general* irony, according to which a paradoxical occurrence, reversing the expected or the coherent outcome of events, is attributed to the "irony of fate." The latter, according to D. C. Muecke's definition, is

> reducible to one great incongruity, the appearance of self-valued and subjectively free but temporally finite egos in a universe that seems to be utterly alien, utterly purposeless, completely deterministic, and incomprehensibly vast. [13]

Other types of modal communication will be enumerated and illustrated in the discussion of each story, that is, those operations going beyond the reception of simple sense, actualizing criticism of targets, and implying certain moral values. This aspect of decoding also concerns the state of cultural receptivity of the reader and the text's capacity to create her skill in actualizing the modes.

Contrary to the fashionable "open" text *(scriptible),* didactic literature is by its nature closed or *lisible* to the extent defined above. It would not be didactic if in a cooperative actualization it could be read in contradictory ways, [14] and so it outlines a limited project and firmly guides its ideal reader. Such a text can be said to be redundant in that many or all of the structures and messages it produces coincide with each other and reinforce each other. They produce all the pathways of their own good reading. [15] Modal communication and structural anaphora are important causes of this restriction of meaning.

---

[13] *Irony* (London: Methuen, 1970), p. 68.

[14] Except in a case like Diderot's work where one of the lessons is method and where various possibilities of ideological resolution are therefore deliberately explored: Carol Sherman, *Diderot and the Art of Dialogue* (Geneva: Droz, 1976).

[15] Eco, p. 9.

Who are the readers? In the kind of analysis I am doing there is no need to subtilize infinitely the distinctions among them. [16] The easiest to see and define is one sometimes addressed by the narrator, one who is not ideal and whom Voltaire does not seek to please. The discourse-relation also establishes the presence of an informed reader of good will. We see ourselves as solicited to resemble that person — implied or represented — and to respond as directed. Whether or not we give ourselves up to this game, we register the attempt to gain our consent to it. The narrator's implied companion is thus not necessarily the same as the real-life subject who actualizes the written text in a given reading. I take into account the appeal made to this good, sympathetic, and cooperative receiver as well as the possibilities of variance taking place in any real-life reader who may or may not identify herself with the one implied by the kinds of guidance given. I am usually not writing of an "average" reader nor of a so-called *naïve* one, but of what I take to be an optimally or maximally actualizing one, that is, me.

I believe that the vocabularies I have named above and in the chapters to follow will be called abstruse only by those unwilling to test their efficacity. These are not new words for old things. They efficiently represent new ways of studying the phenomenon of deciphering the literary text. The processes by which one may make sense of it are my target here and not primarily the meanings themselves: these we already know, and it is often difficult for obstinate interpreters to direct, even temporarily, their attention to process instead. I have tried to be a sensible craftsperson, not a sectarian: I have no gods. This is an eclectic arsenal, and it circumscribes a dynamic view of the literary encounter. It sees it as a meeting of two texts, of two virtualities, the work and its reader. It should then provide its own justification by elucidating the processes of reception in didactic fiction and by showing how the nature of its discourse defines the genre.

* * *

---

[16] For a discussion of some of these varieties, see W. Daniel Wilson, "Readers in Texts," *PMLA,* 96 (1981), 848-63.

I thank Edouard Morot-Sir for reading this work in typescript and for making many suggestions. I gratefully acknowledge the support of the College of Arts and Sciences at the University of North Carolina at Chapel Hill and aid received from the Kenan Research Fund and from the Research Council of that university.

C. S.

Chapter I

MICROMÉGAS *

> But allegories are so much lettuce.
> Don't hide the madness.
>
> Allen Ginsberg, *Reality Sandwiches*

I.1. Competence

1.a. *Initiation and General Competence*

Neither the eighteenth-century reader nor the modern one begins *Micromégas* innocently. The title seems to be a proper name and therefore anounces a tale with a hero; and the subtitle, "histoire philosophique," [1] annuls the idea of a univocal adventure since a philosophical story promises something more than heroic actions. The reader easily registers the fact that actions, adventure, and travel are promised along with a message; that is, a didactic genre announces itself without its specific abstractive procedures being

---

* *Note on editions:* Because of its accessibility, I quote from the Garnier-Flammarion pocket edition of the *contes*. Since the tales are divided into short chapters, I usually cite the chapter-number rather than the page, so that any copy of the text may be used to follow the argument. I have of course regularly consulted the critical editions of the tales, and they are the source of alternate readings and variants.

[1] The subtitle was added by Voltaire in the edition of 1754, the one most carefully reviewed by him and the one in which the most changes were made. Ira O. Wade, *Voltaire's "Micromégas": A Study in the Fusion of Science, Myth and Art* (Princeton: Princeton University Press, 1950), pp. 39-60, 80-82.

immediately revealed. The reader also quickly understands by the title that she will be receiving a story and not a document; she is thus engaged in her role of narratee. The words *Chapitre Premier* correspond to the conventional division of fictions; and the title of the chapter, typically long in the eighteenth century, "Voyage d'un habitant du monde de l'étoile Sirius dans la planète de Saturne," establishes one of the probability-registers of the action and probably recalled to its contemporaries Cyrano de Bergerac (*L'Autre Monde [Les Etats et empires de la lune]*, 1655), Fontenelle (*Entretiens sur la pluralité des mondes*, 1686), and Swift (*Gulliver's Travels*, 1726) to name only the most often cited works in which interplanetary travel and inhabited worlds are imagined. [2] The protagonist here is fabulous in his physical size and abilities, and he will exhibit a superior though human range of intellectual and moral capacities. The *habitant* mentioned in the title of the first chapter is, the reader supposes, the eponymous hero; and his adventure will be offered at the same time as fantastic (*dulce*) and as instructive (*utile*). The manner in which both aspects are received at the same time will be the first subject here (Sections l.a. and l.b.).

One expects the first lines of a short tale to contain exposition, that is, to name the time, the place, and the kind of action. One expects as well to learn the nature of the discourse-situation in which one will be participating as imaginary reader; that is, in addition to the conventional assumptions, instructions for reading will be contained or implied in these lines, the alert to a double reading — "histoire philosophique" — having already prepared the reader for such an apprenticeship. There are several terms for this relation in present critical language: communication-situation, utterance-situation, and so forth, all designating the establishment of written discourse as an illocutionary act, that is to say, as creating context and depending upon it. The title and subtitle of this story announce a combination of fantasy and of truth or a lesson, and they place

---

[2] Wade, pp. 80-82, described these and others in their relation with Voltaire's story. The vogue of the *conte* in the 40's and 50's was remarked by S. Paul Jones in *A List of French Prose Fiction from 1700 to 1750* (New York: H. W. Wilson, 1939). Jacques Barchilon treats the didactic or enlightened tone of the fairy-tale as it appeared after the *Mille et Une Nuits:* "Uses of the Fairy Tale in the Eighteenth Century," *Studies on Voltaire and the Eighteenth Century*, 24 (1963), 111-38.

the work inside a class of literature that includes parables and fables, timeless and familiar. The reader is thus prepared for the fusion of amusement and instruction, and she presumably consents to learning to receive both.[3]

1.b. *Exposition and Instructions for Reading: Specific Competence*

The first paragraph is composed of two sentences; in them a narrative voice says *je* twice and *notre* and *ces* once each. In this way it projects and continues to project with insistence the narrative instance, the act of production of the text or discourse. The locutor *je* and the interlocutor implied in *notre* are consequently assumed to be in contact with each other, one speaking or writing, the other listening or reading. The deictic *ces* — *ces planètes* — implying a common place, *here,* shows them looking, *there,* gesturing and referring together to an object known to them both and at some distance, in thought and in space, from the supposed locus of their encounter.[4] In addition to the space and time common to the narrator and reader, the words *ce* and *ces* imply information that is shared by them both. The narrative voice will designate a specific class of interlocutors with this latter group: algebraists and sculptors (Ch. 1) and grenadiers (Ch. 5). These figurations of possible readers are made by naming them, attributing to them reactions to the story, and reacting to their supposed reactions: "Quelques algébris-

---

[3] Mary Louise Prattt, *Toward a Speech Act Theory of Literary Discourse* (Bloomington: Indiana University Press, 1977); Eco, *The Role of the Reader;* etc. Although speech-act theory is not treated as such, for a recent selected and annotated bibliography of response-criticism, see Susan R. Suleiman and Inge Crosman, eds., *The Reader in the Text* (Princeton: Princeton University Press, 1980), pp. 402-424. Most of the essays edited by Suleiman and Crosman are original; for a reprinting of several older ones, see Jane P. Tompkins, ed., *Reader-Response Criticism: From Formalism to Post-Structuralism* (Baltimore: The Johns Hopkins University Press, 1980).

[4] There is a large lexicon for the pairs author-reader and narrator-reader: emitter-receiver, *encodeur-décodeur, destinateur-destinataire, narrateur-narrataire,* etc. There is an ambiguity belonging to the *conte (conter,* transitive verb) and figuring the writer and the reader at the same time as speaker and hearer. The line between writing and saying, reading and listening is usually rather explicitly erased in most of eighteenth-century fiction and is a clue to its particular illocutionary status. See Carol Sherman, "Diderot's Speech-Acts: Essay, Letter, and Dialogue," *French Literature Series,* 9 (1982), 18-29.

tes ... trouveront que ..." and "tous nos sculpteurs ... conviendront ... que...." Other evocations are by first- and second-person imperatives — "revenons à nos voyageurs" (Ch. 3), "figurez-vous" (Ch. 4, Ch. 5) — by inclusion in a first-person plural statement — "... nous ne faisons pas sur la terre une plus grande figure" (Ch. 5) — and by direct address — "Vous croyez bien que le Sirien et son nain brûlaient d'impatience" (Ch. 6).

The relation in a context between emitter and receiver(s) is enriched by these maneuvers as well as by the frequent presence of other signs of the time and place from which the tale presumably emanates. The categories of deixis that I consider to be signs of *narration*,[5] that is, of the production of the text in the *contes*, are the following: the spatial, that is, personal deixis *(je, nous, vous);* the monstrative *(voici, voilà, ici, là, ce, ces);* and the temporal, the tenses of the verb assigned to the category of discourse by Emile Benveniste.[6] I take as further signs of the narrative instance value-assigning adjectives, comparisons, and atemporal reflections. The tabulations exclude deictics appearing in direct discourse or in what one takes to be indirect or free indirect discourse, attributable to one or several of the characters. My categories of deixis here expand for these purposes the usual spatio-temporal indicators and include indicators of opinion and value which, when assignable to the narrative voice taken as that of an individual, join with the signs of place and time in that the opining consciousness is presumably someplace at sometime.[7] The number in *Micromégas* is on the

---

[5] Gérard Genette, Figures III (Paris: Le Seuil, 1972), p. 72.

[6] *Problèmes de linguistique générale,* I (Paris: Gallimard, 1966), Chapter 19.

[7] It is true, however, that the limits of the term's use are more or less indefinable since all acts of reference can probably be looked upon as deixis, even definite articles. I consider the following description of deictic function to be a useful one:

> ... l'emploi des déictiques permet de référentialiser le discours, de simuler l'existence linguistique d'un référent externe, alors qu'il s'agit en fait d'une corrélation entre cette sémiotique particulière qu'est la langue naturelle et la sémiotique du monde naturel, l'une et l'autre ayant une organisation spécifique (A. J. Greimas and J. Courtès, *Sémiotique: Dictionnaire raisonné de la théorie du langage* [Paris: Hachette, 1979], p. 87).

I have preferred to work with the types just named rather than seeking an absolute or universal definition of deixis. Those I have retained all give a

average between fifteen and twenty per page in the portions attributable to the narrative voice. These signs of the narrative instance will be shown in the form of a detailed chart only for *L'Ingénu* (Ch. 4 below) because that story is the exception to their fairly even distribution in the other tales treated here.

By this use of deixis the narrative voice not only figures itself three times *(je, notre, ces)* in the first sentence as being the reader's informative companion, but it also offers itself as reliable: he actually knew the hero of the story he will tell — "que j'ai eu l'honneur de connaître" — and he is dependable for the mathematical precision of his information: he gives the hero's height in both leagues and feet. The guarantees of truth, reliability, and scientific exactness accompany the traditional expression that begins fairytales, *il y avait,* and that corresponds to the first lines of picaresque travel-literature, folklore, and myth, all of which generally share a brief, preliminary, and concentrated exposition before launching the chronology of adventures and trials. [8] In this sentence, the mixture or alternation is well established by the rapid passage from fantasy, "il y avait un jeune homme," to truth-in-fantasy, "que j'ai eu l'honneur de connaître," to fantasy anew, "dans le dernier voyage qu'il fit sur notre petite fourmilière." Besides observing the conventions of presence and of trustworthiness, the narrator offers early instruction and drill in the two kinds of reading required for the fullest actualization of his written discourse. He makes the reader practice them by offering a simple exercise in meta-literal comprehension: "notre petite fourmilière," implying tiny scurrying inhabitants, refers to the earth. In effecting the translation and in maintaining the parallelism, the decoder registers the narrator's depreciation of the planet and of its inhabitants. This elementary transfer comports an inversion of size and as such immediately presents what will continue to be the fundamental experience of the story. Its principal constant will be reversal, like this one from *petit,* anthill, the sense, to *grand,* earth, the meaning, to *petit* again, anthill, the judgment of sig-

---

specific and same kind of guidance for the reader's reactions. An attempt at synthetic theory is made by Edouard Morot-Sir in "Texte, référence, et déictique," *Text,* 1 (1982), 113-42.

[8] Meir Sternberg, *Expositional Modes and Temporal Ordering in Fiction* (Baltimore: The Johns Hopkins University Press, 1978), p. 25.

nificance. This exercise gives a sample of the relativization that the story both says on occasion and produces constantly. Considering only examples relating to the designation of the earth — *notre tas de boue,* and so on — one notices that when one tries to see the earth as in fact *grand* in both senses of the word, all of those expressions first suscitate the reader's attempt to rectify them and then they sap and refute its greatness.

The reader's first exercise in abstracting meaning from sense is complemented by a second that is even simpler because the instructions are explicit: after naming the hero, the narrator adds a phrase in apposition to his name, "nom qui convient fort à tous les grands," requiring the re-reading of the name, *little-big,* and the subsequent assessment of the aggression contained in the appositive phrase: all those who are taken for *grands* are at the same time *petits.* By asking her to go back to the hero's name and to take it forward to re-name the *grands,* the phrase invites her to perform the reduction by acknowledging the mixed character of all those she encounters in her own life. The reductive or reversing operation will be programmed in several other ways as well. This is a particularly explicit example of the didactic text's broadest message, that of the type "Go thou and do likewise" — here, "belittle the great" — implied in almost all didactic literature. The link with extra-textual existence is given by the quality of generalization of "tous les grands" and elsewhere by specific reference to types of persons — the Sultans, the Caesars, the *barbares sédentaires* (Ch. 7) — who exist in the reader's and narrator's own world.

These frequent moments of second-degree reading, whether their application is intra-textual, extra-textual, or both, characterize it most profoundly; for the lesson extracted or at least available is relativism. The extraction itself requires a relativizing procedure, the revision of a lexeme or sememe in three steps: 1. pause for observation and realization that the first sense needs revision or completion; 2. comparison, reversal or correction; 3. the judgment that the exercise implies. [9]

---

[9] Other manifestations of it and its other functions will be described in Sections Three and Four below.

The narrative voice has presented itself as possessing a didactic communicative intention and as being omniscient; the verbs of its discourse are both in the *passé simple* for the history itself — *voyage qu'il fit, il disséqua, l'auteur eut ordre* — and in the *passé composé* for the recent past still in touch with its own, the narrative present — *j'ai eu l'honneur, le globe qui l'a produit.* [10] The latter reminders of the narrative instance and of its discourse-situation recall the narrator's presence as a guide and the fact that he expects a certain activity in the receiver's grasp of the story's significance.

The first sentence, we have seen, poses the existence of emitter and receiver and defines their relation as well as offering two exercises in significance; it also points to the universe of the action. The second sentence, "Il avait huit lieues de haut: j'entends ..." enriches the narrator's persona by its exactitude, and it offers a sample of this kind of second space and time in the narrative, that of the *histoire.* These are sentences that do not propel the action forward; they are, however, far from being unproductive of meaning pertinent to the didactic purpose announced. The narrator will frequently dramatize himself expressing, for example, his mock scruples, "Je ne prétends choquer ici la vanité de personne..." (Ch. 7) and elaborating the condemnation of one of his targets. The didactic motivations were already clear from the subtitle forward, and this further mix or alternation between passages with propulsive value and those of thematic or didactic expansion, that is, that between passages linking the tale to narration and those linking sender to receiver, are presumably integrated by the reader as coherent with this intent. [11] Different relations between these kinds of passages are possible within the genre, and Voltaire's stories offer examples of several; they will be treated in the chapters that follow. The second paragraph constitutes one development mixing the two relations. It calls upon a particular group of readers and elaborates with them in

---

[10] Benveniste, Chapter 19.

[11] This distinction corresponds to the one made variously by Roland Barthes, "Introduction à l'analyse structurale du récit," *Communications,* 8 (1966), 8-11: *fonctions* and *indices;* by Gerald Prince, *A Grammar of Stories* (The Hague: Mouton, 1976), p. 43: active and stative events; and by Cesare Segre, *Structures and Time,* trans. John Meddeman (Chicago: University of Chicago Press, 1979), pp. 17-21: linear segmentation and linguistic-functional segmentation.

mathematical detail the proportions between Micromégas and his world and earth-dwellers with theirs.

This delight in calculation works in at least two ways to pose the structure of the exercises of proportion and of comparison that diminish the earth and build the thesis. The narrator poses a simple algebraic problem: we are a feet tall and our planet is b leagues around, so if Micromégas is c feet tall, how big around (x) is his planet? The premise, that height of inhabitant and circumference of planet are everywhere in the same proportion, sets a precedent in the story for further analogical reasoning; and it is the model of comparison and relativization everywhere present in it. Further, in this paragraph it presents the earth as minuscule in comparison to the hero's planet (a, Sirius : b, earth) and leads to a reduction of certain individual countries, Germany and Italy, x, being compared to the vast kingdoms of Turkey, Russia, and China, c; thus, a (big) is to b (little) as c (big) is to x (*little*). The delicate omission of France from the group x, the miniscule, is surely noted by the reader, French or otherwise, who revises by placing it anyway into that category. The last phrase of the second paragraph makes the permanent mechanism explicit by remarking that there are "prodigieuses différences que la nature a mises dans tous les êtres," *différences* inviting comparison, and *prodigieuses* expressing the attitude of astonishment in which the comparisons shall be made. It may be noted in passing, and I shall again have occasion to comment on this, that astonishment here as in Aristotle is the beginning of wisdom or philosophy. In the uses of it in eighteenth-century French literature, the evaluation accompanying it may be either grandiosity — "Comment peut-on être Persan?" (Montesquieu) — or humility — "Cet atome m'a mesuré!" (Voltaire) — and when it is the former, some agent will always appear and reduce the utterance by reason or by reversal and ridicule (Section 4, below).

The third paragraph polishes off the presentation of the hero's body and in so doing invokes, although not by direct address, some eventual readers, sculptors and painters, and attributes to them an abbreviated version of calculation by proportions, this time of Micromégas' waist-size, fifty-thousand *pieds de roi*. It pounds the lesson home by adding "ce qui fait une très jolie proportion" in which the word *proportion* has the potential for its technical sense, mathematical relation, and its artistic meaning, esthetic relation. The fourth paragraph presents the hero's mind, expanding the "beaucoup d'esprit" of the first sentence of the tale. Its description is first direct, "un des plus cultivés que nous ayons," then comparative; for it is proportionate to that of Blaise Pascal. It is finally exemplified by an anecdote that expands the information on its scientific abilities and that also criticizes small-minded and politically powerful religious censors *(muphti)* who provide the impulsion or motivation for his leaving his country in the *histoire* and permit starting the series of episodes, the *récit.* [12] A second motivation is added to this exposition and might be said to complete it when the narrator says that the protagonist began traveling "pour achever de se former *l'esprit et le cœur,"* although the italics and the added phrase "comme l'on dit" acknowledge the conventional nature of this pretext for travel in life and for presenting supposedly formative episodes in literature. It may therefore strike the critic as a rare sign of the narrator's breaking both with his protagonist and with his own *récit.* It can seem to be a sort of rift in the union with his admirable hero and in the earnest presentation of him. Wade (p. 22) annotates this phrase with quotations from Voltaire's correspondence, showing the author's scorn for the cliché. This biographical information confirms the impression of disruption that reading pro-

---

[12] Vocabulary for the distinction between "what happens" as reconstituted in its logical and chronological order (fabula, story, *histoire, récit raconté,* content, proposition, ideational function) and the concrete revelation of it in the signifier *(sujet,* plot, *récit, récit racontant,* text, surface structure, textual function) continues to multiply. Some have refined this difference after finding it too simple to cover the real distinctions that are made in the reception of a story (for example, Sternberg, pp. 9-14; Segre, pp. 14-19). Since *sujet* and *fabula* do not have the advantage of being native English either, I have chosen to use Genette's French terms, *récit* for the narrative text or signifier (relaying both *noyaux* and *catalyses)* and *histoire* for the content reconstituted in its logical and chronological order. I shall not regularize or name the further division of the latter concept by which one can distinguish between content in the order given in the *récit,* including the static and purely situational elements, and that reconstituted and emphasizing action (for example, Segre: *intrigue* and *fable).* In addition to employing *discourse-situation* to indicate the relation constituted between imaginary narrator and imaginary reader, I use *narration* (Genette), also called modality or discourse (Roger Fowler, *Linguistics and the Novel* [London: Methuen, 1977] and interpersonal function (Fowler cites the work of M. A. K. Halliday on pages 46-48); *narration* thus includes all the signs in the text of the narrative stance, of the creation of the *récit.*

duces. One might imagine that his dislike for the italcized portion corresponds to his, and to Locke's, refusal of Cartesian dualism; the latter is further ridiculed in the last episode of the tale. Voltaire's remark is perhaps integrated by the receiver as an amusing assimilation of the giant with the average young nobleman whose education included travel, the incongruity arising from the difference in scale: the tour of Europe pales when compared to the hero's tour of the universe. The break may also be seen as pointing to the superfluity of the voyage for such a purpose, given that the hero was capable of the research and of the book mentioned in the preceding paragraph. Reversal of the idea that he could need further formation reflects unfavorably on the censors and on the judges who banished him. The internal or plot-related necessity of the remark will be examined in Section 2.b. below.

Besides being initiated into probability-registers, semantic reversal, and the nature of the hero, the reader has also noted exposition of place and of time in the represented world. The young giant moves through space in the universe on a trajectory between the planets of the star Sirius and the planet Earth. The time of the history is recent since the narrator, who is still breathing while composing the *récit,* once met its hero. Consistent with his preciseness and with his accountability, he will later give an exact hour and exact geographical location of the landing on earth. He will also refer to the places that surround and reinforce the verisimilar aspects of the characters. In keeping with the first impression — algebrists, Germany, Italy — the physical and cultural background of France and of Christian Europe is maintained by mention of the Academy, an archbishop, a *petit-maître,* grenadiers, and of the scientific expedition that contemporaries recognized as that of Maupertuis and a group of scientists who measured a meridian.

Thus by the fifth paragraph, the reader possesses all the traditionally preliminary exposition, that of time, place, and character. Nothing that happens or that is said later will greatly change the primacy effect of the information given about the main character. [13]

---

[13] Primary effect as opposed to the use of recency effect: Sternberg, p. 94. First materials on a given subject fall on an open mind, but further blocks of information on the same topic are conditioned by the anterior effect.

Instead, subsequent episodes will be largely additive to the picture of the protagonist, the demonstration of the abilities attributed to him from the beginning. (The sign of the protagonist's having learned something will be treated in Section Two below: Syntagmatic Process.) One sign of change in the relation between protagonist and reader is a result of omniscient, dependable exposition, that is, of the particular type of relation between narrator and reader. He shares with her what he knows; she believes she has the narrator's advantage over the character, and this prepares change in her relation to him. Her slight advantage must change as the facts of Micromégas' own philosophic competence are revealed: his scientific prowess brings exile (Ch. 1), and his superior powers of reasoning allow him to criticize the Saturnian (Ch. 2); his talents in the represented world are established in that way. The reader thus listens to two authoritative voices, the narrator's which addresses her, and the protagonist's which speaks to the other characters with wisdom guaranteed by the narrator. The relation between reader and protagonist will change slightly when the latter arrives on earth (Ch. 3ff). He seems an uninformed stranger in the place where the reader is an informed inhabitant. This permits a dynamic relation. His lack of knowledge is quickly balanced by his insistence on careful observation, by his cautious reasoning, by his powers of invention, and by the fact that even his ignorance and astonishment effect depreciation of earth and of its dwellers, given the high value that has already been placed upon his intelligence and judgment. The relation between reader and protagonist is thus not fixed like that between narrator and reader. The discourse-situation is created in the first lines and repeatedly emphasized; it leaves only the story itself and the receiver's knowledge of it as susceptible to change. The amount of addition that occurs in this area is small compared to the kinds of revelations that manipulation of point of view can effect in fiction; here it is of a rudimentary sort, but there is one violation of the simplest form of preliminary and concentrated or undispersed exposition.

This exception is an incidental clause in the first sentence, "dans le dernier voyage qu'il fit sur notre petite fourmilière," which constitutes a leap forward in time and space by relation to the time and space of the narrative units to follow; it invokes the end and goal of the voyage to be recounted since it tells us already that the protagonist has been on earth and that he has made more than one visit. Wade called this a lapsus ("For had Micromégas made other trips to the earth, he would not have been so surprised with what he saw on this particular trip" [p. 35]), but it is easy to see it as meaning simply that Micromégas has been back other times since the first trip here recounted and that it was during one of the later visits that the narrator claims to have met him and to have heard the story of the first visit. This clause probably reduces the reader's tendency to rivet her attention upon what happens, and it therefore permits her to give more patient attention to each stage and to the manner of its presentation since she knows from the beginning where he is going. All ulterior developments in the narrative units that follow, right up until the arrival on earth is told, can then be seen as filling the gap formed by this brief expository leap forward.

The artificiality of separating consideration of exposition from that of the relation between reader and narrator, the discourse-situation, is clear; for here the self-conscious (noticeably aware of facing an audience), reliable, unrestricted narrator is responsible for direct, concentrated, preliminary exposition interspersed with explicit repeated lessons on how the reader is to receive it all. The relation between emitter and receiver is often complex. Decoding can be simply mimetic, reconstruction of simple sense, of person, object, or action represented; it can be reception of a generalization or abstraction; and often the sense-making is potentially modal or double, requiring adjustment of the immediate representation or commentary. A value-judgment arises from that act. The competence created by this activity permits passage from sense to meaning and to an assessment and application of significance. The facts delivered, the thematic excursions, and the reversals all form a network of reiteration, in acts represented and in thought-processes invoked. They show that a large part of generic tone is provided by the nature of the narrator's control, the manner in which he dispenses information, and his instructions for grasping meaning and significance. [14]

---

[14] Sternberg, p. 266.

I.2. SYNTAGMATIC PROCESS

2.a. *Temporal and Spatial Distribution*

The linear or horizontal shape of the story is sometimes causal (I.2.b), but the successiveness of its narrative units has chronological and spatial motivation that is more nearly constant than the causal. The events divide themselves formally into seven chapters, most of which fill in the gap left by the early announcement of the end. The last, a conversation between the planetary traveler and some of earth's inhabitants, represents the encounter promised in the first sentence, and the intervening chapters build the flashback that works up to the first visit of Micromégas with ordinary men. In addition to closing the circle of events, the last chapter expands and makes explicit the didacticism — "nom qui convient fort à tous les grands" — that was also present in the first sentence of the tale. The events of the three chapters preceding the last (4, 5, 6) take place on earth also and show the discovery of men (4) and the invention of techniques by which to see (5) and to hear (6) them. Those same chapters, by the actions described and represented, signify the smallness of men.

The chapters report an interplanetary voyage going from Sirius to Saturn (Ch. 1), to Jupiter (Ch. 3), past Mars (3) to Earth (3), and this is the simplest expression of the *histoire*. Since the arrival on earth is told at the end of the third chapter, over half the *récit* is devoted to events that happen on that planet and to its exhaustive devaluation. This distribution in the signifier is proportionate neither to the reconstituted time or story-time passed by the characters nor to space traversed; for example, a stay of one year on Jupiter is related in one sentence (Ch. 3). It confers greatest importance on earth and on its inhabitants even as the fantastic and immense voyage equilibrates by its own marvels the smaller number of pages accorded it and as it relativizes already the absolute importance of the little planet on which most events will be displayed. The planetary framework and its distribution in the signifier are among the transmitters of the relativistic message, for the large number of pages given over to the planet earth is counter-balanced by the opinion of it there expressed, both in the actions — searching for living creatures, eating mountains for lunch — and in the disparaging lexicon employed *(petite lueur, petit pays, petit étang, taupinière,* etc.). The movement or action signified is centripetal, going from the largest radius, one beginning beyond earth, even beyond earth's star, the sun, beyond the planets of another star, and then traveling past stars and planets of decreasing size. This gradation is interrupted by mention of a planet even smaller than earth. Even the steady centripetal movement reinforced by the big-to-little gradation is thus relativized because it encounters an exception that contributes another example of little-but-big compensation: tiny Mars is out of order; it is smaller than earth but is encountered first. Its smallness, however, is compensated for by the fact that it has two moons whereas earth, five times larger, has only one. Other examples of the paradigm of compensation will be treated below in Section Three.

In addition to being motivated by the hero's exile and by his desire for formation, to being chronologically ordered and spatially directed, the events of the voyage that constitute the *histoire* include pauses in the movement. These consist of two long conversations, each of which confronts one or more *grands* with one or more *petits*: Micromégas (big) with the Secretary (little) (Ch. 2) and the hero and his companion (bigs) with earth-dwellers (littles) (Ch. 6-7). The changed status of the secretary underlines the relativistic lesson. These expansions of event-time to equal the duration of the *récit* and the corresponding lack of physical movement transmit by direct discourse a part of the didactic message and complete the idea of formation of the questing traveler who practices continual observation at these moments by interviewing the creatures he meets.

The propulsion in space and time of the action and the space and time of its reciting are also clearly drawn in the signs of the narrative instance: at the end of three of the chapters, it specifically calls attention to its own activity productive of the *récit* (1, 4, 6). In each case the speaker again presents himself as precise, reliable *(rapporterai, ingénument),* and thoughtful of his interlocutor *(satisfaction)* by advertising the tellability *(singulière, intéressante)* [15] of what he recounts: "Je rapporterai ici, pour la satisfaction des lec-

---

[15] Pratt, *Toward a Speech Act Theory,* Ch. 4, sec. 4.

teurs, une conversation singulière que Micromégas eut un jour avec M. le secrétaire" (Ch. 1); "Je vais raconter ingénument comme la chose se passa ..." (Ch. 4); and "Peu à peu la conversation devint intéressante, et Micromégas parla ainsi" (Ch. 6). The endings of the second, third, and fifth chapters are also beginnings in that they mark an action to come and show the other kind of segmentation of the signifier; the first, fourth, and sixth explicitly announce something "interesting" to come; the second, third, and fifth suspend action at a moment — decision of the hero and his companion to travel (2), date and time of arrival on earth (3), the Secretary thinks he has "caught them in the act" (5) — that presumably inspires reading further. The two ways of segmenting the signifier correspond to the two types of discourse, personal (1, 4, 6) and historic (2, 3, 5), that communicate with the reader, *discours* and *histoire* (Benveniste). The narrator's presentation of his material and the breaking up of the *récit* itself freely foreground its status as literature even as it pretends to be also speech.

2.b. *Archetypal Action and Its Succession*

The sheer displacement in time and in space produces a part of the meaning of the story (2.a.); the division of the signifier also creates or produces sense. The narrative units or episodes taken in their sequence and in their content bear traces of the conventional folktale and a certain quality of conventional adventure. Most studies of short tales have been of the natural or primitive forms — folkloric, marvelous, and mythic — and have described either sequence or "structures" of both. Vladimir Propp himself was careful not to extend the claims of validity of his hypothesis: "Nous devons noter que les lois citées ne concernent que le folklore. Elles ne constituent pas une particularité du conte en tant que tel. Les contes créés artificiellement n'y sont pas soumis." [16] I have considered the function of each of the narrative units taken separately and the relation between them, that is the passage from one to the other. The permanent structures, the synchronous aspects of the narrative will be treated in the next section (3). My topic is the sequence of the

---

[16] Vladimir Propp, *Morphologie du conte,* trans. Marguerite Derrida and Tzvetan Todorov (Paris: Le Seuil, 1965), p. 32.

parts of the récit. The Proppian functions have revealed themselves
to be useful in many areas other than that of Russian folklore, and
they have stood up against efforts at their so-called improvement
or alteration by A. J. Greimas. [17] Ulterior attempts to modify his
functions have done nothing to invalidate their usefulness. Their
application to the "artificial" creations by Voltaire isolates the
constants, and their adaptation to his satires shows how the units
contribute to the transmission of a particular philosophical message
even as they correspond to a pattern that is timeless. Propp's functions are useful, and the points of deviation in their application to
the philosophe's stories mark the difference between the didactic
tale and the traditional framework of heroic adventures. [18] Their
scheme represents an abbreviated version of the action, the skeletal
line of codable events, *event* being understood in Propp's sense of
function, an action having a result. This spare list is itself capable
of signifying as well as of meaning, and in the same didactic direction
as that of description and commentary. The division of the tale into
episodes appears at the left of Figure IA below; the Proppian
function to which each corresponds, at the right. The notation
of functions has been unified as follows, and Propp's symbols as
they were translated in the first American edition appear in paren-
theses. [19] INITIAL SITUATION AND PREPARATORY FUNCTIONS: O, initial
situation, (α); 1, distancing, departure (β); 2, order or prohibition
(γ); 3, execution of order or transgression of prohibition (δ); 4,
interrogation of hero by aggressor or vice versa (ϵ); 5, information

---

[17] "Eléments pour une théorie de l'interprétation du récit mythique," *Communications*, 8 (1966), 28-59; *Sémantique structurale* (Paris: Larousse, 1966);
Du sens (Paris: Le Seuil, 1970); *Maupassant, la sémiotique du texte; exercices
pratiques* (Paris: Le Seuil, 1976), etc.

[18] Fredric Jameson remarks (p. 71) that Propp's diachronic functions do
not define the folktale as genre and suggests substituting a "rather Hegelian
analysis ... reducing the individual events ... to some basic idea" (pp. 69-70).
He prolongs the old concept of genre as content or representation even though
he seeks its most abstract expression, "central notion," "single timeless concept"
(p. 70): *The Prison-House of Language: A Critical Account of Structuralism
and Russian Formalism* (Princeton: Princeton University Press, 1972). I think,
however, that genre may be most convincingly and usefully defined by the
kind of discourse-relation it invites.

[19] I am using the unified numbering suggested by Jean Verrier, "Notes de
lecture" on Propp's *Morphologie* in *Le Français Aujourd'hui*, 43 (Sept. 1978),
97-99.

given or received (ζ); 6, aggressor tries to deceive victim (η); 7, victim is deceived (θ); and FUNCTIONS OF THE ACTION ITSELF: 8, misdeed or lack (A); 9, mediation, connective incident (B); 10, hero consents to act (C); 11, hero departs (↑); 12, test(s) or trial(s) imposed by the donor of the magic object (D); 13, reaction of hero (E); 14, reception of the magic object (F); 15, transfer of hero (or the way is shown to him) (G); 16, combat by hero against the aggressor (H); 17, hero receives a mark or wound (I); 18, victory of hero (J); 19, reparation of initial misdeed or lack (K); 20, return of hero (↓); 21, pursuit of hero by aggressor (Pr); 22, aid brought to hero (metamorphosis, transport) (Rs); 23, arrival of hero incognito at his home or starting place (o); 24, pretensions of false hero (L); 25, difficult task(s) imposed on the hero (M); 26, task(s) accomplished (N); 27, recognition of hero by others (Q); 28, denunciation of false hero (Ex); 29, transfiguration of hero (T); 30, punishment of false hero or of aggressor (U); 31, reward of hero (marriage, kingdom, power . . . .) (W).

FIGURE I.A

FUNCTION, EPISODE & CHAPTER	FUNCTION-NUMBER	
Description of hero: young, intelligent 1	0	
Implicit prohibition: publishing books inimical to religion 1	(2)	
Transgression of prohibition: publication of book on insects 1	3	*Preparatory Functions*
Interrogation of hero by aggressor: M. is prosecuted 1	4	
Information given: M. defends himself	5	
Misdeed and lack, hero consents to act, hero departs: M. banished, begins travel for formation	8^1, 10, 11	*Nœud*
Combat by hero against aggressor: M. converses with Secretary of Saturn, notes defects in his expression 1, 2	16^1	
Lack, hero consents to act, hero departs: M. and Sec. decide to take a philosophical trip 2	8^2, 10, 11	

Combat by hero against aggressor: M. and Sec. seek inhabitants of earth 3, see them 4, hear them 5, and pick them up 6. M. notes defects in Sec.'s observations and reasoning	16^2	
Victory of hero (in combats, 16): Sec. avows that finally he has no opinion 6	18^1 & 2	
Combat by hero against aggressor: M. and Sec. discuss with men, supposing ignorance to correspond to size 6	16^3	
Defeat of hero: M. and Sec. learn men's mathematical skills 6	18^3 neg.	
Reparation of misdeed or lack: M. revises his opinion of proportions 6	19	*Dénouement*
Difficult task imposed on hero: M. tries to find in men wisdom proportionate to their mathematical skills 7	25	
Pretensions of false hero: men claim to have answers to metaphysical questions 7	24	
Task (25) accomplished and denunciation of false heroes: M. discovers men's lack of ability in metaphysics 7	26 neg., 28	
Task (25) accomplished bis: only the little disciple of Locke speaks with M.'s and Sec.'s approval 7 (denunciation of others implied) 7	26, 28	
Pretensions of false hero: theologian speaks 7	24	
Denunciation of false hero: M. and Sec. laugh at theologian 7	28	
Punishment of false hero or of aggressor: all men fall into Sec.'s pocket 7	30	
Punishment of false hero or of aggressor: M. denounces their pride 7	30	

In his enumeration of the spheres of actions, Propp distinguishes between two types of hero for any given story: the questing hero and the hero-victim, like the philosophe of the eighteenth century. According to Propp's functions, in Voltaire's story Micromégas is described as a victim during two-thirds of the first chapter, the persecution and trial giving the impulse to departure and to the encounter with new and potentially instructive situations. That aggressor or victimizer then disappears from the *récit;* and having it both ways, the narrative voice almost reluctantly pronounces the phrase providing motivation for the conversations and displacements which follow, "pour achever de *se former le cœur et l'esprit,*" transforming the hero into a quester even though it is clear that he possesses already *(achever de)* the highest philosophical talents. The conversations would not follow from his persecution, and they thus require a new motivation. The only internal changes the hero will undergo will be the acquiring of information, the result of this involuntary quest. Because the type of hero changes, the sphere of action of the aggressor contains two persons: the muphti, cause of exile of the hero-victim, and the purveyors of ignorance, obstacles to information-gathering by the questing hero. The episode of banishment is thus, by the addition of the remark on forming heart and mind, the moment of a sort of cross-over in the type of hero and in the designation of aggressor; it corresponds as well to the first "discriminated occasion" (Sternberg, passim) which occurs after the preparatory functions (0, 2, 3, 4, 5). The latter constitute the exposition.

Propp's hypothesis includes the possibility of more than one character's being charged with a single sphere of action and of a single character's occupying more than one sphere. The Secretary first plays the role of aggressor ($16^{1\&2}$), then joins the sphere of hero (16^3) against ignorance in the quest. The hero acts as his own mandator; the sphere of false hero contains the group of philosophers, including the theologian, but excluding Locke's disciple. The spheres of donor and of magic auxiliary are not represented. In Propp's system, the donor submits the hero to tests (12) before giving him the magic aid (14); I find no unit corresponding to these functions. To the degree that Micromégas is helped in 18, 19, and 26, some of the functions in which the auxiliary often plays a role, it seems to be his own intelligence and skill that bring the happy results. That this is "magic" and enabling for a philosophe is undeniable, but the story itself does not represent the invention or endowment of the hero with these qualities; they are given from the beginning onward. The second combat, the one with the supposedly ignorant little men (16^3), brings about the defeat of the hero, for it is there that he must correct his idea of direct proportions: the little creatures' power to measure is in inverse proportion to their size. Micromégas' amazement marks this reversal of his expectations.

This functional schema does not take into account the changing role nor the particular lustre of the Secretary-dwarf, inhabitant of Saturn. He can be seen at times as a double of the hero since they decide together to take a philosophical voyage, and he is thus joined to the quest. However, in the conversations between him and the larger giant, he is inferior in wisdom. [20] Since he changes ($18^{1\&2}$), one can see him as an aggressor defeated, but it would also be possible to code his transformation as 19 (reparation of misdeed) for a questing hero whose lack (8) was of powers of observation and of reasoning. Three separate individuals and groups occupy the aggressor's sphere at different moments. The first group is that of the judges and theologians who banish the hero-victim from his homeland. The hero then being transmuted into a quester, the Secretary is the second aggressor, or the first one for the questing hero, and engages twice in combat. In those encounters, Micromégas is victor, for he succeeds in making the Secretary more cautious and humble. The third group to occupy the aggressor's sphere is that of the earth's philosophers. By the mathematical tour de force, the hero is defeated in his suppositions. The men then pass into the sphere of false hero, and their pretensions are revealed when the battleground becomes metaphysical. This kind of doubling of persons in the hero's sphere of action and their re-assignment to other functions in the course of the story occur also in *Candide* and in *L'Ingénu*.

The transcription into discursive prose of the Proppian coding shows that reading of events expressed as *histoire* and detached from the *récit* does not exhaust the text's capacity to signify, no more than the isolation of its spatial dimension accounted for all its potential for producing sense. Since the quest is seen as philosophical, it does, however, account for the representation in the *characters* of the main didactic point of the story; that is, it is possible to code the apprenticeship of vanity and of lack of proportion, the hero's formation through "combat" — conversation — and re-

---

[20] The probable allusion to Fontenelle is part of the information concerning the author's intentions that we possess about this story; Wade, p. 24.

sponse to it. The quest codes the devaluing of certain men's views of themselves and of the universe by showing them to be aggressors and false heroes. It codes the punishment of their pretensions in *events* instead of in commentary. [21]

This examination shows the particular ways in which *Micromégas* differs from the reiterative pattern of trial and reaction (12, 13) that characterizes *Zadig* and *Candide*. Although the values opposed are nearly the same in every scene — science against metaphysical or poetic pretensions — there is a great deal more flexibility in the kinds of actants transmitting that confrontation. They change spheres; the aggressor's sphere changes characters; and the hero changes his type. He also loses as well as wins in combat; and he finally (Ch. 7) leaves the sphere of the hero altogether and becomes the archetypal observer, participating only at a great distance in the deflating of man's pretension: he ceases to be personally concerned in the outcome of any struggle and rises, laughing, to assume the role of cosmic ironist, that is, of an observer who shares the perceptions of author and reader, reversing the *Sorbonnard*'s pretensions and finding him ridiculous.

I.3. PARADIGMS: OPERATIONS, OPPOSITIONS, INTERTEXTS

Certain paradigms, that is totalizing grids or vertical structures, are everywhere present in the story. They organize for the reader both the experiences represented in the story and those produced by it as she actualizes its meanings. There are constants in the operations that Micromégas performs and that the reader is led to repeat,

---

[21] This view of Voltaire's stories as traced on the folkloric model does not exclude the possibility of their reception as parody of the *romanesque*. Françoise Barguillet is categorical on the subject: "*Zadig* and *Candide* tournent en dérision le roman romanesque, les contes orientaux, et les romans exotiques. *L'Ingénu* se moque du roman sentimental tel qu'il a pu surgir chez Prévost, Mme de Tencin ou dans la deuxième partie du siècle tandis que *Micromégas* persifle les romans du voyage imaginaire" (*Le Roman au XVIII*ᵉ *siècle* [Paris: Presses Universitaires de France, 1981], pp. 95-101). It seems doubtful that their author's intent was primarily parodic given the heavy hints and restrictions that I am examining, all of which transmit a philosophical lesson. The multiplication of chance encounters, while potentially mocking of novels, may be inherent in the short tale's compression or in the purely comic effort. Carefully prepared causalities are not a requirement of folk-genres.

and in the oppositions or relations proposed by both those areas of action. The relation represented in the text and produced by it is traced after the several avatars of the *règle de proportion* (I.3.b), and the operation is that derived from Lockean sensualism and Newtonian observation and experience: 1. observation of more than one sense-impression makes possible 2. comparison, which leads to a choice, that is, to 3. judgment about value or worth. Comparison, the second step of this process, is the one most explicit in the largest quantity of signifier in *Micromégas*. Most comparisons are expressed by mathematical proportions; the fundamental and permanent comparative exercise is most often presented in the mathematical language of the time. It appears in all aspects of the text — lexical, semantic, syntactic, representational, diegetic, and extra-diegetic discourse; and it undergoes variations, one of which coincides with the narrative climax of the story, the reversal of the expected proportion and of the emotion or judgment that is usually associated with it. Before illustrating the presence of the paradigm in all those aspects of the text, I shall group and examine the small number of emotional expressions attached to the operation just described.

3.a. *Operation and Feeling*

A "philosophical story" does not necessarily include torrents of affective phrases, and so those sentences in which strong feeling is represented make themselves noticed in a particular way. The use of the *naïf* in French and English didactic literature of this period is well known. Micromégas' naïveté is a limited sort; he is discerning and intelligent, but has never before left his own planet; so everything he sees is new and prompts comparison between what he is used to and what he encounters in his voyage. The observation of difference bears with it immediate comparison, and comparison results in preference and judgment. [22] The judgments are often ex-

---

[22] A nearly contemporary expression of this pattern was made by Condillac whose *Essai sur l'origine des connaissances humaines* (1746) and whose *Traité des sensations* (1754) presented Lockean sensualism and postulated the awakening of mental activity through sensual experience. In the *Traité,* the statue is capable of attention from which derives memory, the capacity to recall past sensations, and can thus compare them with present ones; and "dès qu'il y a

pressed first through the emotion they inspire: the hero's finding
difference between himself and others sometimes suscitates scorn,
which is translated by a smile or by laughter; one time, the difference releases amazed and admiring judgment. In the second paragraph, the narrator alerts the reader in an indirect statement of the
fundamental observation of difference and of the act of comparison:
"Les Etats ... comparés à l'empire ... ne sont qu'une très faible image des prodigieuses différences que la nature a mises dans tous les
êtres." Three paragraphs further on, the protagonist, although he is
used to new things, says the narrator, cannot resist smiling upon
seeing the tiny creatures of Saturn: "... il ne put ... se défendre de
ce sourire de supériorité qui échappe quelquefois aux plus sages."
The demonstrative adjective *ce* reflects the supposition that the reader
also knows the smile. The judgment of superiority is prolonged by
the phrase "Il s'en moqua un peu d'abord avec ses gens ..." but his
intelligence permits him to understand that even a dwarf can be
"un être pensant." This expression renders vulnerable the strict and
direct relation between size and value (small size equals small value)
and thus prepares by relativizing it the greatest suprise represented
in the story, that showing the smallest creatures accurately taking a
giant's measure. The movement thus sketched goes from astonishment to a first judgment, scorn; then upon closer examination and
reflection, it passes to a second, revised judgment, to acceptance,
and even to admiration. Yet another reversal will form the last
judgment made by the protagonists: the theologian's astonishing
claims will revive their scorn. In all cases, it is clear that the statement of difference and its attendant feeling of surprise can result in
either deflation or inflation in the value-judgment assigned to its
source. The emotion caused in the Sirian by the Saturnians' startling
difference is reciprocal. He also surprises *them*: "Il se familiarisa
avec les Saturniens, après les avoir étonnés." Near the end of the
fourth chapter, seeing men in their boat perched on his thumbnail,
the protagonist begins to laugh "pour la seconde fois" — the nar-

---

comparison, il y a jugement," says Condillac (Chapitre II.15), judgment
consisting essentially of perceiving relations *(rapports)*. Astonishment plays a
part in the statue's apprenticeship also, making it feel more sharply the difference between its mode of being and leading to greater care in the comparison
of sensations and the judgment of their relation (II.18).

rator is counting — this laughter is deflating since its cause is "l'excès de petitesse." In Chapter Five the pleasure of discovery makes the hero cry out with joy as he manages to see the creatures better with the aid of the microscope he has devised; novelty is one of the reasons: "... par le plaisir de voir des objets si nouveaux." The reciprocity of astonishment continues in the reaction of this new set of tiny creatures; like the Saturnians amazed by the sound of Micromégas' voice, the earthlings are astonished: "Si jamais il y a eu quelqu'un d'étonné, ce furent les gens qui entendirent ces paroles" (Ch. 6).

In the next paragraph, the Saturnian dwarf is stupefied when the "atoms" measure him and the hero draws an explicit lesson from this fact: "Je vois plus que jamais qu'il ne faut juger de rien sur sa grandeur apparente." He thereby completes a step toward this principle, the step made in his according the category of *être pensant* to the Saturnians who were much smaller than he. In the second paragraph of the last chapter (7), he once again insists on the astonishment provoked by his observation, and this time pity is the emotion that results from contrast and comparison: "... ému de pitié pour la petite race humaine, dans laquelle il découvrit de si étonnants contrastes." The Saturnian also continues to be astonished ("étonné de leurs réponses") before the scientific knowledge possessed by the earthlings. The greatest amazement is attained when the theologian declares that all the universe was made uniquely for him and for his kind. The most violent emotion of the story is released, and the demonstrative pronoun once again supposes the reader's recognition of the reaction and her complicity in it, "ce rire inextinguible qui, selon Homère, est le partage des dieux." The attendant movements of the two giants caught in uncontrollable laughter pronounce severe judgment on the theologian and signify true philosophy.

3.b. *Relation and Proportion*

Surprise associates itself with the process of observation, comparison, and judgment in the diegetic part of the story. The three-step process is also represented by the narrator and produced by the reader; and in its second step, comparison, it is often expanded and even quantified by an elaborate and at the same time tongue-in-cheek use of various mathemathical rules of proportion.[23] The constant relating, opposing, comparing, and contrasting occur in all aspects of the text: it is stated by the narrator, lived and stated by the characters, and performed by the competent reader who recognizes the echoes and correction of the Pascal-like statement of proportions, the infinitely great and the infinitely small. The comparisons invoked and performed are of two kinds: good and bad. The good are those made by the narrator, the reader, and the hero; the bad, by the Saturnian dwarf — a character — and by Pascal — a presence not incarnated. I shall illustrate these assertions by following again the very first lines of the story. I continue to assume that this sort of analysis discovers another kind of instruction given to the reader, that of the profound paradigms the tale can impose.

The description of the protagonist in the first paragraph is made in absolutes, except for his name which is the emblem of relativity. Then from the second paragraph onward the signifier is imbued with the relativizing brought about by comparisons, and it thus constantly transmits considerations of proportions both in what is said and in what is done. The narrator there attributes an exercise to algebraists (to geometers instead in the editions before 1754); it requires using the rule of proportions: a (man's height) is to b (the earth's circumference) as c (Micromégas' height) is to d, where d is the unknown, the circumference of Sirius. This is a mathematical model of reasoning by analogy (article "Proportion," *Encyclopédie*, tome XIII, 466b). Wade called attention to the fact that Voltaire read at Cirey and mocked in a letter to Maupertuis portions of Christian Wolff's *Elementa matheseos universal* (Geneva, 1735) in which the German philosopher used the rule of proportion in several steps in order to calculate the probable size of the eventual inhab-

---

[23] For serious definitions and examples of this simple rule, one may consult the articles "Proportion," "Règle (de trois)," "(de trois inverse)," and "Progression," of the *Encyclopédie*. Voltaire's own remark, made in the twenty-fifth of the *Lettres philosophiques,* seems to comment both on the Secretary-Fontenelle's poetic comparisons and on the narrator's mathematical playfulness in the philosophical story: "Une comparaison n'est preuve ni en poésie ni en prose: elle sert en poésie d'embellissement, et en prose elle sert à éclaircir et à rendre les choses plus sensibles. Les poètes qui ont comparé les malheurs des grands à la foudre qui frappe les montagnes feraient des comparaisons contraires si le contraire arrivait." See also Jean Sareil, "L'Exagération comique dans les contes de Voltaire," *French Literature Series,* 2 (1975), 50-63.

itants of Jupiter (Wade, pp. 55-58). In the article "Planète" of the *Encyclopédie* (vol. 12, 1765), D'Alembert later translated a portion of Wolff's calculation and also made fun of it. The language of the computations attributed to the algebraists in the story shows well enough that it ridicules them and their methods: "gens toujours utiles au public," possible antiphrasis; and three expressions showing their presumptions — "sur le champ," "qu'il faut absolument," and "au juste." The statement "Rien n'est plus simple et plus ordinaire dans la nature." is also potentially antiphrastic and can be read as "Nothing is in fact more extravagant than this kind of calculation." The narrator says that the algebraists will reverse the direction of Wolff's proportion, for they know the height of Sirius' inhabitant and calculate its circumference from the proportion of man's height to the circumference of their planet. The narrator improves upon the foolishness by stating the "answer" not as an absolute number but as another proportion: the circumference of Sirius calculated by this method is twenty-one million six-hundred thousand times that of the earth.

Propositions accumulate as a third and a sort of fourth appear immediately, and they complicate considerably the kinds of production of sense in this paragraph: "Les Etats de quelques souverains d'Allemagne ou d'Italie, dont on peut faire le tour en une demi-heure, comparés à l'empire de Turquie, de Moscovie ou de la Chine, ne sont qu'une très faible image des prodigieuses différences que la nature a mises dans tous les êtres." One notes *quelques,* which was used to modify *algébristes* at the beginning of the paragraph and which modifies *souverains* here; its meaning, "a small or a certain number of," has minimizing value in both cases, considering especially the scorn of the algebraists expressed in the ways already mentioned and given this repetition of the locution. The first proportion that was partially given in the sentence quoted is $a:b::c:d$; the half-hour tour is to Germany and Italy as a lengthy one is to the three great empires. These two groups of states are compared to each other — the word *comparée* is embedded in the middle of the sentence — their confrontation seen as a proportion forms a merely feeble image of the prodigious differences between all creatures. This last relation is offered as a permanent or archetypal structure, and all things shall thus be seen through their difference from others, in proportion to each other, and in comparison.

The tour that one can make of these countries recalls the figure of the circumference of the planets mentioned just before; and it introduces another tour or circumference, Micromégas' waist, of which it is a question in the new proportions that follow in the next paragraph. This new calculation is attributed to "our" sculptors and painters, and it is truncated. The steps — a man's height is to his waist as Micromégas' height is to his waist — are being spelled out, but the answer presumably obtained in this way is given as soon as the problem is posed. If the reader wishes to amuse herself by working backwards in the problem, 120,000 *pieds de roi* are to 50,000 as 5 are to 2, she sees that this time the narrator supplies what was unknown in the problem posed (the giant's waist) and does not say what was presumed given, the earthling's waist. Following the operational schema described above (I.3.a.), this comparison also leads to judgment — "ce qui fait une très jolie proportion" — and the judgment is double. The words *jolie proportion* are probably first understood as the esthetic valorizing of the giant's body, but it can also be understood as a sign of the mind's — ours and his — satisfaction with the amusement of such mathematical manipulations performed both forward and backward.

The editions published before 1754 contained another sentence stating other proportions and inviting calculation of the length of the hero's nose. The joke was wearing thin, but Voltaire had once again varied the form. It was not a true proportion, but it expressed two relationships (*rapports* or *raisons,* art. "Proportion," *Enc.*): "Son nez étant le tiers de son visage, et son beau visage étant la septième partie de la hauteur de son beau corps, il faut avouer que le nez du Sirien a six mille trois cents trente-trois pieds de Roi plus une fraction, ce qui étoit à démontrer" (Wade, p. 120). The good student finds there a problem of this type: given Micromégas' height and the fact that his face is to his height as one is to seven and his nose to his face as one to three, how long is his nose? The reader of Rabelais will find familiar the comic preciseness, and everyone recognizes the playful variants on a powerful mathematical tool.

The "quant à son esprit" of the fourth paragraph shows recognition of the Cartesian and conventional distinction between mind and body, and it announces another comparison. His body is marvelous, and now here is his equally extraordinary mind; the relation (*raison* or *rapport*) is a direct one. The mind, one half of that comparison (equal proportion) is presented also by two other direct comparisons: the first, that with all other minds, results in a superlative — "un des plus cultivés que nous ayons"; and the second, that with the single mind of Blaise Pascal, results in another direct relation in which the giant emerges again as superior, the seventeenth-century genius fading by comparison: Micromégas invented fifty of Euclid's propositions compared to Pascal's inventing only thirty-two.

Before 1754	1754 and after
... c'est dixhuit de plus que Blaise Pascal, lequel après en avoir deviné trente-deux en se jouant, à ce que dit sa Sœur, aima mieux depuis être un assez médiocre Métaphysicien, qu'un grand Géomètre. (Wade, p. 120)	C'est dix-huit de plus que Blaise Pascal, lequel, après en avoir deviné trente-deux en se jouant, à ce que dit sa sœur, devint depuis un géomètre assez médiocre, et un fort mauvais métaphysicien.

In both versions the devaluation of Pascal is expressed as a comparison. In the change from "un assez médiocre Métaphysicien, qu'un grand Géomètre" to "un géomètre assez médiocre, et un fort mauvais métaphysicien," Voltaire replaces the comparison that treated Pascal with respect by two absolute condemnations of him in both his roles. The protagonist presumably looks even better *by comparison*. The reversal of the order giving metaphysician before geometer permitted *métaphysicien* to be the last word in the sentence preceding the description of the hero's research. In this way it sharpens the contrast, another comparison that is permanent in the story, between useless metaphysics and interesting, sure scientific research. The long sentence describing his observations and his being persecuted for having published them prolongs the contrast with metaphysicians by re-introducing them in the figure of the *muphti* (theologian), his persecutor, who is concerned about the "forme substantielle" of fleas and snails. His language points to Aristotle, to Aquinas, and to scholasticism.

Inviting the reader's performance by giving statistical information suggests comparison with her own world: Sirius' smallest insect is one hundred feet in diameter and can scarcely be seen with a microscope; the trial lasted two hundred and twenty years; the banishment, eight hundred. Another comparison is prepared by the narrator and responded to by the reader; he proposes the emotion — astonishment — no doubt aroused at the view of the conveyances used on Sirius. Insisting on the difference, he diminishes the reader's ordinary vehicles with the *ne ... que*: "Ceux qui ne voyagent qu'en chaise de poste ou en berline seront sans doute étonnés des équipages de là-haut...." The narrator continues to instruct the reader in the proper reaction to radical difference and thus develops his epistemology of astonishment. We have seen that in addition to inducing it in the reader, the narrator also depicts it in his heroes. During the telling of the astral voyage the narrative voice makes another comparison, this time between the hero's method of observation, "sur les lieux," and Monsieur Derham's distant view through his telescope; once again, Micromégas is valorized by a contrast.

The end of the first stage of the voyage corresponds to the end of the chapter and releases a frenzy of comparisons or relations and of proportions as well. The hero himself makes one on arrival, that between his own planet and Saturn. The narrator takes over and fills in part of a new proportion: Saturn is to earth, 900 to 1, as its inhabitants are to earth's, that is, one-thousand *toises* to x, where x is something we already know but which he leaves uncalculated in *toises*. It would be one and one-tenth *toise,* but like this proportion, all the others in the story, is approximate — 1.1 *toise* equals about 6.6 feet. A banal or "poetic" comparison follows: "Il s'en moqua un peu d'abord avec ses gens, à peu près comme un musicien italien se met à rire de la musique de Lulli quand il vient en France." The sign of it here is the word *comme,* and the proportion implied is this: Micromégas' mockery is to the Saturnians' worth as an Italian musician's is to Lulli's music. That is, the alert reader understands, initial scorn results from novelty or difference and is subject to revision or correction if the musician, like the giant visitor, has a "bon esprit." The parallel should be prolonged since the Sirian's modification of his first impression ("... il comprit bien vite que ...") can be proportionate to the musician's change of opinion, and so on. This has biographical confirmation in the fact that Voltaire liked Lulli's music (Wade, p. 151). A final comparison is conducted, this time between the hero and his new friend, the Secretary, who is first described with the phrase applied to Micromégas himself at the beginning of the chapter, "homme de beaucoup d'esprit"; this briefly puts them on equal footing. The narrator's further description of the Saturnian gradually separates the two, however; and the direct depreciation of the Secretary makes him fade considerably in the comparison: "qui n'avait à la vérité rien inventé," "qui faisait passablement de petits vers et de grands calculs." The lexical opposition between *petit* and *grand* is abnegated by the sense of the adverb; both epithets diminish the noun they modify.

The contrast between the two thus established, it will be used to compare the investigatory methods and reasoning powers of both; and judgment favoring the hero implicitly and explicitly will each time be pronounced. For instance, as they search for the inhabitants (Ch. 4) and begin to communicate with them (Ch. 5, 6), the Sirian and his companion converse, and their exchanges form a fragmented, that is, distributed discourse on method. Micromégas criticizes the Secretary's hasty enthymemes or truncated syllogisms; his observations are cursory and he rushes to a deduction. His reasoning follows the pattern (b) I don't see anyone; therefore (c) there is no one (Ch. 4). He expresses only the second and third steps of a syllogism the premise of which — (a) not to be seen is not to be — might be viewed as the negative reversal of Berkeley's *esse est percipi*. The Secretary's premise makes as little sense to the hero as Berkeley's made to Voltaire (*Traité de métaphysique*, 1734). In Chapter Six the unrepentant Secretary executes a similar deduction, again omitting the premise — (a) not to be heard is not to speak — and saying only the last two steps: (b) I don't hear them speaking; therefore (c) they cannot speak: "il n'entendait point parler nos atomes, et il supposait qu'ils ne parlaient pas." Throughout these exchanges, Micromégas shows himself to be a better observer; the opposition between the two giants is implicit in these juxtaposed replies: "Mais, dit le nain, j'ai bien tâté. —Mais, répondit l'autre, vous avez mal senti" (Ch. 4). He is also better at forming judgments: "En vérité, ce qui fait que je pense qu'il n'y a ici personne, c'est qu'il me paraît que des gens de bon sens ne voudraient pas y demeurer. —Eh bien, dit Micromégas, ce ne sont peut-être pas non plus des gens de bon sens qui l'habitent" (Ch. 4). [24] The narrative voice continues using

---

[24] As the *être pensant* quoted above could be received as an echo of both Descartes and Pascal, so this repetition of *bon sens* could eventually recall

the language of comparison and instructs the reader to take the hero
as a model of method; he calls him a "bien meilleur observateur
que son nain" (Ch. 6). The comparison between the two protagonists
is carried throughout the story explicitly by the narrator. The relation itself involves their uses of comparison. One type of it is
condemned and its practitioner reprimanded. It constitutes a further
variant of the Saturnian's poor use of analogy. Micromégas himself
condemns his friend's attempts at poetic comparison, rejecting his
use of *comme* to define nature: "... encore une fois, la nature est
comme la nature. Pourquoi lui chercher des comparaisons?" He
replaces the Secretary's repeated poetic *comme* by a mathematical
combien (Ch. 2).

Another way to appreciate the pervasiveness of the comparative
structure is to understand the kinds of decoding it inspires. There
are many comparisons explicitly made by the narrator, those already
mentioned and others to which he calls attention by naming them
or by reinforcing them. In these cases the mere registering in consciousness of the first sense causes the comparison to be grasped in
an immediate way. To criticize Castel's belief that Mars has no
moons, he invokes a comparative reasoning that implies an inverse,
although approximate proportion — earth is to one moon as two
moons are to a five-times-smaller Mars — guaranteed by "ceux qui
raisonnent par analogie." In the sentence that follows he mocks
this kind of reasoning even as he uses it to mock Castel: "Ces bons
philosophes-là [those who reason by analogy] savent combien il
serait difficile que Mars, qui est si loin du soleil, se passât à moins
de deux lunes" (Ch. 3). The last implies yet another proportion,
and it confirms the necessity of more than one moon; not only is it
smaller (inverse proportion), but it is also farther from the sun and
so in need of more light (direct proportion). In the same paragraph
the narrator employs "poetic" comparison: "... ils passèrent leur
chemin comme deux voyageurs qui dédaignent un mauvais cabaret
de village et poussent jusqu'à la ville voisine." The juxtaposition
between the little planet Mars and a bad hotel is piquant, and it is
so partly because *comme,* which signifies sameness, succeeds once

the first sentence of the *Discours de la méthode,* which bears the potential
for relativism, the major lesson of Voltaire's tale.

again in exacerbating difference instead. I would call this a kind of antiphrasis, or one might call it *anticomparatio*. Other examples of the narrator's performing and naming his comparisons exist in Chapters Four and Five. Comparing the picture wherein the Saturnian pants to keep up with the Sirian to the scene in which a lapdog follows a captain of the Prussian guard, he names his act and asks the reader's indulgence: "(s'il est permis de faire de telles comparaisons)" (Ch. 4). When he depicts the giants' astonishment and pleasure at seeing the earthlings (Ch. 5), he compares it to the *étonnante découverte* made by Van Leeuwenhoek and Hartsoeker, thereby assimilating the two couples by the emotion and the instrument common to them and depreciating mankind by the implied proportion: spermatozoa are to Leeuwenhoek as mankind is to Micromégas.

Another type of comparison is that made by the characters in the story in their own words. In Chapter Six, the hero discovers with surprise the principle of inverse proportion when he learns that the infinitely small men have a mind superior to that of the great animals he has seen in the sky. This comparison between size and worth that marks the climactic series of things the hero learns in his quest (Section 2. above) stands out from almost all the other comparisons; they were between one size and another size, both of beings and of planets. At the same time, the comparison is not entirely new since a rather frivolous version of the inverse proportion between size and worth occurred in Chapter Three where we were reassured that the small size of the Secretary's mistress, 660 *toises,* was compensated for by "bien des agréments." Further, when the Saturnian began making mistakes, the reader had already learned that bigger was not always better. Of course, in the *histoire* he is smaller than the hero anyway, and so the latter expects little from him. This preparation for reversal operates only for the reader. The compensatory principle in comparison is put to vaster and more serious didactic purpose in the last episode. The double inversion discovered by the hero — certain small bodies are to their large minds as certain large bodies ("ces superbes animaux que j'ai vus dans le ciel") are to smaller minds — is expanded to both extremes of size by one of the earthlings who speaks to him: a dive toward the infinitely small — "il est en effet des êtres intelligents beaucoup plus petits que l'homme" — and a shot up to the infinitely large, passing by a repetition of the infinitely small and making, by the use of proportion, an infinite progression of large to small, large to small relations that relativize everything: "Il lui apprit enfin qu'il y a des animaux qui sont pour les abeilles ce que les abeilles sont pour l'homme [little animals: bees: : bees: men], ce que le Sirien lui-même était pour ces animaux si vastes dont il parlait [little animals: bees: : Sirian: big animals], et ce que ces grands animaux sont pour d'autres substances [little animals: bees: : big animals: other substances even bigger] devant lesquelles ils ne paraissent que comme des atomes." This development extends comparison to the entire chain of being in the universe. In Chapter Seven the hero tries to reason from what he has just learned by employing proportion and analogy: since mankind has so little matter and seems entirely mind, it must thus have very pure joys and spend its life in loving and thinking. They tell him he is wrong. He tries another time: since men know so much about physical nature, they must know a lot about ideas and the soul. He learns that they do not and says that though small bodies have big minds and this is good, the same small bodies also have infinite pride and this is deplorable. In this way the *récit* in its successivity reveals the paradigm; it is displayed additively instead of simultaneously, and its sequence permits the comparison of two comparisons — body and mind with body and pride. It thereby leaves man thrice relativized. The hero's two failures in analogical reasoning — pure joy, ideas and soul — or rather the failure of analogy itself, confirms and imposes the climate of uncertainty produced by the inversion according to which size and intellect are not proportional to each other. Analogy and proportion break down when Micromégas has to learn about mankind. What their break-down does to his and to the narrator's apparently successful use of them earlier in the story surely offers another paradigm, that of the text's deconstructing itself (Section 5, below). The lack of proportion makes man jar, clash, and contrast with the order of the universe, and he seems out of place in the chain of being. The contrast he creates by comparison condemns him.

Several comparisons occur only upon the reader's decoding of meaning; they are explicitly represented neither in the narrator's discourse, extradiegetic, nor in the characters', diegetic. The images and gestures of the giants and important parts of the narrator's vocabulary require a more active decoding for their potential meaning to be actualized. For example, one can understand either that the visitors' eyes are too big to see the little men, or that the men are too small to be seen without microscopes. The giants' voices are too loud, or it is men's ears that are too fragile. Micromégas' hands are too large or man's boats too small, and so on. Similar reversals and reflections are prompted in reception of certain words themselves: *étang, mare, taupinière* for the Mediterranean, the ocean, and the earth require translation or substitution and thus constantly offer the comparative structure by inciting its performance. These words juxtapose two referents that are felt to be incommensurate. [25] Their incommensurability is stressed in gesture and in lexicon by this juxtaposition of unassimilable things. Comparison is forced upon the reader again and again; and by showing that "there's no comparison," it makes man insignificant by comparison. These are not the places of infinite expansion described at the end of Chapter Six, where big and little are relativized by each being seen as at the same time big and little depending on the things to which they are compared. On the contrary these movements and the lexical juxtapositions are absolutes, and they reduce absolutely the pretensions of mankind.

3.c. *Pascalian Intertexts*

It is now a commonplace that all literary works contain in some way other texts, that they imply their existence, and that they at the same time suppose, absorb, and transform certain of those that precede them. The relation that the new work maintains with its past may take many forms. It can imitate or repeat a past text in different ways: 1) affirmative: by taking the earlier formulation seriously for its own ends; 2) negative: by refusing or deforming it even while invoking it; 3) conflictual, by citing or implying it while actively dialoguing with it. The elucidation of the kinds of

---

[25] Wade drew up lists of all the words and expressions associated with smallness and those with bigness, pp. 94ff. Jean Sareil studies this phenomenon as well as commenting on its Pascalian aspects and on the use of comparison in general in "Le Vocabulaire de la relativité dans *Micromégas* de Voltaire," *Romanic Review,* 64 (1973), 273-85.

relations literary discourse maintains with its past and even with its own future is far from complete, but this rough categorization is usable.[26] During the seventeenth and eighteenth centuries, a great many authors of all sorts expressed astonishment and wonder at the infinitely large worlds revealed by the telescope and at the infinitely small worlds seen under the microscope later. Wade gives samples of the contemplations that plunged their minds into the microcosmic and raised it to the cosmic (pp. 66-77). He isolates from them four key words that were always accompanied by the expression of their inconceivability — *divisibility, abundance, proportion,* and *relativity* — the last two naming the concepts that I identify as structuring the principal meaning derivable from *Micromégas.* Voltaire read many of these meditations and was himself an experimenter, the owner of microscopes, as is well known. It would seem that inside this generalized, collective "text" that marveled while contemplating greatness and smallness, the *expression* of the drama of it that most attracted and repelled him was Blaise Pascal's, particularly that fragment called "Disproportion de l'homme." The comparison developed there and in Méré's famous letter to Pascal was repeated in the *Logique de Port-Royal* and elsewhere before Voltaire gave to it his own formulation (Wade, pp. 65-66). It is thoroughly exploited in his story: its expression is in some ways affirmative, for his text presents man's disproportion as fact; there is also a parodic presentation of part of it, and it is thereby refuted; finally, part of it is omnipresent in a conflictual relation, in a "Yes, but" that nuances both the acceptance and the refutation of other parts and that enters into dialogue with Pascal's view of man in the universe.

Before passing to examples, we may note that in this aspect also the text can create a certain competence in the reader. Those grasping the specific reference to Pascal certainly draw a different kind of enjoyment or annoyance from its presence, but the reader who is thoughtful but ignorant of Pascal's text has the wherewithal to see what is at stake, for the refuted extremes or conclusions that

---

[26] Suleiman, "Le Récit," p. 481, follows Julia Kristeva, "Le Mot, le dialogue, et le roman," in *Séméiotikè* (Paris: Le Seuil, 1969); and both follow Mikhail Bakhtin, some of whose essays have been translated as *Esthétique et théorie du roman* by Daria Olivier (Paris: Gallimard, 1978) and whose *Rabelais and His World* has existed in English since 1968 (Cambridge, Mass.: MIT Press).

might be drawn from the fact of disproportion are present in their own condemnation. The fact that the story announced itself as *philosophique* leads even that kind of receiver to expect that by its very didacticism it is written in relation to something else, against or for that something, but definitely in the company of an idea or a doctrine that was expressed *elsewhere*. In this regard, Wade presents the fact of similarities with a group of thinkers including Pascal, Malebranche, Fontenelle, Locke, Leibniz, and Réaumur. Since Pascal's thoughts are the most likely then and now to be recognized as such, and since my perspective is reception and not genesis of the work, I shall not be concerned here with *influences* — Mandeville's bees, Réaumur's insects — but with the relation of concepts expressed in the text and referred to by its own conceptual structures. The *roseau pensant* (Pascal) or *être pensant* (Voltaire) does not seek its dignity in space, where it is insignificant — *roseau* — but in the regulation of its own thought-process — *pensant*. To the degree that any reader is aware of this text's being reflected in the dominant discourse — "Cet atome m'a mesuré! " — she is probably conscious of its affirmative nature, of the fact that its authority guarantees the dominant discourse in the new or more recent work. There is deviation from that authority, however, for the story restricts man's glory to that derivable from mathematical calculation. Despite a certain selectivity, text and intertext remain on this point univocal. The use of disproportion is in both cases humbling of man's pride. Pascal speaks of "une présomption aussi infinie que leur [men's] objet [first principles]"; and Voltaire, of "un orgueil presque infiniment grand." Furthermore, the spatial construct that Pascal's text inspires corresponds in some ways with Voltaire's. The Pascalian scheme of disproportion puts man directly in the center of infinitely small and of infinitely big multiple universes that he can imagine going off in both directions, "un milieu entre rien et tout." He is seen as big by relation to the microcosm and as little in relation to the macrocosm. To this situation and to these proportions in space, the geometer adds that in neither sense of the verb does man *comprehend* either extreme, and that he can never attain first principles. To try is to bear witness to presumption. The two areas, physical and metaphysical, are delineated by Voltaire's text as well, but man's exact place in the schema is different and the relation

FIGURE I.B

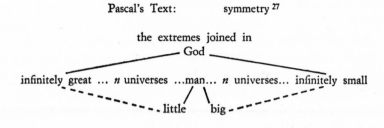

Pascal's Text: symmetry [27]

the extremes joined in
God
infinitely great ... *n* universes ...man... *n* universes... infinitely small
little big

$n = \infty$

Voltaire's Text: compensated asymmetry

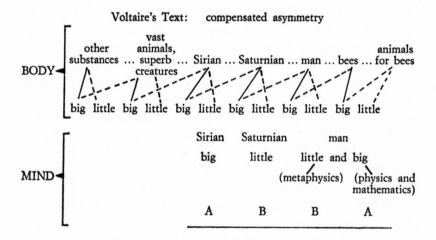

BODY

vast
other animals, animals
substances ... superb ... Sirian ... Saturnian ... man ... bees ... for bees
creatures
big little big little big little big little big little big little

MIND

	Sirian	Saturnian	man	
	big	little	little and big	
			(metaphysics)	(physics and mathematics)
	A	B	B	A

---

[27] Note that the word *symmetry* refers only to the words and concepts used to contrast man and the universe, the infinitely great and the infinitely small. It is clear elsewhere that in Pascal's view, the infinite is everywhere, in the great and in the small; that is, there is no infinite, for all is infinity, non-finite. The world is therefore not infinite in the sense that God is; it has a fundamental imperfection, the impossibility of unity. Large and small are concepts in this world, but God is an absolute infinity where they have no meaning. Pascal's thoughts on spatial infinity and its significance are not transmitted by the signified of the passage treated here. It is also true that Pascal disliked symmetry: in style, he condemned it. The symmetry of the passage being treated is imposed by its antithetical movement. My schematic interpretation of the word *milieu* should also be nuanced: man is not, for Pascal, the middle of a medieval hierarchy of creatures; he uses *milieu* here in a geometric or proportional sense.

between physical and metaphysical is not as simple. The intertextual space thus created is dialogic or conflictual since the two discourses differ from each other by displacement and not by opposition or refusal.

The space imagined by Pascal's *text* puts man in the middle of a straight line that is infinite. The line extends between two extremes; and man can never comprehend them. The resulting anguish can be assuaged by the line's becoming a circle, another line without end, where God contains and thus reconciles the extremes. Pretension to a human solution is vain. Man's place differs in *Micromégas*. He still stands between two extremes, but to one side of the continuum that joins them. The point of focus is off-center, the pattern asymmetrical, and the line finite at each end. The triad of named creatures defines individuals of three sizes. Their mental differences reverse the gradation in size and prevent the center, the Saturnian, from balancing the two sides. Man encloses two of the four members of a chiasma formed by aligning, according to size and to order of presentation, the three agents of the eighteenth-century cosmic plot. The affirmation and displacement of Pascal's scheme finally end in denial, for the weak and small creature of this particular text possesses in Voltaire's scheme *both* greatness and smallness in the exercise of mind. It is thus he instead of God who embraces two extremes.

How do these two views (Figure I.B) imply each other in the movement or unfolding of the story? The story begins with Micromégas; he is the first measure, and man is invoked from the start and repeatedly as smaller and inferior in the back-and-forth comparative movements. The giant seems by his name to be a middle term since like Pascal's man he is big by relation to some and small by relation to others. Dimensions greater than his are mentioned near the beginning — "... j'ai vu des mortels fort au-dessus de nous; j'en ai vu de fort supérieurs" (Ch. 2) — and they are stressed near the end (Ch. 6). This lesson is not elaborated at the beginning, for the text does not seem to humble its own hero as Pascal's does. The "superbes créatures" and "ces animaux si vastes" that dwarf him are themselves dwarfed by "d'autres substances devant lesquelles [ces grands animaux] ne paraissent que des atomes." Similarly, there are two degrees smaller than the hero; they are imagined at the other end of the scale, bees and what are "animals for bees." There is thus at the end a certain symmetry between Micromégas' situation and man's — each is two degrees from infinity in his own direction — and this resemblance reinforces the similarities of intellect that contrast with their difference in size. The resemblances are, however, only potential in the case of mankind; but the giant's being absolutely "human" in all but his size permits him to serve as a model of thinking for the little and inferior men, and this is another important difference with Pascal's scheme. The story's first creature is big and little only with respect to size, not to mind; the hero's intellect is presented as entirely admirable. Although he lacks certain information, he knows how to search and to reason and is not guilty of the *présomption* that Pascal assigns to his focal creature, man. [28] When Voltaire's text elaborates the nature of mankind, the mixture of little and big holds again for size, but the little-and-big paradox of mind is divided much differently. Pascal establishes symmetry between mind's and body's capacity: "Notre intelligence tient dans l'ordre des choses intelligibles le même rang que notre corps dans l'étendue de la nature." In the story, it is not that man's mind is great with respect to some other dimension and small with respect to another; it is big or little according to the proportion between its aim and its grasp in the physical sciences and to the disproportion between them in metaphysics.

In a passage written and then crossed out at the beginning of the *pensée* on disproportion, Pascal alluded to scientific discoveries, thus to man's capacity for knowledge of nature where nature is susceptible of being known by him if anything can be. This fragment shows a point of departure and an assignment of credit that resembles Voltaire's. Furthermore, the truth of the facts, the discovery of which permits grudging acknowledgment of man's powers, leads nonetheless to his humiliation in Pascal's thought: "Voilà où nous

---

[28] "C'est une chose étrange qu'ils [les hommes] ont voulu comprendre les principes des choses, et de là arriver jusqu'à connaître tout, par une présomption aussi infinie que leur objet. Car il est sans doute qu'on ne peut former ce dessein sans une présomption ou sans une capacité infinie, comme la nature" (*Œuvres complètes,* ed. L. Lafuma [Paris: Editions du Seuil, 1963], Fr. 199). It is, however, well-known that Pascal elsewhere sees man's glory in the fact that he is a *roseau pensant* and is capable of scientific discovery, as show the texts on progress in the *Opuscules.*

mènent les connaissances naturelles. Si celles-là ne sont pas véritables, il n'y a point de vérité dans l'homme; et si elles le sont, il y trouve un grand sujet d'humiliation, forcé à s'abaisser d'une ou d'autre manière." Voltaire, on the contrary, makes of this effort one of man's few glories and has his hero expand the inverse proportion between size and grasp of knowledge about the universe: "... s'il est possible qu'il y ait des êtres plus petits que ceux-ci, ils peuvent encore avoir un esprit supérieur à ceux de ces superbes animaux que j'ai vus dans le ciel ..." (Ch. 6). This extension of the inverse proportion to other worlds and beings goes with a vision of spots of intelligence sprinkled throughout the universe, and it conflicts richly with Pascal's idea according to which the sole repository of intelligence is pitiful man's almighty God. [29]

Pascal's text is merciless. Voltaire's mitigates the absolute nature of its condemnation by displacing and by specifying the limited incompetence. He positions yet another variety of mental and physical bigness and littleness: the Saturnian's place is between the two parallels-with-difference, Micromégas and man. The "dwarf" is bigger than one and smaller than the other, and he demonstrates philosophical weaknesses found also among mankind. He thus shares a trait with the domain above by his body, and by his mind with that below him. The story negates the picture of little man at the center of the universe and avoids Pascal's oxymoron of the insignificant center; it thereby rejects that particular kind of inverse proportion. By its definition of man's situation and skills, it also negates the idea that this insignificant little center — Pascal wrote but then crossed out the terms *humiliation* and *s'abaisser* — needs big-and-everywhere God: "... la réalité des choses ... une sphère infinie dont le centre est partout, la circonférence nulle part. Enfin c'est le plus grand caractère sensible de la toute-puissance de Dieu, que notre imagination se perde dans cette pensée." The circle is closed when the center that looks for itself finds itself in God: "Ces extré-

---

[29] This is *l'homme abandonné,* but elsewhere in Pascal one sees that intelligence is, approximately, God in man and makes man capable of salvation. Similarly, the concept of the insignificant center, which is presented in the text on the two infinities and which I mention below, must be completed by Pascal's famous phrase quoted on this page, that there is no center, and that the circumference is nowhere.

mités se touchent et se réunissent à force de s'être éloignés, et se retrouvent en Dieu, et en Dieu seulement." The absence of absolutes in the philosophical story defines yet a wider intertextual space, for its discourse contains no hint of the declaration of man's impotence, and so it actively denies that crucial part of the text that it equally overtly recalls, both lexically and in its comparative and astronomical structures. Voltaire's tale maintains a relation of maximum complexity with the discourse it echoes: it affirms portions of it — the fact of man's disproportion — denies its conclusions — man's impotence without God — and develops and sustains a conflictual confrontation with it by tracing, displacing, and elaborating its spatial scheme.

I have compared the relationships among the figures posited in each of the two texts (Figure I.B). This static view showed the symmetry of man, universe, and God depicted in Pascal's text; the asymmetrical status of relations produced by Voltaire's story had a sort of dynamic potential. In fact, the represented notion, the un-schematized movement depicted by the narration in both texts, marks another of their differences and poses the question of using the term *irony* to describe a part of their relation to each other. The term taken in any of its meanings — antiphrasis, situational, circumstantial, and mention or echo — seems inadequate to account for the complex relation that the story maintains with the thought that it mentions in many ways.

What relation does each provide for its reader? Pascal's narration is an injunction; it tells man what to think as it puts him on stage and dramatizes a certain movement. The first sentence — "Que l'homme contemple donc la nature entière dans sa haute et pleine majesté, qu'il éloigne sa vue des objets bas qui l'environnent" — launches an imaginary voyage of the eyes; they are directed first to the infinitely large, and then man, *revenu à soi*, is ordered to examine the prodigiousness of the infinitely small. The author, *meneur du jeu*, makes him pivot on his own center and then tells him that seeing himself between two abysses, he will be afraid and will tremble. The eighteenth-century story's center is a giant, not an ordinary man, but one having human characteristics. The movement in space goes in the opposite direction from that of the *pensée*. From far out in space, the hero moves gradually toward man, who is repeatedly relativized because implicit in all the comparisons made from the very beginning. Furthermore, the reader is in a freer and multiple relation with this text. Instead of finding places to hide, in the *pensée* she has her head turned this way and that and is subjected to the rude lesson of a director who has an overtly authoritarian narrative voice. In Voltaire's story she follows discourse offering various nooks and crannies of identification and play; she is free to let herself be spoken to by the narrator when he says *we* and *our,* to see herself in Micromégas' admirable character, or to consent to being part of ordinary humanity invoked in contrast to the hero, to his planet, and to both their proportions. The successive *emboîtements* that mark both texts go in two different directions in each signifier, and man's *mise-en-abyme* is itself considerably relativized in Voltaire's by the directions and by the place accorded to the infinitely small by relation to him. With which figure shall we identify Pascal's *homme* who contemplates? with Micromégas, the narrator, the reader, or the atoms? The actualizer of the text is plunged into a scientifico-ludic universe [30] seen through all the eyes *except* those of man, the represented character dwelling on earth.

I.4.   DEVALUATION AND MODAL COMMUNICATION

By making certain criticisms the didactic text functions in several disparaging modes as well as by direct statement. I understand modal communication to be that inviting one or more operations beyond simple reception of the sense of words: for example, caricature, parody and so on, all deprecatory. The operation can fully actualize the meaning or meanings of a given phrase, sentence, commentary, or scene. Voltaire's didacticism can express itself in direct verbal aggression [31] needing no adjustment of sense by the reader. In the first chapter, "Micromégas, nom qui convient fort à tous les grands," has as its target the great; its method is direct, demanding only the deciphering of the proper name, but not inviting a re-reading of the condemnatory utterance itself. Its agent is the

---

[30] Duisit, p. 29.
[31] I have borrowed this and other terms and concepts from Duisit, *Satire, Parodie....*

narrator's voice; and discounting the great promotes the relativism
that is the value put forward in all aspects of the story. Phrases like
"un géomètre assez médiocre et un fort mauvais métaphysicien,"
aimed at Pascal, "grand vétillard, et fort ignorant," aimed at theologians, and "... car nous autres nous ne concevons rien au-delà de
nos usages" are also of this openly hostile type. The narrator is agent
in each case; and a particular person, Pascal or the *muphti* or
mankind, undergoes the criticism. These instances of direct aggression are most frequent in the first chapter: there are six examples
against one or none in those that follow. It is possible that this
difference obeys a law by which the first lines of a short didactic
narrative, having no context to count on for more elaborate deval-
uations, move in a direct and rapid-fire manner to orient the reader
in the system of values being put forward. I summarize briefly other
examples of such direct attack; they are attributed to various agents
in the rest of the story. A direct lesson is drawn in Chapter Three.
By stating a fact, the narrator makes censorship the target: certain
beautiful secrets the hero learned on Jupiter would be available
except for *messieurs les inquisiteurs,* for which words one may read
French royal censors. The verb in the conditional tense is a further
sign of the narrative instance (Benveniste's *discours*). In Chapter
Five, the narrator chastises the Saturnian's mistaken perception and
expands the target of the reproach to persons outside the tale:
"... mais il se trompait sur les apparences; ce qui n'arrive que trop,
soit qu'on se serve ou non de microscopes." In the name of those
values, careful observation and good judgment, the hero also makes
didactic pronouncements of a direct sort: "... il ne faut juger de rien
sur sa grandeur apparente" (Ch. 6). In the last chapter, one of the
philosophers being interrogated ridicules directly his own kind and
its love of war: "... cent mille fous de notre espèce, couverts de cha-
peaux." Some of the terms he uses require translation and have as
targets men's pretensions — *cent mille autres animaux* (men) and
quelque tas de boue (disputed territory) — but the expression of
the ideas remains univocal, direct criticism.

  In a zone between direct criticism and satiric devaluation, one
finds already in the first chapter two remarks that require slight
adjustment in their reception; the same remarks and adjustments
will appear frequently in the chapters that follow: "sur notre petit

tas de boue" presents an image that must be translated by the finding of a simple *equivalence,* the earth, and by assignment of reduced value to the latter because of its continued co-presence with its reductive equivalent, the mudpile; and "algébristes, gens toujours utiles au public," demands a different sort of operation, *substitution* instead of co-existence and equivalence of two referents. The decoding of "gens toujours utiles" invites the substitution of its opposite, "not very useful." The principal instructions for this reversal are the appositive nature of the phrase, possible common-sense rejection of algebrists as being of public utility, and the extravagant calculations that follow the incidental clause and that are attributed to them.

A more extended devaluation, one demanding several kinds of manipulation of sense, occurs near the end of the first chapter.

> Il parcourut la voie lactée en peu de temps, et je suis obligé d'avouer qu'il ne vit jamais à travers les étoiles dont elle est semée ce beau ciel empyrée que l'illustre vicaire Derham se vante d'avoir vu au bout de sa lunette. Ce n'est pas que je prétende que Monsieur Derham ait mal vu, à Dieu ne plaise! mais Micromégas était sur les lieux, c'est un bon observateur, et je ne veux contredire personne.

Even a reader innocent of biographical or historical information does not hesitate to situate the target of the passage in Derham and in his idea of the heavens as a celestial sphere *(empyrée)*. The narrating *je* ridicules the vicar's idea in the name of a value, observation *sur place;* and he gives the advantage to the giant, the only creature able to perform a close examination. The phrase "je suis obligé d'avouer" announces something disagreeable for someone. Without the obligation, the speaker claims, he would certainly keep his remarks to himself. The demonstrative adjective *ce* makes possible the relativization of the *beau ciel empyrée* seen by Derham, and *se vante d'avoir vu* confirms his sky's status as ridiculous. The word *illustre,* appearing between *ce* and the verb, is not antiphrastic for those who know that he was illustrious, but it does not quite indicate merit either because of the sabotage — *je suis obligé, ce, se vante* — all around it. It thus transmits a certain hyperbolic sense that the reader corrects downward, thereby diminishing Derham. The exclamation that follows is susceptible of reversal; given the mockery preceding it, one may freely understand its opposite, "I do claim that M. Derham saw poorly." The two positive values of the hero, whom the narrator contrasts with the vicar, follow; and the brusque "je ne veux contredire personne" is literal for Micromégas and antiphrastic for Derham. In his careful study of references and sources, Ira Wade was concerned with Voltaire's feelings about Derham, and he noted that since it confirmed views the philosophe included in his own *Traité de métaphysique* (1734), it seems that the philosophe read the vicar's *Astro-theology* (1715) for its theological content. However, Wade also cites another author whom Voltaire knew and who was critical of Derham's archaic and metaphysical view of the *empyrée* (p. 23). I add that, if we care to consider Voltaire's probable intentions in the passage, a clue supporting them is given by a small change he made in it: in 1754 he replaced "étoiles dont on la croit semée" with the more positive "étoiles dont elle est semée" and thus sharpened the contrast between what Micromégas saw, a universe of fragments, and what the vicar brags about seeing, a solid sphere.

Most of the techniques of mockery in the first chapter consist of direct verbal aggression, but the two others just cited signal the possibility of re-reading and of translation, with or without replacement or substitution. In the remaining chapter the kinds of signals for devaluation of persons, of methods, and of opinions are mostly of the broad second type, inviting or making possible some operation in their reception, and in each case the optimal reading discerns both an agent and a patient or target as well as a positive value implied in the target's devaluation. In their details the methods vary, and I shall continue to classify them according to the kind of process necessary for their reception. I shall have little recourse here to the unstable term *irony,* although most of the concepts called *ironic* are fundamental to Voltaire's art. [32] The few other instances of direct verbal aggression are divided between the narrator and the hero. In Chapter Two, Micromégas is the agent; the Secretary, the patient; and the criticism is made in the name of objectivity

---

[32] The struggle to define types of irony continues, and the bibliography is vast. For recent debates, see the second number of the series "Linguistique et sémiologie," *L'Ironie* (Lyon: Presses Universitaires, 1978) and the number 36 of *Poétique* dedicated to that matter (1978).

in instruction: "... la nature est comme la nature. Pourquoi lui chercher des comparaisons? ... je veux qu'on m'instruise." Again in Chapter Four, he criticizes the Secretary's manner of reasoning. Although
the hero's voice has been added, extradiegetic didacticism also continues in full force and seems to direct itself, once and gently, against
even the protagonist himself: the narrator says that the pair of
giants told each other a little of what they knew "et beaucoup de
ce qu'ils ne savaient pas .... " The criticism of vain discussion is
made in the name of speaking only of what one truly knows.
A favorite target, the Secretary's manner of comparing and judging,
is attacked by both voices in the same chapter: the narrator says that
he "jugeait quelque fois trop vite," and the hero politely makes him
feel that "c'était raisonner assez mal." The lightest criticism of this
sort is a reference to the *père* Castel "qui écrira contre l'existence
des deux lunes de Mars" (Ch. 3), which may be understood as not
good since there is no reason for bringing it up otherwise, and
which seems to be said in the name of nothing in particular except
the author's irritation against Castel, historically verified (Wade,
p. 156). Nevertheless, it is consistent with the narrator's as well
as the author's steady attack on the wrong-headedness of churchmen
who meddle in science.

The passages requiring translation by reversal that results in
doubling or in substitution increase in frequency throughout the
story. The entire first conversation between the hero and the Secretary (Ch. 2), their exploration of the earth (Ch. 4), the exploits
needed to see and to hear man (Ch. 5), all devalue the earth and its
inhabitants and suscitate in the reader the continuing act of comparison that I have already described. All the astonishment over the
dwarf's *peu* — senses, time, properties of matter — invites seeing
how much grander his *peu* is than mankind's *beaucoup*. This exercise
ends in a *chute,* the fact that the two plan a *petit voyage philosophique* through the galaxy. Once more *petit* must be read at the
same time as *grand*. This and all the expressions that invite such
corrections and create relativization — *petite lueur, petit atome, tas
de boue,* etc. — maintain the receiver in a constant state of alert,
tending to make this flexibility in reception a habitual way of seeing,
at least while she is reading the story.

From the third chapter onward the methods of devaluation require increasing activity by the reader, and one-sentence remarks gradually give way to a preponderance of longer discourse and entire scenes that provide more complex sense-making even before they give rise to various operations of substituted, parallel, or reversed meanings. Two descriptions of inconsistent behavior — the Secretary's mistress who faints at his departure, then rapidly consoles herself with someone else, and the archbishop whose church persecutes an author for certain writings, but who keeps them at home anyway and lets the narrator read them — leave the reader to see the contradiction and to consider that in both cases hypocrisy is being condemned (Ch. 3). The narrator promises to relate frankly his travelers' first exploration and adds that he does so "sans y rien mettre du [s]ien: ce qui n'est pas un petit effort pour un historien." The historians' lack of objectivity is the target, and the reader has to grasp this in two steps: first, through *pas un petit effort,* a litotes for a *big effort,* the affirmation being expressed by the negation of its opposite; and second, if objectivity is a big effort for a historian, members of that profession are not inclined to make the effort, this meaning coming from a reversal required to arrive at an enthymeme — historians are not objective; therefore, they are bad. The missing premise is "objectivity is good," the positive value that one may infer from the remark. These acrobatics are surely instantaneous for the trained receiver, but the point here is to describe the moderately elaborate steps of such comprehension.

Another kind of potential for devaluation arises from situations in which a protagonist by innocent remarks and questions transmits criticism of the object he investigates. The Secretary's speculations do this at the same time as they reveal the defects in his own reasoning (Ch. 6); by the nature of his own discourse (*indirect libre*) — "D'ailleurs, comment ces êtres imperceptibles auraient-ils les organes de la voix, et qu'auraient-ils à dire?" — and by his method of devaluing men, he himself appears ignorant and unskilled. The reader has grasped the fact of an inferior creature's scorn of man, and the superior hero explicitly confirms the reader's condemnation of the Secretary's impulsive judgment. A simple use of the same technique consists of certain questions the hero asks of men in Chapter Seven; his interrogative makes him another agent of this version of Socratic irony, although it is impossible to decide if his character supposedly includes the deliberate pose of ignorance (Socrates) or if consciousness of the devaluing effect of innocence is shared only by author and reader (Rica in the *Lettres persanes*). The reader takes as false the innocent supposition that Micromégas addresses to the creatures sitting on his thumbnail; the statement "Puisque vous savez si bien ce qui est hors de vous, sans doute vous savez encore mieux ce qui est en dedans." flatters mankind; and the reader replaces it by its correction — men have no good and single answer to questions about the soul. The correction performed by the reader predicts the confusion displayed by the philosophers' contradictory answers. Two positive values, metaphysical modesty and consciousness of limits, are implied in this criticism; and they are incarnated three paragraphs later by the disciple of John Locke.

The narrator excels in putting on stage people who ridicule themselves. In a simple scene of this type, he evokes a hypothetical reader, an army captain, and imagines that upon his reading criticism of virtually fruitless battles, he will raise the hats of his troops by two feet. The narrator then states explicitly the lesson to be drawn from the captain's supposed effort to be *grand:* "... mais je l'avertis qu'il aura beau faire, et que lui et les siens ne seront jamais que des infiniment petits" (Ch. 5). Just before the portrait of the captain, he had made other (diegetic) targets render themselves ridiculous: he painted the agitation exerted to no effect by sailors and geometers when they were moved into the giant's hand. The moral quality that is criticized in the targeted creatures is still man's pretentiousness; the positive value implied, modesty. The narrator once again draws the lesson, both from the image of vain agitation and from the scene: a tiny ship is seen by the giant only with the aid of a microscope. The moral made explicit by the dramatization requires an operation in its reception, for it is another of the rare examples of antiphrasis: "Je ne prétends choquer ici la vanité de personne, mais je suis obligé de prier les importants de faire ici une petite remarque avec moi ..." and what follows is another instance of comparison of proportion: man is to earth as an animal of one six-hundred thousandths of an inch is to a ball two feet around. The antiphrasis presenting the proportion can be translated as "I want to shock the vanity of the important by pointing out that they are nothing"; and the narrator, by the antiphrase, by his reluctance *(je suis obligé),* [33] and by the modesty *(petite remarque)* of what he must say, makes a triple play for conveying the idea that the demonstration is being dragged out of him. It is in fact direct and violent, lifting the game of proportion out of the safety of diegesis and making it concern the emitter and receiver themselves: *nous* and *vous* appear twice each and *les nôtres,* once. The represented action is only a pretext for representing proportion, the fundamental problem of the text.

The powers of agitated humans to ridicule themselves are deployed twice more, once in each of the last two chapters. Their reaction to the voice of the hero resembles the agitation unleashed earlier by his moving them, but this scene is expanded to include the tics of other professions: sailors swear, the chaplain prays, and the philosophers invent systems (Ch. 6). The images isolate one trait of each and thus may be named parodic or burlesque. The representation of such characters by a single gesture has the effect of ridiculing them but alone does not bear the strong implication of an opposing positive value. The third example is even more lengthy and includes the direct speech of the targets, various philosophers (Ch. 7). In answering the hero's question about the soul, each man devalues himself and the philosophy he represents by exaggeration, sweeping claims, faulty logic, and so on. The parody here is that of their discourse, not of gestures alone; and so the opposing value is once again clear — philosophical modesty. This didactic measure repeats itself in two more steps. For once, the positive value itself appears instead of remaining implicit. Lockean discourse is valorized: "Je ne sais pas . . . ." The *petit disciple* appears truly *grand* by the contrast between his speech and the preceding, ridiculous ones. The receiver's tendency to approve him is confirmed by the Sirian's smile, by the narrator's litotes, "... il ne trouva pas celui-là le moins sage," and by the Saturnian's impulse to hug him. The third moment of the didactic climax brings the return of a negative portrait. The devaluation of the Roman Catholic theologian depends upon a cluster of operations to be performed, and this fact gives all the more reason

---

[33] A similar use of obligation and reluctance occurs in Chapter Five, "... je suis obligé d'avouer ..." (p. 66 above).

for applying neither the single word *ironic* nor *satiric* to any stretch of discourse. The conjunction *mais* introduces the portrait and announces opposition; the phrase *par malheur* reinforces it and asks the reader's condemnation; the lexeme *animalcule* is pejorative. Further, the gesture and the speech contradict each other: he looks the giants up and down and then declares the universe made for his own race of little men. That guidance is given by the narrator and by the target's pretensions; the protagonists also take their turn in destroying the speaker's claims to importance, for they cannot stop laughing. Finally, the cosmos itself takes over as agent of ridicule. Crushing circumstance makes the boat on which the theologian stands fall into the pocket of the smaller giant's pants. The detail of the pants was added in 1754, their pockets presumably being the most degrading kind. The boat cannot be found for a long while.

Just in case the point is not clear by now, the narrator has the hero declare his anger before the infinitely great pride of infinitely small creatures; this explicit reaction was added to the edition of 1754 and shows Voltaire pounding his lesson home. He also expanded at that time the last episode of the story, which employs yet another didactic method. It is itself a short parable, a complete though miniature story inside the story, including a setting, complication, and resolution. In words added in 1754, Micromégas promises to give to the mites a book of philosophy written in very small characters for their use. In it, and this was also added, they would see the *bout des choses*. This promise, the rising action, is kept; and the book is brought to the Academy (complication or climax) and found to be empty (resolution or falling action). This parable and *mise-en-abyme* reinforces the lesson of philosophical modesty by containing in itself both the hope or pretension of metaphysical knowledge and the main story's answer to it, the fact that it cannot be found. The reader easily draws this repeated and concentrated lesson from the juxtaposition of the promise — the knowledge of ends — and of its result — a blank book. [34] Further-

---

[34] The blank book recalls Locke's *tabula rasa* and the possible equivalence between the page and the mind; the metaphor was used by eighteenth-century empiricists. The negative wiping-away has a positive consequence in this view, for saying that one knows nothing is the beginning of science. The Book, or received knowledge, is thus subordinated to experience; and language and

more, one character plays the receiver's role in the parable, saying "Je m'en étais bien douté," flattering her by crediting her with the same prescience. This is the prize handed out to the skillful reader; her suspicions were surely aroused by the hero's promise, "le bout des choses" having long since been dismissed as a valid goal of reflection; and she can say with the final speaker that she too suspected as much. The short rapidly related fable is a deviation from the discourse to which one has become accustomed, but it ends in a new fusion by assimilating the reader to the spokesman in it.

The modes of criticism — direct abuse, litotes, antiphrasis, and the dramatization of the targets' autodestruction — necessitate a variety of measures in their reception. They also form certain patterns among themselves. Invective is more abundant at the beginning, and the messages require more complicated decoding as one approaches the end. The last three chapters repeat the staging of ridiculousness, and the triple alternation of those scenes and the lesson to be drawn from them reinforces condemnation of metaphysical pretension. Each of the last scenes is longer than the preceding one, and each is more specific in the ridicule of human vanity. The accumulation and reinforcement of the same opposition is finally re-distributed in a new, short story at the end of the principal one. The hope from which issue pretentious acts and discourse is isolated and exhibited by Micromégas' promise to let them see the end of all things, and it is shattered as such by the image of the empty book, a potentially destructive image finally pure of any trait *ad hominem*.

I.5. THE FRAGMENTED SUBJECT. DECONSTRUCTION AND SIGNIFICANCE

The reader, the deciphering subject, is also a text. Initial reception by the critic-reader is probably absolute adherence to the written discourse and to the intentions it teaches. At some time or in some

---

experience are thus opposed to one another. Book and mind are blank; on them experience will write, constructing its truths. The book of the world shall be read in nature and no longer in books.

place of herself, the subject substitutes differentiation for adherence, and reading becomes a mediated act. Thus, not only may writing be called rewriting at the moment of the text's creation — absorbing, altering, and opposing discourses that precede it — but reading includes successive or simultaneous re-readings. In a Gestalt-like perception, the successive parts acquire sense, meaning, and significance in relation to each other and to the whole configuration that is gradually constructed by re-reading. [35]

In the sections above, I was describing reading-processes. The text was object and subject since I looked especially at the possibles of reception where discourse stimulates sense-making, operations, and judgment. Here I shall expand the concept of the text as subject in its encounter with the reader-subject as text, as meta-reader, that is, as truly critical. Looking for failures in the system of constraints the text puts on its actualizer, I pass from the structures and processes in the sign, the *conte,* to the structures of its reading-writing by the subject; and I try to elucidate the play between the absence and presence of structures and of constraints as the deciphering subjects perceive them. Deconstructive actualization seems to occur or to be encouraged in three regions of the story: 1) the juxtaposition of certain anecdotes offers the potential for weakening the analogical structure; 2) the doubling of the represented subject, the hero, diminishes the mythic force of the folkloric syntagma; and 3) the foregrounding and vacillation of certain words themselves is always already sapping the reading subject's confidence in the narrative voice and in its very language.

(1)   Certain of the anecdotes in *Micromégas* put forward a text on analogy as deception. There is more than a trace of counter-text in the narrator's criticism of Castel's belief that Mars has no moons. In finding fault with the churchman, the narrating voice invokes comparative reasoning implying an inverse and approximate proportion — earth is to one moon as a four-times-smaller Mars is to two — two moons being the given, the fact seen by the hero. The verity of this proportion is undermined by its being attributed to "ceux qui

---
[35] For a brief introduction to these ideas, see Carol Sherman, "Response Criticism: 'Do Readers Make Meaning?' " *Romance Notes,* 18 (1977), 288-92. For bibliography on the correlation between Lacanian theories of the self and Derridian theories of the text, see Suleiman, *The Reader...,* pp. 41-42; 419-22.

raisonnent par analogie." The next sentence also incriminates this kind of reasoning even as it is used to mock Castel: "Ces bons philosophes-là savent combien il serait difficile que Mars, qui est si loin du soleil, se passât à moins de deux lunes" (Ch. 3). A certain slippage diminishes the vigor of the refutation of Castel. Of the two proportions offered to oppose him, one is inverse — the size of Mars (less) is in inverse proportion to the number of its moons (more) — and the other is direct — its distance from the sun (more than earth's) is directly proportional to the number of its moons (more than earth's). Besides having their origin in the anthropomorphic "needs" of the planet, their diverse theoretical expressions, direct and inverse, seem to contradict each other, for "those who reason by analogy" are needed to shore up the second proportion ("ces philosophes-là"), but "ceux qui" has often been used in the story to present a group for condemnation. An additional erosive element persists from the comparative exploits performed by the narrator only four pages before, where the playful variants of proportion were deceiving. The hero's attempts at analogical reasoning also result in its depletion. He, like the narrator, tries one of each kind, inverse and direct. He says to men both "since you have little matter, you must have much mind" (inverse), and "since you have much knowledge about nature, you must also have much about soul" (direct). He is wrong on both counts. The hero's apparent failure (he may also be seen as a conscious eiron in these questions) to grasp fact and proper use of proportion with regard to men has the potential to weaken further the process in the mind of the synthesizing subject as she assimilates them to the narrator's largely destructive uses of them earlier in the story. Another factor of doubt and erosion arises from the possibility for the subject to hesitate among several ways of reading: that the hero makes poor use of analogy, that man himself is ajar from a truly proportioned universe, or that the external and universal paradigm of mathematical proportion suffers deconstruction, the failure of analogy itself in nature. The philosophy of relativism that is the overt lesson of the story depends upon the analogical structure that suffers deconstruction. There is a slippage from mathematical proportion to natural analogy; it is explicit in the phrase mentioned above — "mais je m'en rapporte à ceux qui raisonnent par analogie" — which occurs in a passage that presents proportions. This epistemological assimilation of the two is one of the most interesting traces in *Micromégas*. The seventeenth and eighteenth centuries saw the gradual exclusion of analogical thought from mathematics, analogical reasoning being finalistic and thus criticized in the name of scientific objectivity. The text combines them, the dressing of proportion compensatory for the loss of analogy's prestige, criticized, in the phrase above, but upon which depends the relativistic lesson. The analogies — giants to men, real skills to pretensions, etc. — are treated seriously and thus receive importance by the stress on proportion, which gives in turn a scientific allure to relativism. From Locke onward a difference had been marked between juxtaposition (metonym) and resemblance (metaphor). What is most evident in this deconstruction is that Voltaire imitates mathematical language in an area where it is not applicable; he implies resemblance by simple juxtaposition.

(2) To the degree that the tale overtly offers itself as bearing a lesson ("histoire philosophique"), it proposes itself as one term of comparison, that is, of an equal proportion, between the reading subject and the hero, or between the world outside the tale and the world within it. This claim to equivalence or to allegory becomes increasingly clear as the hero repeatedly reacts according to values presented as positive and as worthy of emulation — thorough observation, prudent and methodical comparison, reasoned judgment — and as the narrating voice approves him — "bien meilleur observateur que son nain." Some part of the interpretant registers the appeal to compare her usual way of thinking with his and to pass to analogous acts. [36] The various claims to analogical performative force range from the subtitle of the story to the repetition of the paradigm of proportion in all parts of the signifier. This homomorphous quality attaches the story to the category of myth; that part of it seems engendered by mythic patterns of cycle and repetition. At the same

---

[36] I shall not distinguish among the terms *myth, allegory, analogy, metaphor,* and so on. In his *Allegory,* written for the series "The Critical Idiom" (London: Methuen, 1970), John MacQueen begins by using *allegory* and *myth* interchangeably. In an article on Diderot's use of allegory, Georges May combines *métaphorique* and *analogique* in a sentence marking allegory as a simpler form of representation ("Diderot et l'allégorie," *Studies on Voltaire and the Eighteenth Century,* 89 [1972], 1052). For the discussion here, the idea of representing one thing by another should be sufficient.

time, the phrase "once upon a time" and others present the tale as news, as a once-in-a-lifetime chance-occurence unregulated by patterns or cycles. However, even its linearity, the movement represented in space and going from one planet, from one size, from one discovery to another, includes a mythic aspect by the repeated confrontation of large and small and by their constant revision. The mythic qualities predominate over the idea of singularity and encourage the application of the tale to the reader's existence. [37]

Further tension in the mythic, didactic, exemplary pretensions and structures occurs in the violation of the category of hero as a single actor. His sphere of action is shared off and on by the dwarf from Saturn. Whether we assign logical or historical priority to the cyclical or mythic text, or whether we simply see that aspect of this story as engendered by cultural memory (author's and reader's) or by persistent unconscious need, it is true that linear paraphrase of a (potential or past) cyclical text often bears two or more distinct figures in the hero's sphere (Lotman, p. 164). The hero's dwarf at first plays the role of obstacle, aggressor in the first combat (Chapter Two; 16^1 in Figure I.A above). When he and Micromégas decide to take a philosophical trip together (end of 2, beginning of 3), he becomes the hero's double, but then breaks away again to return to the category of obstacle, poor observer and poor judge in the hero's quest for formation (Ch. 3-6). When the two interrogate earth's creatures, the dwarf again acts as one of the heroic character-doubles in their (its) fight against ignorance, and he remains there until the end. He moves back and forth between the plot-space of the immobile resisting enemy and the domain of the mobile questing hero. The breakup of the hero's person pulls the reader or actualizing subject toward perceiving the story as news instead of myth even as she senses its mythical attributes. The dwarf's shifting status traces another figuration of analogy's breakdown. The mythic force of a single admirable hero would have been maintained if characters in different areas were simply different names for the same person, but the relation or proportion from giant to dwarf

---

[37] The distinction between news and myth as a tension in most modern plot-texts is described by Jurij Lotman, "The Origins of Plot in the Light of Typology," *Poetics Today*, 1 (Autumn 1979), 161-184. Some of the terms and concepts I apply here are his.

does not remain constant in each episode, A is to B not being as A'
to B'. At the same time mobile subject (hero) and immobile object
(aggressor), the Saturnian changes the analogical game by destroying
the integrity of the mythic paradigm of heroic proportion.

(3)   The third type of perception available to the fragmented
subject is performed by the attack on linguistic confidence through
the semantic retraining of the decoding reader. By the time she
reaches the end of the story, the words *little* and *big* are totally
relativized, cut loose from any essence as well as from their habitual
signifieds which attained at least provisional stability in contexts.
Now even context is removed since it constantly shifts and multiplies. The perceptual slipping of these terms subverts even the
Saussurian thesis by which terms have meaning with respect to
each other and not to fixed reality outside their system. Here in a
miniature enactment of the Derridian objection to Saussure, neither
term can signify with regard to the other since each is ceaselessly
redefined in a new context by relation to new physical or verbal
elements. [38] Two of the most banal words in any language are thus
charged with (their own) absence, being emptied of absolute or
referential sense as well as of relative or contextual moorings. They
have the capacity to provide or to stimulate wide and thorough
investigation of unstable context. In so doing, they command a *mise-
en-abyme* of themselves, requiring fine scrutiny for the establishment
of their (big or little) value. Each time one reads *small* or *large,* the
sense is absent; and one must resort to context in order to determine
meaning, which is nonetheless ephemeral. The significance derivable
is thus both relativization and evaporation of meaning.

Through the mediating act of reflection all these persistent and
exhaustive underminings of the credit of analogical thinking succeed
in deconstructing the text's reiterated arguments and reinforced
structures. According to the mathematicians of the time, the thing
it signals and the processes it requires were growing weaker. Proportion kept its status in Euclidian geometry and in formal logic, but
the story bears the trace of analogy's wearing-out there and in other

---

38 Derrida, *De la grammatologie,* pp. 58ff.

areas as well. Society and its beliefs often follow the prescient edge of the literary work. Those who see intent in the universe, users of the argument-by-design, are also victims of the destruction of analogical vision.

CHAPTER II

ZADIG

> ... l'arithmétique mène à la philologie, et la philologie au crime ....
>
> Ionesco, *La Leçon*

II.1. COMPETENCE

1.a. *Initiation and General Competence*

The preparation of the reader begins with the title. It offers three bits of information: a proper noun, presumably the name of the hero; a subtitle, "Histoire orientale," confirming the exoticism of the name *Zadig* and announcing a well-known genre of tale that had circulated in France for over thirty years; [1] and the words *ou La Destinée,* which could be an alert to allegory, to the posing of eternal teleological questions, the conjunction *ou* being seen as signifying the presence of both the protagonist and destiny in the story. However, the juxtaposed proper noun and the vague possibly dramatic abstraction contrast with the words *oriental story.* Because of the title and the subtitle, one suspects already that this

---

[1] For Voltaire's reading on the Orient, see Georges Ascoli's critical edition of *Zadig* (Paris: Didier, 1962), pp. IV-V. The *Contes des mille et une nuits,* transmitted to France by Galland in 1704-1717 are mentioned in the "Epître dédicatoire" of the tale. Jacques van den Heuvel devotes a chapter to "Zadig et le conte oriental" in his *Voltaire dans les contes* (Paris: A. Colin, 1967), pp. 183-200. For the names, see Pauline Kra, "Note on the Derivation of Names in Voltaire's *Zadig,*" *Romance Notes,* 16 (1975), 342-44.

is not a simple oriental tale. If we hesitate to succumb to this early
irony, we could then think that an abstract topic will be joined to
the concrete adventures of an oriental hero; but destiny itself is a
cliché of the novel — heroes and heroines follow their destiny or
are destined to some condition, etc. — and the word may not immediately deter us from the conventional idea of an exotic tale with
fated heroes. On the other hand, the latter may be the parody or
mocking echo of the serious novel and not themselves equivocal.
All these ricochets are available to the reflective reader and immediately alert her to the possibilities of complex decodings.

The *Approbation* that follows mocks the usual form by echoing
it — "Je soussigné..." — and by showing a voice that ridicules
itself — "qui me suis fait passer pour savant." It exhibits contradictory reasoning: having found the tale amusing, moral, philosophical, and so on, the censor declares it detestable. The tale's first
reader has thus already been charmed in spite of himself, and he
sets an example of giving in to its power and then of using his own
power in order to decry it.

The dedicatory epistle that follows mentions exotic traits, objects, and places; and in the sultana addressed, it depicts one ideal
reader of the tale to follow. Far from being only implied, she is
constituted by her description and by being invited to extract possibly plural meanings from the "ouvrage qui dit plus qu'il ne semble
dire." The work, says its modest "translator," was written by an old
sage. In the paragraph, he repeats the word *sage* three times, once
in the course of a compliment paid to the figured reader, who
herself possesses "un petit fonds de philosophie," and who thus
causes him to believe that she would take "plus de goût qu'une
autre à cet ouvrage d'un sage."

This compliment ends a development that began a series of six
concessive phrases *(quoique)* pretending to oppose the sultana's
beauty to her capacity for philosophy; the sentence ends however
by joining the two: "cependant," she has "l'esprit très sage et le
goût très fin." Even though the world has no right to expect such
perfection, she can "raisonner mieux que de vieux derviches à longue
barbe et à bonnet pointu." This mention of creatures who are her
opposites launches four statements contrasting traits she possesses
and those she avoids ("Vous êtes discrète et vous n'êtes point dé-

fiante," etc.), which give way to two fully negative statements of things she never does, it being understood that those with whom she is being contrasted, the *vieux derviches,* do possess these vices: "Votre esprit n'emprunte jamais ses agréments des traits de la médisance; vous ne dites de mal ni n'en faites, malgré la prodigieuse facilité que vous y auriez." The outline of the perfect reader sharpens as it is contrasted with those whom the author-translator would not want as his public. At last, a positive and admiring phrase permits beauty to rejoin philosophy in the portrait of the lady: "Enfin votre âme m'a toujours paru pure comme votre beauté."

In the paragraph that follows, the translator nests another depiction of an ideal reader, this one drawn for the benefit, emulation, and flattery of the addressee of his epistle. The sultana is invited to compare herself with a much earlier reader of this very story, Ouloug, for whom it was translated into Arabic and who could not understand the others' interest in stories "sans raison," those that sought only to amuse. He too contrasts with a group of bad readers, the silly sultanas who surrounded him. The translator has thus created for any real reader's instruction two pictures of the audience he does not want and two portraits of his ideal readers, philosophically intent persons who prefer, as he does, stories and conversation in which one can *parler raison.*

The positive depictions of readers assert the serious purpose of the tale and invite the search for meaning beyond simple sense. Signs of folklore and fairytale persist nonetheless side by side with these assertions. Among the initiatory signals perceived by the reader is the conventional beginning, "... il y avait ... un jeune homme." This kind of opening bears rich literary and pragmatic presuppositions, among which is the possibility of its own parodic nature. It usually identifies the story with conventions of the fairytale and prepares the reader to take certain attitudes toward it, but here the preceding epistle has also prepared her for other complex attitudes receptive of moral lessons. Both kinds are now mixed and held in readiness. Traditional also, the ending will be an extremely insistent form of "they lived happily ever after": "L'empire jouit de la paix, de la gloire et de l'abondance; ce fut le plus beau siècle de la terre," and so on. However, the reader has an unconventional experience of the conventional ending because of what happens on the way to it.

At the start, the subtitle and the phrase *Once upon a time* encourage and maintain expectations of a certain tradition; they are more or less fulfilled as the hero falls in love with the heroine, loses her and, after many trials, finds her again. The eighteenth-century listener and the modern one both know, as all children do, what a story is. That this particular one will tell more than adventures has been abundantly hinted at in the title, in the approval, and in the dedication. The first lines of the tale already alert the reader to the kind of response that will actualize multiple meanings.

1.b. *Instructions for Reading: Specific Competence*

No marked narrative voice is heard in the first sentence; it is historical and neutral: "Du temps du roi Moabdar il y avait à Babylone un jeune homme nommé Zadig, né avec un beau naturel fortifié par l'éducation." In the second, the concessive *quoique* returns, expressing opposition; it betrays the presence of an opinion — "Quoique riche et jeune, il savait modérer ses passions" — containing the presupposition that young and rich men are usually prone to excesses that are remarkably absent in the hero. The sentence continues, "il n'affectait rien; il ne voulait point toujours avoir raison, et savait respecter la faiblesse des hommes." The third sentence varies in two ways the procedure of valorizing the hero by describing his foppish opposites; it employs *on* for the wise persons of his time who expected less of the young and rich men and who were astonished, once again, at the absence of certain vices in him. Demonstrative adjectives insist upon those vices, and this use of deixis establishes a place or state of mind common to the here and now of the narration. The narratee is invited to join in this narrative space and time by following with the mind's eye the gesture implicit in the four *those* and in the *that* setting off traits supposedly known equally well by her and by her guide:

> On était étonné de voir qu'avec beaucoup d'esprit il n'insultât jamais par des railleries à ces propos si vagues, si rompus, si tumultueux, à ces médisances téméraires, à ces décisions ignorantes, à ces turlupinades grossières, à ce vain bruit de paroles, qu'on appelait *conversation* dans Babylone.

Both the second and the third sentences oppose Zadig's positive traits — *riche et jeune, beaucoup d'esprit* — and the evil that usually accompanies them. One is exposed by the *quoique* ("quoique riche et jeune") that may be attributed to the narrator; and the other, by naming, though vaguely, the agent — *on* — of the second opinion expressed, *étonné*. In the fourth sentence, the hero himself is made to assume responsibility for the criticisms emitted, although he did learn them from a sacred authority: "Il avait appris, dans le premier livre de Zoroastre, que l'amour-propre est un ballon gonflé de vent, dont il sort des tempêtes quand on lui fait une piqûre." The fifth makes the bald statement about another vice he does not possess; this sentence would return the discourse to the historical or neutral except for the second word, *surtout,* revealing once more the presence of an opining voice which is here stressing the importance or rarity of this particular abstention: "Zadig surtout ne se vantait pas de mépriser les femmes et de les subjuguer." The rest of this first, expositional paragraph tells of the hero's knowledge of "natural philosophy"; and the overt narrator allows himself a direct hit on the target of metaphysics — Zadig "savait de la métaphysique ce qu'on en a su dans tous les âges, c'est-à-dire fort peu de chose." He briefly puts on stage the *mages* who refuse heliocentrism among other true things, and he has them make themselves ridiculous by the attitudes he attributes to them.

The exposition of the hero's situation and of his knowledge is completed by the first sentence of the second paragraph which summarizes his qualities and contains another meta-commentary:

> Zadig, avec de grandes richesses, et par conséquent avec des amis, ayant de la santé, une figure aimable, un esprit juste et modéré, un cœur sincère et noble, crut qu'il pouvait être heureux.

The *par conséquent* is another economical way of making a criticism; it assumes that the relation between wealth and friendship is one from cause to effect. The phrase *consequently* constitutes logical parody, for it accents an appearance of logic and implies a syllogism that is both trivial in its content (burlesque) and aggressive in its reference to mankind's self-interest (satire): the rich always have friends, Zadig is rich, therefore he has friends. The reader is by now practiced in understanding the kind of guidance the narrator is likely to provide; and, failing other indicators, she probably consents to consider him trustworthy. This same sentence can thus safely effect a distance between narrator and protagonist, and it begins to define the reader's particular reaction to the character also. A list of qualifiers separates the subject of the sentence, Zadig, from its verb, *crut;* and the items in the list would in other positions render the *crut qu'il pouvait être heureux* perfectly plausible. However, the length of the enumeration, the fact that it delays the arrival of the verb, and the preterit of the verb *croire* all conspire to create damaging surprise in the inhabitual sequence. The presence of the comment "et par conséquent avec des amis" contributes to giving the impression that this sentence with its unusual order is not neutral, that is, not innocently historical. The delayed verb, its tense, and the presence of comment make it possible to see the narrator as taking his distance from the protagonist and as showing that although the latter believed happiness possible, he was mistaken. This is the first clue to the narrator's transmitting the superiority of his own knowledge over that of his hero (as well as creating the limited suspense of the tale) and his willingness to let it show and to guide the reader, who learns from it to be wary before espousing the hero's sentiments and predictions.

The initiation this sentence provides is reiterated at other moments throughout the tale. Narration has already betrayed itself in the deictics, the signs of a space and a time common to narrator and narratee. The demonstrative adjectives of the third sentence have already been mentioned. The conditional mood, sign of *discours,* appears in the middle of the second paragraph: "... dans les emportements de leur violence ils la blessèrent, et firent couler le sang d'une personne dont la vue aurait attendri les tigres du mont Imaüs." A generalization given in the present tense and placed near another demonstrative occurs at the end of the second paragraph and thus reiterates the narrative locus: "Jamais bouche plus ravissante n'exprima des sentiments plus touchants par ces paroles de feu qu'inspirent le sentiment du plus grand des bienfaits et le transport le plus tendre de l'amour le plus légitime." The pointing *ces* and the generalization "paroles ... qu'inspirent le sentiment et le transport" refer to information and to an opinion (*idée reçue* or cliché) sup-

posedly shared by speaker and listener. The reliable narrator intervenes to interpret, not by explanations or asides as Fielding does,
for instance, but often by a single word — adjective, conjunction,
or adverb — he points to the exemplary quality of his story. Several
signs of the narrator's interventions erupt in his otherwise largely
historical (preterit and imperfect tenses) recital of events.

Like *quoique* and *par conséquent* in the sentences quoted above,
the *cependant* of " ... on l'admirait, et cependant on l'aimait" com-
poses a pessimistic commentary around the uncommon affection
Zadig inspires. According to the narrator, the irony already obtains
in the condition described, and *cependant* points to that ironic condition by expressing surprise at the opposition between what happens to Zadig — "on l'aimait" — and what usually happens, represented by the implied syllogism: if people have to be admired, they
are not liked; Zadig is admirable; therefore, he is not likeable. The
conclusion of the syllogism is overturned by Zadig, and *cependant*
has the double effect of pointing to mankind's usual pettiness and
of valorizing the hero. The opinion expressed by presupposition
enriches the relation between narrator and reader and seems to
confirm again, although briefly, the early announcement of multiple
meanings in the story. At other moments later in the story, the
narrator orients reception of certain facts by employing a value-
charged adjective: a widow's throwing herself on her husband's
funeral pyre is a "coutume affreuse," says the narrating voice, and
the protagonist also finds it so, showing his master how "cette
horrible coutume" is contrary to the good of humanity ("Le Bûcher"). In two other ways, that voice confirms certain of the protagonist's thoughts. Twice an overt *en effet* and the word *vrai*
specifically approve Zadig's meditation. The approval includes the
reader also by the words *nos, notre,* and *ces,* which enjoin her to
participate in this moment of sane expression:

> Il admirait ces vastes globes de lumière qui ne paraissent
> que de faibles étincelles à nos yeux, tandis que la terre, qui
> n'est en effet qu'un point imperceptible dans la nature,
> paraît à notre cupidité quelque chose de si grand et de si
> noble. Il se figurait alors les hommes tels qu'ils sont en
> effet, des insectes se dévorant les uns les autres sur un
> petit atome de boue. Cette image vraie semblait anéantir
> ses malheurs. . . . ("La Femme battue")

Once, the narrator even imitates the hero's propensity to statements of cause and effect as they operate in his life; but whereas Zadig's teleological lamentations (below) are often felt to be naïve and simple, he is momentarily justified when the narrator takes on the same expression of cause-to-effect; and the reader is led to feel destiny's absurdity in a way similar to that often expressed — absurdly — by the protagonist himself. The first example takes the form of an oxymoron attributable to the narrator — "par une bizarrerie ordinaire de la fortune" in "Le Chien et le cheval," and the second appears much later, in the sixteenth chapter: "Ainsi, après avoir été toujours puni pour avoir bien fait, il était près de périr pour avoir guéri un seigneur gourmand." One cannot make this (very) free indirect discourse attributable to Zadig because he never learns the information there given; the arrival of Astarté's letter and its summons take him away from the table just in time. The narrator is fully accountable for the statement. He keeps a moment longer his foregrounded position as he exhibits again his amusement before these chance happenings by concluding that "[q]uand on est aimé d'une belle femme, dit le grand Zoroastre, on se tire toujours d'affaire dans ce monde." ("Le Basilic"). [2]

Besides seizing these small (adjectives) and large (statements) opportunities to comment on *le monde comme il va,* the narrating voice also provides the reader with information that is available to the protagonist at the moment in the *histoire* he is recounting. These instants mark a clear separation between the *récit* and the *histoire,* for they are in fact small but critical flash-forwards allowing the reader to share in the narrator's superior knowledge about the outcome and placing the protagonist in the light or shadow shed by dramatic irony: he is doubly helpless, both facing the events them-

---

[2] It does happen that the narrative voice emits opinions that must be attributed instead to a character; in the phrase "Ce blasphème effroyable fit frémir les juges" neither the narrator nor the protagonist finds the opinion expressed to be blasphemous; the judges do. Quotation marks could surround the words *blasphème effroyable;* they are citational irony, for their use outside the original context and in the impertinent context makes them ironic. Another example occurs in "Le Basilic": "C'était Astarté elle-même, c'était la reine de Babylone, c'était celle que Zadig adorait ... c'était celle dont il avait tant pleuré et tant craint le destinée." Here, an imitation of what could be the hero's breathless exclamations combines in the same sentence with descriptions of him.

selves *(histoire)* and before their prediction by the *récit*: "La reine le regarda dès lors avec une complaisance qui pouvait devenir dangereuse pour elle, pour le roi son auguste époux, pour Zadig, et pour le royaume" ("L'Envieux"); "Le roi acquit la réputation d'un bon prince, qu'il ne garda pas longtemps" ("Les Généreux"); "... elle finit par laisser tomber sa jarretière; Zadig la ramassa avec sa politesse ordinaire; mais il ne la rattacha point au genou de la dame; et cette petite faute, si c'en est une, fut la cause des plus horribles infortunes" ("Les Disputes et les audiences"). This last example appears two sentences before another sort of correction, a contradiction of the hero's expressed opinion: "Zadig disait, 'Je suis enfin heureux!' Mais il se trompait." All these extradiegetic comments occur in the first section of the tale, the one relaying the rising action, before the formation of the *nœud*. Yet another form of dissociation between narrator and *histoire* opens the chapter entitled "La Jalousie," where the crisis forms, the misdeed occurs, and the lack is made manifest. The narrative voice never more explicitly interprets the sense of the hero's adventures: "Le malheur de Zadig vint de son bonheur même, et surtout de son mérite." These last two instances of the narrator's volubility occur within five paragraphs of each other, and in their midst another sort appears. It is opposite in its content — he claims *not* to know something — but it is fully as constitutive of the discourse-relation: "D'autres dames se présentaient tous les jours. Les annales secrètes de Babylone prétendent qu'il succomba une fois, mais qu'il fut tout étonné de jouir sans volupté, et d'embrasser son amante avec distraction." Here information is not guaranteed but is referred to as uncertain. By this conventional hesitation concerning actions that may render the hero less admirable to some, the narrating voice feigns a position outside historical knowledge of its material and coquettishly relinquishes responsibility for the truth of what is reported. This transmission of hypothetical information is a rare event in the *contes* where the narration is typically authoritative.

Another sort of intervention by the narrator is motivated by technical considerations related to ease of exposition and of reception rather than by the desire to guide the reader to second meaning or to distance her further from the protagonist. In two of the three tales inserted and told to Zadig by other characters, the narrator avows a violation of the chronology of the *histoire*. In "Le Pêcheur," the fisherman's recital of his life was, we learn, punctuated by the exclamations of its listener, but the narrator has the speaker relate it in one block and then says that it was in fact often interrupted: "Le pêcheur ne fit point ce récit tout de suite; car à tout moment Zadig, ému et transporté, lui disait: 'Quoi! vous ne savez rien de la destinée de la reine?' " In "Le Basilic," the disordered nature in the *histoire* of the intercalated tale, Astarté's, is explained before she relates her adventures:

> Elle reprenait vingt fois des discours que ses gémissements interrompaient; elle l'interrogeait sur le hasard qui les rassemblait, et prévenait soudain ses réponses par d'autres questions. Elle entamait le récit de ses malheurs, et voulait savoir ceux de Zadig. Enfin tous deux ayant un peu apaisé le tumulte de leurs âmes, Zadig lui conta en peu de mots par quelle aventure il se trouvait dans cette prairie.

After the interruptions occurring in the *histoire* are told, her long story follows without interruption in the *récit*. Since the end of the fisherman's story concerns the heroine, it as well as her own is naturally portrayed as prompting the excited and vocal interest of Zadig, but from the point of view of the narrating author the maintaining of the reader's interest seems to make monologue preferable. Since it does not concern the protagonist directly, the first intercalated tale, that of the brigand, can be offered without accounting for interruption in either *récit* or *histoire*. The exemplary nature of all three stories manifests itself by their very mass and by the density of unmerited fortune or misfortune. They do not need punctuation by the cries of the hero in order to be inserted by the reader into the didactic paradigm (Section 3, below).

The greatest density of deixis, that is, of reference to the here and now of narrative instance, occurs in the section containing the largest number of references to specific abuses present in the specific culture in which the work was created. It applies itself to the targets in the second half of Chapter Four, "L'Envieux." An addition, critical of an archbishop and made in 1752, also includes a large number of deictics associated with the same mode of satiric communication (Section 4, below). In this account of the narrator's relation with his interlocutor and with his text, it should be noted that the eighteenth chapter ("L'Ermite"), the second longest, contains only one reference to narration, a single deictic that is the use of the conditional mood — "Le portier, qu'on aurait pris pour un grand seigneur, les introduisit ..." — that all the other verbs are in the preterit or the imperfect tenses, and that the proportion of true theatrical dialogue is larger than in the other sections, leaving the reader much more to her own devices. The narrator's abstention here is one of the important reasons for the reader's perplexity before this episode, which thus clearly dissociates itself from the kind of discourse that characterizes the rest of the tale. I shall return to this difference below.

The narrator gave preliminary and concentrated exposition, like that in *Micromégas*. Here, however, its topic is limited to the protagonist's character, his goodness and intelligence; and it does not summarize events of his past as is done in *Micromégas*. This section, that is, the first paragraph and one sentence of the second, establishes a discourse-relation including an authoritative, reliable narrator, writing in the historical imperfect tense, descriptive of a state in the past, showing by deixis his consciousness of writing or of speaking to an audience in a narrative present. The first discriminated occasion begins, "Il devait se marier à Sémire," and brings the first verb of action in the preterit, "... ils virent venir à eux des hommes armés." The nature of the exposition, Zadig's character, and the lack of flash-forward prepare the reader for learning *what* happens to him and not only for seeing the *how* of events already predicted. Contrary in this to *Micromégas,* the outcome is not clear in advance, and one is encouraged to expect the events themselves to be interesting and significant. The last phrase of exposition, he "crut qu'il pouvait être heureux," permits predicting that he will not be, but what exactly will happen to someone so obviously meritorious is not clear. In the perceptual set thus formulated, the reader's interest will mostly be offered events of unmerited suffering. A certain suspense inside a generally unpleasant necessity is thus maintained rather than being abolished as it is in *Micromégas*.

This particular experience of the text — punctual surprise inside generalized certainty — is the primary one productive of exemplary meaning, and it results from the double relation that the narration arranges between the reader and the main character. The first im-

pression of the protagonist will remain — good, earnest, and eironic — and the primary effect will be the only effect.[3] What we
know about him will be largely unchanged in nature or kind
— he will almost always seem good — or in scope (quantity).
Nothing will be added to his flatness; he will not be a rounder
character at the end than at the beginning. A pleasure that the
traditional fairytale offers is recurrent recognition of the pattern
of trials, looking forward to the certain future development of misfortune that is uncertain only in its precise content. The narrator's
sometimes flaunting his superior knowledge ("mais il se trompait")
leaves no doubt that it is he who has the situation under control;
so our very moderate anxiety for the hero, the simple curiosity deployed in reading a novel as well, can be tempered to allowed appreciation of the comic aspect of events.

The reader, elevated to a degree of awareness similar to that of
the narrator, has an advantage over the character that could turn
either to comic or to tragic awareness by the same conditions, and
which constitutes dramatic or situational irony. Which one, which
tone she feels or responds to is determined in part by the particular
manner in which misfortune is received and deplored by the character. The agent of lamentation is Zadig, its object is himself, and in
this he acts the parts of hero and of Greek chorus. In this he also
speaks for Job and for all of suffering humanity, as will Candide.
However, his method of doing so is not only steadily unenlightened
but often repetitious and puerile in its deductions. For most receivers
the manner as well as the previous diminishing of his stature by the
narrator's distance prevents a solely tragic reading.[4] There are
roughly two sorts of discourse attributed to the proper name of the
hero:[5] tragic, the refrains and recapitulations that follow the episodes of misfortune — summary, exclamation, and complaint — and
comic, most of the moments in which he reasons out the lesson he

---

[3] Sternberg, p. 99.

[4] For an illuminating discussion of defining tragic and comic in relation
to each other instead of as absolutes, see Edouard Morot-Sir, "La Dynamique
du théâtre et Molière," *Romance Notes,* 15, Supp. No. 1 (1973), pp. 15-49.

[5] Seymour Chatman summarizes various ideas of character in fiction. My
view, for Voltaire's philosophical stories at least, seems to be close to that
of Tomashevsky. Chatman, *Story and Discourse: Narrative Structure in Fiction
and Film* (Ithaca: Cornell University Press, 1978), pp. 107-45.

has learned and makes its application to future situations. Both types — and they are sometimes two parts of a particular moment of reaction — affect the reader's construction of the character, and their mixture prevents her entire emotional and ideological adherence to him even as she recognizes the potential dignity and the universality of his lamentations.

One example of the first type, the *épiphonème,* occurs after the hero has renounced his love for philosophy and for natural science. Injustice is visited upon him in spite of the wisdom he acquired from science; and he exclaims,

> Grand Dieu! ... qu'on est à plaindre quand on se promène dans un bois où la chienne de la reine et le cheval du roi ont passé! qu'il est dangereux de se mettre à la fenêtre! et qu'il est difficile d'être heureux dans cette vie! ("Le Chien et le cheval")

Shortly thereafter, he cries, "A quoi tient le bonheur! Tout me persécute dans ce monde, jusqu'aux êtres qui n'existent pas" ("L'Envieux"). An example of his reasoning is reported immediately: the sentence "Il maudit les savants, et ne voulut plus vivre qu'en bonne compagnie" expresses the rejection of one way of life in order to embrace exclusively another. After the parrot saves him from death, and after the narrator says that the queen's affection is dangerous for him, we are told that "Zadig commençait à croire qu'il n'est pas difficile d'être heureux." The glibness of his unjustified conclusion and its proximity to the narrator's warning combine to remind us that he makes unreliable judgments. One time, he gives a sign of having learned something and of being prepared for misfortune in the bosom of ease: "... je suis maintenant sur le lit de roses, mais quel sera le serpent?" ("Les Disputes"). His next refrain consists largely of recapitulation that he performs after apostrophizing virtue:

> Qu'est-ce que donc que la vie humaine? O vertu! à quoi m'avez-vous servi? Deux femmes m'ont indignement trompé; la troisième, qui n'est point coupable, et qui est plus belle que les autres, va mourir! Tout ce que j'ai fait de bien a toujours été pour moi une source de malédictions, et je n'ai été élevé au comble de la grandeur que pour tomber dans le plus horrible précipice de l'infortune. ("La Jalousie")

Just when we could begin to be impressed by the understanding shown in this tirade, the *chute* makes the character ridiculous even though in the strictest sense he may be right: "Si j'eusse été méchant comme tant d'autres, je serais heureux comme eux." This cynical assessment corresponds to the ordinary wisdom of the principled person who has failed or been fooled, the *à quoi bon?* typical of self-righteous losers. The temptation to be *méchant* like the winners in order to gain the advantages they have, as Zadig expresses it over and over again, opposes itself to an intertext, that of Christianity's promise that the last shall be first; the first, last; and that accounts shall be paid at the Last Judgment.

The hero's continuing preoccupation with the action of seemingly insignificant causality in his life is reflected in this typical recapitulation found in Chapter Thirteen:

> Quoi! disait-il, quatre cents onces d'or pour avoir vu passer une chienne! condamné à être décapité pour quatre mauvais vers à la louange du roi! prêt à être étranglé parce que la reine avait des babouches de la couleur de mon bonnet! réduit en esclavage pour avoir secouru une femme qu'on battait; et sur le point d'être brûlé pour avoir sauvé la vie à toutes les jeunes veuves arabes! ("Les Rendez-vous")

Summaries of cause and effect alternate with exclamations concerning the rewards of the wicked and the punishment of the just: "... ô fortune! ô destinée! un voleur est heureux, et ce que la nature a fait de plus aimable a péri peut-être d'une manière affreuse ou vit dans un état pire que la mort" ("Le Brigand"). This particular kind of discourse is sometimes transmitted indirectly: "Zadig marchait inquiet, agité, l'esprit tout occupé de la malheureuse Astarté, du roi ... enfin de tous les contretemps et de toutes les infortunes qu'il avait éprouvés," or it is only referred to: "... il répétait la liste de ses infortunes, à commencer depuis la chienne ... jusqu'à son arrivée chez le brigand Arbogad" ("Le Pêcheur"). Most of this language with its apostrophes — *ô vertu, ô destinée,* etc. — could be read seriously if taken out of context; it could come from a Gothic novel or from tragic or lyric poetry. The context — *la chienne,* etc. — gives it parodic potential even as it echoes our reaction to serious dilemmas. As I said above, it does happen that the narrating voice takes upon itself the kind of reasoning at which Zadig is adept —

"Ainsi, après avoir été toujours puni pour avoir bien fait, il était près de périr pour avoir guéri un seigneur gourmand." It provides momentary fusion by presenting causality in the eiron's terms, but even authority and voice seems to be ridiculed when, at the end of the section following, the hero again engages in the same exercise and is sabotaged by the familiar *chute* into a concrete detail of his own speech: "... et il fut tenté de croire que tout était gouverné par une destinée cruelle qui opprimait les bons et qui faisait prospérer les chevaliers verts" ("Les Combats").

The second kind of discourse typical of the eironic hero is that by which he plans his future behaviour: "*Puisque* j'ai essuyé, dit-il, un si cruel caprice d'une fille élevée à la cour, *il faut* que j'épouse une citoyenne" ("Le Borgne"; my emphasis). After the failure of that adventure, he chooses to reject love for the study of the *librum mundi*: "Rien n'est plus heureux, disait-il, qu'un philosophe qui lit dans ce grand livre que Dieu a mis sous nos yeux. Les vérités qu'il découvre sont à lui: il nourrit et il élève son âme, il vit tranquille; il ne craint rien des hommes, et sa tendre épouse ne vient point lui couper le nez" ("Le Chien et le cheval"). The last phrase can be seen as ridiculing the reasoner, but it also has the potential to show a Zadig whose wit is increasing by making the *chute* into concrete detail that belies the elevated and universal sentiments that precede it. Our mild hesitation may give us time to reflect that the nose may have been in any case a mere euphemism for another part of the body, the healing powers of which might have been thought great.

The hero draws the same kind of literal lesson from the next misfortune: "Zadig vit combien il était dangereux quelquefois d'être trop savant, et se promit bien, à la première occasion, de ne point dire ce qu'il avait vu" ("Le Chien et le cheval"). This kind of lesson-learning corresponds to a folk-tradition; someone, usually a child, takes advice given on the occasion of one error and misapplies it to the next, but inappropriate circumstance ("Little Black Sambo"). The first type, recapitulation, also has its equivalent in children's literature: the *Little Orley* stories and "The Little Red Hen."

These two kinds of speeches in which Zadig appears as eiron, unconscious or deliberate, keep the reader from attributing to the character either richness — more than one trait — or a large capacity for change. The moments of foolishness continue to chip away at our habitual efforts to grasp and to compose him as a unified and literarily believable whole. To avoid further suffering, he thinks, it suffices to do exactly the opposite of what he did previously; this conviction is continuously and infelicitously applied: he is happy that unlike his first master, his new one has no wife; he is surprised that a dog and a horse caused him harm but that a parrot did good; and after the theft of his suit of armor, he says, "Voilà ce que c'est ... de m'être éveillé trop tard; si j'avais moins dormi, je serais roi de Babylone, je posséderais Astarté." I repeat that these speeches may, however, be received two ways: as comic simplicity, ironic mention of childish reasoning; or, in the context of the incomprehensibility of evil and in the light of the narrator's occasional espousal of this kind of statement, these conclusions about the immediate cause of a given misfortune may be registered seriously since their content, the sense of injustice, echoes typical human reactions to unpleasant predicaments. Even as they block identification with the hero, or because they block it, they may seem to reveal a certain truth about the ridiculous, scandalous, arbitrariness of reward and of punishment. In this light, and in that of a certain folk-wisdom according to which "for want of a nail the (shoe, horse, soldier, battle) war was lost," it is perhaps believable that if he had slept less, he would have been king.

The dialectic between destiny and accident thus constantly receives both expression and incarnation. Pascal had remarked on so-called destiny's relation to small accidents, to chance — Cleopatra's nose — and the eighteenth century still believed in accidents ("l'accident fatal") even as it began looking for broader historical explanation of events. This view was anti-Bossuetian and anti-Christian in its refusal of a necessary continuity, ascension, progression.

These moments in which the hero exclaims, summarizes, and reflects constitute pauses in the action, a sort of counterpoint to suspense. They make the reader dwell with him on the meaning to be derived from the elemental sense of experience, on the unmeritedness and absurdity of events, but also on the distance between her and the hero's simplistic expression. The pauses are not propulsive or actional (Sternberg, p. 169), but thematic, relating to the exemplarity announced by the dedicatory epistle. They are related to it because they seem to incarnate a search for meaning, but am-

biguity is maintained since the situation that we seem encouraged
to grasp as unjust is nonetheless reviewed by a fool. These moments
are also after-the-fact counterpoint to the narrator's own predictions
of evil and of his wry comment ("bizarrerie ordinaire de la fortune").
The latter confirms Zadig's astonishment but never quite imitates the
lesson he draws. Until the episode of the hermit we wait in vain for
the narrator to guide us to a "grown-up" lesson, and in that supposedly explanatory episode itself almost all signs of narration
disappear. However, the correspondence between a part of the relation between narrator and reader and part of that between hero and
reader is one of the areas of redundancy of the tale's reception, that
is, the feeling of scandal before the spectacle of life's accidents.
By his meditative pauses, Zadig mediates his own assimilation of
those events; and the narrator mediates our reception of the hero's
reception, sometimes confirming the fact of a scandal, the serious
side of his clown, but often weakening the hero's authority by
ending his speeches with descents into isolated concrete details.
Furthermore, at those moments the narrator rarely gives guidance to
replace the hero's faded power.

II.2.   Syntagmatic Process

2.a.   *Distribution in the Signifier*

Zadig is an exception to the usual universal consent about the
meaning of a didactic story. Its ending is the primary cause of all
the discussion since it frustrates the expectation of resolution and the
desire for it. However, in the tale's unfolding, in the *histoire,* its
constants are just as clear as those of the typical philosophical story.
I except for the moment the peculiar kinds of coincidence and
disjunction in the relations discussed in 1.b. above. The description
of the integrative and assimilative processes of receiving a narrative
includes isolating the parts of the signifier and their contribution to
meaning. The reader's attempt to make sense of the text builds structures that are linear, a gradually accumulating sequence of events,
that I call here *distribution,* and those that give a sense of the
components or dimensions of each moment in the series; I call
the latter *paradigms* (Section 3, below).

The rough quantification of the segments according both to setting and to sense reveals in a general way their conformity with the
ordinary reader's expectations of what a folktale will be, and it
also gives the measure of their violation. The distributional logic
of the episodes includes traditional situations of happy stasis at the
beginning and at the end. My perception of the arrangement is based
on joining the episodes according to whether they recount good or
bad fortune, a concern reiterated in the entire story, according to
their geographical location, and according to the apportionment of
traditional dramatic action — rising action, the *nœud,* and falling
action; Figure II.A schematizes this description. The broadest division that those criteria suggest is one in three parts, the chapters
one through eight, nine through sixteen, and seventeen through
nineteen. [6] The group consisting of one through eight, the Babylonian
episodes, can be subdivided into one to three and four to eight; the
second group, including the hero's foreign wanderings (9-16) can
be seen as nine to thirteen (voyage and adventure) and fourteen to
sixteen (three persons encountered), and it thereby reverses the
division into three plus five of the first eight, making it five and
three.

The first three chapters recount misfortunes, the successive failures of the aristocratic woman, the common woman, and philosophy
to bring the happiness that the hero thinks he can have. The next
five have in common their situation in the king's court, and the
first four (4-7) have happy endings. The first two episodes at court
make Zadig think "qu'il n'est pas difficile d'être heureux" ("L'Envieux"), and "Je suis donc enfin heureux." The narrator, however,
corrects the latter perception for the reader ("Les Généreux"). The
third of the four, "Le Ministre," ends with Zadig's pronouncement
approved by the narrator; and the next, "Les Disputes et les audiences," continues the approbation by stating the subtlety of his genius
and the goodness of his soul. Later in the same chapter he commits
what the narrator calls a fault, and at its end the hero has a dream
from which he also acquires some of the sense of impending evil to
which the reader and the narrator have already been privy. In the

---

[6] I have used the numbers of the chapters as they appeared in the edition
of 1752.

FIGURE II.A   Distributional Logic

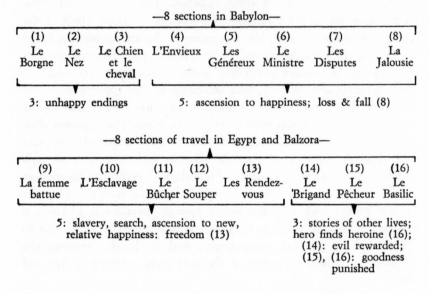

(0) Epître dédicatoire

—8 sections in Babylon—

(1)	(2)	(3)	(4)	(5)	(6)	(7)	(8)
Le Borgne	Le Nez	Le Chien et le cheval	L'Envieux	Les Généreux	Le Ministre	Les Disputes	La Jalousie

3: unhappy endings   5: ascension to happiness; loss & fall (8)

—8 sections of travel in Egypt and Balzora—

(9)	(10)	(11)	(12)	(13)	(14)	(15)	(16)
La femme battue	L'Esclavage	Le Bûcher	Le Souper	Les Rendez-vous	Le 'Brigand	Le Pêcheur	Le Basilic

5: slavery, search, ascension to new,   3: stories of other lives;
relative happiness: freedom (13)   hero finds heroine (16);
                                               (14): evil rewarded;
                                               (15), (16): goodness
                                               punished

—3 sections in (17), outside (18), in (19) Babylon—

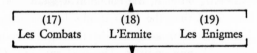

(17)	(18)	(19)
Les Combats	L'Ermite	Les Enigmes

3: trials and reward
(17) & (19): tests to be king
(18): tests to obtain understanding

eighth chapter, the fifth of the group taking place at the court of Babylon, the *nœud* is formed, the threats of the preceding sections having borne their fruit. After the three initiatory and rapid rises to happiness and falls from it (1-3), the longest-lasting conflict is formed, traditional in that the hero and his beloved are in danger of losing each other and their lives (4-8). From that moment on, the hero travels through a number of episodes equal to the number leading up to the loss, eight, that is, the group going from Chapters Nine to Sixteen in which he finds the heroine.

The voyage maintains the sense of the quest throughout episodes that have also their own point to make: intolerance, corruption, cruel

custom, etc. Geographical displacement makes manifest the existence
of a search. It is a magnifying technique belonging to many fairytales. The equilibrium between the group of eight static, Babylonian
episodes and that of the next eight in which the hero is in motion
or quest in Egypt and Balzora was achieved only in 1756 when
Voltaire divided in two what had been a single chapter containing
"Le Ministre" and "Les Disputes."

Each group of eight can be seen in two sections. The first three
chapters of disappointment and of injustice done to the hero are
followed by the five taking place at the court and establishing a
temporary happiness. In the second block of eight, five recount the
adventures of the hero as a slave; and three, his encounters with
three persons, each of whom tells the story of his or her own
adventures: the brigand (14), the fisherman (15), and the heroine (16). As the first block was amplified from seven parts to eight
by the author's dividing one chapter into two (6 and 7), the division
between the first five and the last three in the second group also
involves a change, but only a projected one. Because of the names
of their characters, the chapters called "La Danse" and "Les Yeux
bleus" belong to the group in which Zadig is slave to Sétoc, and
after Voltaire's death the editor Kehl inserted them into the story
in that place; but the fact that their author refrained from introduc-
ing them preserved the symmetry between the two blocks of eight,
and it maintained also their internal proportions as mirror-images
of each other: the arrangement of Chapters One through Eight and
Nine through Sixteen in blocks of three and five, five and three
respectively produces compensated asymmetry, frequent in Voltaire. [7]
One can also see compensated asymmetry in the final groups of three
each, 14-16 and 17-19. The fact that Fourteen, Fifteen, and Sixteen
participate in each of the two ways of cutting up the signifier — they
are the last three of the five plus three forming the second group
of eight as well, and they are a triad of similarly inserted stories
balancing the final triad — serves to highlight the exemplarity of
those concentrated inserted tales. They concentrate three times the
hero's thematic of Chapters 9 through 13, and the density of their

---

[7] Jean Starobinski, "La doppietta di Voltaire," *Strumenti Critici,* I (1966-
67), 13-32.

events puts into relief the simplicity of the return of focus to the hero and the corresponding dilution of three kinds of adventure into the three final chapters of testing.

The intercalated stories told by the three persons encountered in those three chapters expand to other lives the feeling of struggle and of injustice that the hero has been living and upon which he has been commenting. Similar in this one way to the old woman's tale in *Candide,* they constitute synchronic repetitions of the configuration spread out over all the previous chapters. They serve as generalizing devices related to the didactic purpose announced, both by their topics and by the repetition they provide. Two of them, the fisherman's and the queen's, illustrate his observation that the good are often punished. The brigand's incarnates the same general irony and poses the moral problem of Leibniz,[8] but it does so by confirming the other half of Zadig's complaint, that the evil are rewarded. His tale and the advice he gives to Zadig are very funny in that context:

> Puis-je vous demander, dit Zadig, depuis quel temps vous exercez cette noble profession? —De ma plus tendre jeunesse, reprit le seigneur. ... j'étais le grain de sable, je résolus de devenir diamant. Je commençai par voler deux chevaux . . . .

The brigand is a great success in his chosen field, so his tale proclaims the accuracy of the hero's lament even as it parodies the moral autobiography of success. This is another way in which the author-narrator repeats a view or structure that the events of the narrative illustrate and that the hero, the victim involved, articulates. The last three chapters, "Les Combats," "L'Ermite," and "Les Enigmes," return the hero to his geographical starting point where two aspects of folkloric, medieval, and courtly custom — combat and riddles, two forms of contest — appear in parodic form and surround the episode telling of his experience with the hermit-angel outside the city. The latter is supposedly a moment of revelation.

Re-reading the groups, one sees that the expansion of unmerited misfortune (1-3) contrasts with the respite of gradually acquired

---

8 Muecke, *Irony,* pp. 66-77.

temporary happiness (4-8); struggle toward new success returns and multiplies in the same proportion (9-13) as in Chapters Four through Eight. The tale then illustrates in other lives (14-16) the lack of reason that the hero feels in his. These concentrated stories make all the more noticeable or contrastive his final, formal trials, their successful outcome, and his apotheosis (17-19). The segmentation of the episodes is in itself meaningful.

2.b. *Order in the Signified*

The application of Vladimir Propp's functions confirms the existence of a folkloric plot-type, reveals the presence of micro-sequences of action in the *histoire,* and permits one kind of description of the horizontal forward-moving thread of the principal actions. Although this method of observing records a simple kind of sense, it also ultimately arrives at a reading or at an interpretation, part of this being that the story is against interpretation. This hypothesis about how the text invites certain readings and then alters and limits them leads to an examination of the deployment of the signifier in time and to a consideration and comparison of the paradigmatic structures generated. It tries to describe the ways in which the story guides and determines the boundaries of an inductive process.

The proper name *Zadig* is the principal signifying link between all the episodes. Another way of saying this is that the hero of all of them has the same name. We consent to think that the signified of that name is a person whose adventures and meditations are a constant of the attention we pay to what is told; we lend coherence to that lexeme. Thus continually constituted by the reader, Zadig is seen to combine the two types of hero that Propp identifies, questor and victim; in the folktale the two kinds can be combined (Propp, p. 103). In the overt, represented action he is a questor since he loses, looks for, and regains Astarté (Quest I in Figure II.B). The other link between the episodes in the signified is the conflictual structure of evil rewarded and goodness punished; in these oppositions, the questing hero also thinks himself, until the very end, a victim of general injustice. For this reason, he also conducts a second quest (II in the Figure), a philosophical one, that of understanding. Because a certain kind of discourse — wonder,

FIGURE II.B Proppian Coding

Chapter and Title		*Quest I (happiness)*	*Quest II (understanding)*	*Sub-sequences (other heroes)*
Le Borgne	1a	8^{1a}		
	1b	12, 13, 14neg. (Sémire)		
	1c			
Le Nez	2	12, 13, 14neg. (Azora)		
Le Chien et le cheval	3	12, 13, 14neg. (knowledge of nature)		
L'Envieux	4a	12, 13, 14neg. (philosophy)		
	4b	12, 13, 14neg. 19^{1a} (friendship)		
Les Généreux	5	19^{1a}		
Le Ministre	6	19^{1a}		
Les Disputes et les audiences	7	6, 7, 21		
La Jalousie	8	8^{1b}, 9, 10, 11, 22	8^{II}, 12, 13, 14neg.	8^{s}, 14^{z}, 19^{s}
La Femme battue	9	12, 13, 14neg. (Missouf is hostile donor.)		8^{s}, 14^{z}, 19^{s}
L'Esclavage	10a	12, 13, 14neg. (Sétoc is hostile donor.)	12, 13, 14neg.	8^{s}, 14^{z}, 19^{s}
	10b			
Le Bûcher	11a	16, 17, 19		
	11b			

Le Souper	12	21		8^S, 14^Z, 19^S
Les Rendez-vous	13	22		
Le Brigand	14		12, 13, 14neg.	8^A, 12, 13, 14, 16, 17, 18, 19, 21, 22, 25, 26, 28, 30, 31
Le Pêcheur	15		12, 13, 14neg.	8^P, 12, 13, 14^Z (present) 8^P, 12, 13, 14neg. } (past) 8^P, 12, 13, 14neg. }
Le Basilic	16a 16b	19^{Tb} 21, 22	12, 13, 14neg.	8^A, 12, 13, 14^Z 8°, 12, 13, 14^Z
Les Combats	17	23, 24, 25, 26, 11, 12, 13, 14neg.		
L'Ermite	18	15	12, 13, 14neg. (book) 12, 13 12, 13 } visits 12, 13 12, 13	
Les Enigmes	19	27, 25, 26, 28, 30, 31	[14] [19]	

surprise, lamentation — is in Chapter Eight and after it constantly assigned to the name, we synthesize under it not only the concrete search but also the abstract one; not only the quest for a person and for happiness but also that for understanding and wisdom.

One more general statement on the order of the actions needs to be made: the tale proceeds by multiple episodes of loss and of reparation. Propp describes this kind of doubling of sequences, saying that after any 22, help given to hero, there exists the possibility of a new misdeed (8 bis) followed by another sequence that moves toward a new reparation. He goes on to say in his terms what is commonly known, that many tales are composed of more than one series of functions, a new misdeed giving rise to a new sequence, and that thus sometimes one story unites a whole series of tales. This is precisely the case in *Zadig*.[9]

The individual anecdotes, the episodes of certain chapters, may be looked upon as stories or as fragments of them; that is, their inner events as well as their entirety as event, are codable in Proppian functions. For example, in the first episode after the broad requirement for happiness is posed (8^{Ia}), the two and one-half sentences going from "Il devait se marier à Sémire" to "lorsque, se promenant ensemble," constitute the description of the initial situation of the episode (0). The struggle with the aggressor (16) and the wound received by the hero (17) result in victory (18) and temporary reparation (19): Sémire is safe. Her rejection of the wounded hero and his denunciation of her could be seen as a denunciation of the false heroine because she might be seen to share the hero's

---

[9] The Brazilian critic Maria Pandolfo has published exercises analyzing the story by the methods of Propp and of Greimas. A literary supplement printed the first articles: "La Morphologie de Zadig (1)," *Minas Gerias. Suplemento literario* (Belo Horizonte) 22 November 1975; and (2) in the issue of 29 November 1975; "O Model greimasiano e as estruturas narrativas," 26 June 1976; "As Estruturas narrativas e o ideologema do signo," 21 February 1976. A book then appeared: *Zadig: Análisè da narrativa* (Rio de Janeiro: Vozes, 1978). She provides a good example of a rich and ideologically satisfying *interpretation,* but the latter is the result of a strong desire to make a coherent and unified sense of all the elements of the text, and this decision requires bringing to it many outside factors and creations such as personified Evil who "learns things" about Zadig and who sets traps. The insistence on organic unity weighs on her enterprise, not only in the presupposition of a fundamental coherence but also in her efforts to find an action in the story to correspond to every single one of the functions.

sphere of action since her conquest was not in question. She thus shares the sphere in which the second struggle occurs, the fight against the blindness resulting from the wound; but she gives up and leaves him alone. Her pretensions would thus be *mensongè-res* (24) when she ceases to be loyal, and one infers her denunciation (28) from the fact that punishment of the false hero (30) comes at the end of the entire story where one learns that she never found consolation for the error of having left Zadig. The end of this chapter, "Le Borgne," and the whole of the next, "Le Nez," constitute another micro-sequence. In it Azora, presumably part of the heroic sphere since she is joined to the hero in marriage, seems frivolous and false (24). Zadig tests her, she fails, and he denounces her (28); her eternal punishment (30), regret, is told at the end of the tale along with Sémire's. In the next episode, "Le Chien et le cheval," the hero combats aggressors three times in the conversations about what he saw. The first two end in victory (16, 18). In the third, he loses and pays a fine (16, 18neg). Beginning with the fourth section, "L'Envieux," and continuing through the group of five chapters that I labeled in Section 2.a. as *ascension towards happiness,* the micro-codings include true misdeeds or lacks (8) and real reparation (19). Thus, they correspond to a general impression of the hero's increasing well-being. In the first of these the broken tablets cause him to be accused (8); saved by chance and by the parrot, he becomes the king's friend (19, reparation). The act of reparation is reiterated: the bestowal of the cup at the end of "Les Généreux" and his being named prime minister at the end of the sixth chapter. These three reparations occur in the three sections that show the temporary happiness of the hero, a state from which, although he remains in favor, the fall is prepared in the two episodes following: in "Les Disputes et les audiences," the wife of the *jaloux* interrogates him by a gesture (6, aggressor tries to deceive victim), and his failure to respond as she wishes (7, the victim allows himself to be deceived) will make her inform the king of Zadig's and Astarté's love for each other. This precipitates the second principal misdeed (8[Tb]), the one told in "La Jalousie," where the king threatens the lovers, thus separating and pursuing them (21). The dwarf divulges this plot to Zadig (9, mediation: divulgence of misdeed); and he leaves the palace (10, hero consents to act; 11, departure of hero), forced to do so by Cador and aided in the transport by him (22, aid brought to hero). Propp observes that departure (11) sometimes takes the form of flight from danger.

This misdeed and this lack of the desired object will not be repaired until Chapter Sixteen. The intervening episodes will depict the hero fleeing and encountering diverse adventures until he finds again what was lost. One can see the misdeed, the loss of Astarté, in Chapter Eight as repeating and incarnating the hero's initial requirement, the lack coded 8^I, which was that of happiness; for the eighth section, happiness has come to equal possession of the queen, but it was posed from the final line of the initial description of the hero according to which he "crut qu'il pouvait être heureux." When the two expectations are combined and viewed as a quest for happiness, Quest I in Figure II.B above, the micro-or sub-sequences, which are themselves codable as fragments, can then be re-coded as incidents related to the widest view of the total action. In the context of this quest, the incidents concerning Sémire, Azora, and the animals appear as tests of the hero (12) and as records of his reactions (13). In each case, because none brings happiness, and because he states his disappointment, the result may be called a *14 negative* (magic object not received); for despite his efforts, he does not receive the magic or enabling object that would open the way to acquisition of his goal. The first half of the fourth chapter, the controversy about eating griffons, shows the same pattern of test, reaction, and negative outcome: "A quoi tient le bonheur! tout me persécute dans ce monde...." The second half relates the first happy episode in the pattern of trial, reaction, and reparation (12, 13, 19), the reparation being, temporarily, that of the first lack, happiness (8^{Ia} repaired by 19^{Ia}): "Zadig commençait à croire qu'il n'est pas si difficile d'être heureux." Two more successes in each of the next two chapters combine to make a triple victory: "Je suis donc enfin heureux." After a further successful episode — he settles a dispute about the way to enter the temple — the seventh chapter, "Les Disputes et les audiences," returns to certain functions (6, aggressor tries to deceive victim; 7, victim is deceived) preparatory to loss, and by which the wife of the envious one and chance (the garters) combine to pursue Zadig (21) by attempting to harm him in the king's eyes. The beginning of Chapter Eight announces his new unhappiness: "Le malheur de Zadig vint de son bonheur même et surtout de son mérite," says the narrator. This lack is that of the object (8^{Ib}) become necessary to his happiness (8^{Ia}). The dwarf divulges the imminent misdeed (9), and Cador helps him to depart (10, 11, 12).

It is at this moment, at the end of Chapter Eight, that Zadig himself starts posing the larger question, one going beyond his own state of contentment or discontent: "Qu'est-ce que donc la vie humaine? O vertu! à quoi m'avez-vous servi?" From this point onward we can code a second quest, that of understanding. The trial and reaction shown here do not give an answer to this desire either (12, 13, 14neg, under Quest II, Figure II.B). In the first paragraph of Chapter Nine, the hero continues to pose the cosmic question: "Son âme ... contemplait ... l'ordre immuable de l'univers." The event of this chapter, his saving an Egyptian woman from the man who is beating her, has the same form of trying his courage and generosity (12), of reaction — he kills the oppressor — (13), and of failure (14neg.) since the woman (Missouf, hostile donor) reproaches him his valiant act and since it advances him not at all in either quest: he is no closer to finding Astarté (8^{Ia}), and the inexplicable reaction of the woman merely confirms the strangeness (8^{Ib}) he finds in events and creatures. The chapter "L'Esclavage" contains two incidents: 10a, Zadig's being put into slavery (12, 13: discussion and trial with the Egyptians) and Sétoc's acting as hostile donor of the refused magic object (14neg.); and 10b, the solving by the hero of a dispute about a debt owed Sétoc. This is the first in a series of episodes in which Zadig can be seen as magic auxiliary, 14, for the person he helps, Sétoc, his master. These also may be coded as microsequences. The next two, 11a and 11b, show Zadig solving a conflict about the celestial army and another concerning the burning of the widow Almona. Each may be coded 8^s, Sétoc's lack (of knowledge, of wisdom, etc.); 14^z, Zadig's aid; and 19^s, reparation of the lack. In the last of this type, "Le Souper," Chapter Twelve, Zadig performs the same wise and peace-making function and then learns abruptly that he will be burned to death (21, pursuit of hero by aggressor). This fact returns him to the hero's sphere, and the actions rejoin the principal plane of the hero's quests.

Before following the rest of his story, we may ask what kinds of meaning are produced by those episodes in which Sétoc is the one with the problems, and where Zadig has all the answers. None of the three episodes 10b, 11a, 11b advances the widest action of the tale (Zadig's love-plight and his philosophical one); they are probably easily accepted by the reader because they coincide with the conventions of certain types of stories and because they enhance the superior qualities that she expects to see in a hero. The kinds of tale echoed in these episodes include the picaresque, where the wandering hero encounters persons and situations that belong to the category of *nouvelle,* news, and of which novelty is the only interest. They also include the ancient types of riddle or problem, the oracle, sibyl, and so on, found in medieval romances and in Rabelais and in which a hero's talents are tested or displayed in ways not necessarily physical: dilemmas, cases to adjudicate, disputes among groups, and so on. These conventions also include the creation of a sense of epic delay; the hero is on his way somewhere, and although these incidents do not contribute to the advancement of the principal action, his finding the queen and wisdom, they do *take time* and give an impression that space as well as time has been traversed before he arrives at his goal.

The story of Almona's saving the life of Zadig occupies the next chapter, "Les Rendez-vous," and like the incidents preceding, it highlights certain common social abuses as it dwells four times on lecherous and hypocritical ecclesiastics who allow themselves to be tricked into clemency by the beautiful widow's promises. Zadig was condemned to death (21), she saves him (22): each kept the other from being burned. He is now free to leave Sétoc, and if one re-reads the previous micro-sequences in their totality (episodes 10a, 10b, 11a, 11b, 12, 13), they can all be seen as another long trial-by-combat over a secondary adversary, slavery, from which he emerges victorious (18). The hero takes up again his wanderings, and the sentence telling this movement also re-poses his two goals, 8^{Ia} and 8^{Ib}, confirming by this repetition the eccentric nature of the anecdotes preceding: "Zadig marcha du côté de la Syrie, toujours pensant à la malheureuse Astarté, et toujours réfléchissant sur le sort qui s'obstinait à se jouer de lui et à le persécuter." He then recapitulates his adventures, their recitation enriching this part of his perpetual lament, the fact that fate persecutes a good man.

The next three chapters, the ones containing three tales told to the hero by three people he meets, can be coded internally with their tellers as heroes; and they can also be placed as uncoded entities under Quest II since each teller can be seen as a potential donor in the principal hero's search. Zadig still hopes to understand his life; and he undergoes the test of listening, 12, and, in the first two, reacts, 13, by exclamations relating to his failure to understand:

> ô fortune! ô destinée! un voleur est heureux . . . . (Ch. 14)

> O puissant Orosmade! . . . vous vous servez de moi pour consoler cet homme; de qui vous servirez-vous pour me consoler? . . . il répétait la liste de ses infortunes, à commencer depuis la chienne de la reine jusqu'à son arrivée chez le brigand Arbogad. (Ch. 15)

In the last of the three, since he has found Astarté, and since the episode thus represents reparation of the lack of 8^{Tb}, he tells his story to her "en peu de mots" and then asks to hear hers. This lengthy stretch of delayed exposition catches up both reader and hero on the adventures that the heroine has undergone in the meantime, and it offers further fragmented commentary on various social abuses. In this chapter, in which one element of the quest for happiness has been attained, the end has the hero again pursued by the (an) aggressor (21), and he is saved (22) by the arrival of the letter. The fact that the stories are told and that he listens may thus be seen as test and reaction with a negative outcome, no enabler (magic object) having been obtained toward Quest II; Quest I is partially served however in the person of the third tale-teller, the queen. When one codes as micro-sequences the tales told, one discovers schemes similar to those found in episodes 10b, 11a, and 11b where some other creature having suffered loss or misdeed (an 8) and having undergone some test and having reacted, Zadig himself appears as the magic object permitting resolution of the dilemma. The story told by Arbogad is particularly rich in codable events (Figure II.C). The fisherman's story recounts two past lacks, the search for understanding, all this may be coded as 12, 13, 14neg. twice). However, his entire encounter with the hero in the present of the *histoire* can be coded as a 14positive: that is, Zadig acts again as enabler: he gives the fisherman half of his own money and sends him to Cador in Babylon for more help. In the third of this group of chapters, the one where the queen is found, Zadig also acts as enabler for someone else, for Ogul, the tyrant in need of a basilisk $(8^O, 12, 13, 14^Z)$ and for Astarté also whose life he saves and whose liberty he obtains by the exploit of healing Ogul. The functions $8^O, 12, 13, 14^Z$ would all be included in the 14 healing Ogul. The functions $8^O, 12, 13, 14^Z$ would all be included in the 14 (reaction) of Astarté's $8^A, 12, 13, 14^Z$; and the latter group of functions seen from the point of view of Astarté's loss is what makes 19^{Tb} (reparation of lack) possible in Zadig's own long sequence.

In spite of these similarities the three chapters are nonetheless varied in the location and attribution of the sequences that they contain. The fourteenth contains the illustration, in Arbogad's life-story, of the hero's negative observation that the wicked are rewarded; its entirety may thus be coded as leading in form — test and reaction — but not in substance toward the goal of Quest II. Its sub-sequence coded with the brigand as hero shows the details of the lawless man's victory. The fifteenth illustrates in the fisherman's story the hero's observation that the good — or even those who simply mind their own business — are punished. It contains three sub-sequences, two out of the fisherman's past, with him as hero, and one in his present, where the result of his telling his tale is that Zadig helps him. The sixteenth also illustrates the hero's lament about unmerited suffering, and its whole forms part of his own adventure; but its sub-sequences are even more complex than those of the two previous episodes. One consists of the heroine's past; one, of her present with Zadig as enabler; and one introduces yet another hero of a sub-sequence (Ogul) in whose adventure, illness, Zadig also plays a critical role. The redundancy plays itself out without being redundant in the *histoire* — different heroes, lives, places — and by varying even the use of the *récit* — the narrative *now,* its past, and the past of its past. Zadig's experience finds replication in other experience, other times, and other places. It is given universality by these repetitions.

These three chapters are thus similar because each enriches the temporal planes and the personnel of sequences; and they are remarkable for their reiteration of a sequence that is the expression of Zadig's dilemma according to which one is tested, reacts valiantly, and gets nothing in return. The sub-sequences also present Zadig's function as destiny for others; even as fate harms him, his movements and reactions impinge on the fortune of others and sometimes have a positive effect.

If for the moment we omit considering Chapter Eighteen, "L'Ermite," the end of the story corresponds neatly and rapidly to Propp's final functions. In Seventeen, viewed in the perspective of the quest for happiness, the hero returns incognito (23), hears the claims of a false hero (24), performs difficult tasks, the combats (25, 26), is tricked (6, 7) and departs again (11). In the domain of Quest II, the search for understanding, all this may be coded as 12, 13, 14neg. again. After the episode of the hermit, the hero is recognized (27), undergoes another difficult task, the riddles (25, 26). He denounces the false hero (28) who is punished (30); and he receives his reward, the throne and the hand of the queen (31). After that there is nothing to code under Quest II, for he asks no more questions. This application of Propp's functions is not designed to prove that *Zadig* is a story, for the functions taken out of any context can also be seen to show that the tale is a parody of a story.

Discussions about interpretation of the story have tended to focus on what I just left out, "L'Ermite." Its nature and its placement must be examined in order to see some of the ways they affect the reader's experience of the tale. The chapter constitutes an interruption in the falling action just summarized. I have already pointed to two of the ways in which it sets itself apart from the others, by its length and by the virtual absence of deixis. More obvious traits that distinguish it are its main character, who is a supernatural visitor, and the rapid succession of four similar events in which the hermit is actor and Zadig spectator and which were preceded by a pact and announced as revelatory. The presentation to Zadig of enigmas that he is invited to interpret resembles the enigmatic discourse of the chapter itself which the reader confronts without guidance from the narrator. This intermediary chapter deals only with Quest II, understanding, "le livre des destinées" offered to the hero. It separates the two halves of the tests that permit choosing a king and that will give to the hero what he sought by

Quest I. This is the first time since the introduction of the search for understanding in Chapter Eight that the two threads have been separately represented in the signifier. After solemn preliminaries — the august appearance of the hermit, Zadig's immediate knowledge that he must show signs of respect to the old man, the view of the traditional book containing The Answers, and so on — the hero undergoes again what may be seen in the Proppian coding as test and reaction: this inability to decipher the book in the first 12 (test), 13 (reaction), 14neg. (failure to receive magic object) of the episode. He then responds four times in four visits to a test of the type "Stick with me no matter what happens," the terms of the pact proposed to him by the hermit: "...jurez-moi par Orosmade que vous ne vous séparerez point de moi d'ici à quelques jours, quelque chose que je fasse." The form of testing and the offer of reward are clearly present. The reader has a sense of the structure in which a hero is usually seen to have earned the right to special knowledge or special powers (the magic object, 14). She expects that he will attain access to understanding, but although the form of discovery, of resolution, of gratification is there, its normal content is absent. By the trappings — angel, proclamations, puzzles, "You alone deserve to know" — we are made to think that something has been transmitted, but the hero's response does not permit us to feel or to know that clearly. It represents on his part both protest, "Mais," and submission, "Zadig, à genoux, adora la Providence, et se soumit." The circumstances and the discourse made us think that something was to be transmitted (14), and that there was to be thus reparation (19) of the lack (8^{II}) of comprehensibility.

All these means of isolating the episode make it seem to come out of nowhere; and, by giving it the importance of an exception, they seem to crystallize the second parallel quest. The part of the title "ou la destinée," the exclamations and interrogations about happiness and about justice, and the long series of misfortunes, all have presumably combined to make the reader share in some way the hero's feeling of perplexity. At the angel's disappearance into heaven and at the hero's submission, the reader may conclude either that the examples and the discourse of the heavenly visitor are convincing explanations or that they are equally incomprehensible to her and to the hero, that the explanation of everything is that one can explain nothing.

The book of destinies which Zadig could not decipher before the hermit took him in hand remains mysterious. It would seem to resemble the blank book of the end of *Micromégas* as well as the attack on theodicy in *Candide,* the modesty of Lockean epistemology, and Voltaire's hatred for metaphysics; however, this book is *not blank:* "Il mit le livre dans les mains de Zadig, qui, tout instruit qu'il était dans plusieurs langues, ne put déchiffrer un seul caractère du livre." The presence of a *blank* book would constitute a *referential* statement according to which there is no answer. This one, on the contrary, is simply unreadable and shows the hero's ignorance. Similarly, Voltaire's tale itself may be seen as the book of destinies, as promised by the title; it too is unreadable. Both are, however, eminently writable.

II.3. Paradigms

Another way of approaching a description of the reader's experience of the several endings interrogates each of the episodes in its entirety in addition to studying their succession as I have just done in Section 2.b. Every whole text is a combination of an analogical component and a sequential one; that is, it can deny its own progress by paradigmatic repetition, or it can seek its own progress by stressing movement and change in time. My goal here is the description of the kind of balance or imbalance that obtains between the two tendencies. One kind of analysis produces a scheme of the forces at work in the plot. In the figgure below (II.C), square brackets enclose the formal or "grammatical" occupants of the spheres of action, but I do not believe them to be usefully viewed as substantial or "rhetorical" agents of those spheres. I shall explain this later.

The episodes telling the hero's desiring, losing, and finding the object of his happiness and those showing his search for understanding must appear in the order given (1a, 4b, 7, 8, 16a, 17, 19); but the larger group, the episodes 1b, 1c, 2, 3, 4a, 5 and 6 (which reiterate 4b), 9, 10, 11, 12, 13, 14, 15, 16, 18, recount self-contained adventures and possess little necessity in the quests and little

FIGURE II.C   Spheres of Action

SPHERE	QUEST I	QUEST II
1) Object	happiness, Astarté	understanding
2) Mandator	Zadig	Zadig
3) Hero	Zadig	Zadig
4) Aggressor	wife of the envious one, king, priests, etc.	fate? chance? destiny?
5) Donor	(all hostile) Missouf, Sétoc, all those at 14neg. in Fig. II.B	[hermit]
6) Magic Auxiliary	Z. never finds one	[the book of destinies]
7) False Hero	Itobad	———

connection among their components. There are some ties between parts of the *histoire;* for example, the figure of Missouf first appears in the incident of "La Femme battue," Chapter Nine, and at that moment the hero notes her resemblance to the queen. She is indeed carried off by soldiers who, one guesses, think that she is Astarté. Her name reappears seven chapters later when the queen tells her story in which Missouf figures in several ways (Ch. 16). In a more perfunctory manner the first loves of the hero (Chapters 1-2) are mentioned again in the last chapter, and they thus contribute to the tying off of all loose ends as tradition requires. The sense of progression given by the hero's desiring, losing, and finding the heroine is seconded by these repetitions that stress the linear movement of the *histoire*. A backgrounded sense of relation is provided by the reported movement from one place to another, but this displacement has virtually no value as *theme* or *structure,* two terms often used to refer to *voyage* in Voltaire's stories. The fact of travel has very different degrees of integration and different capacities for generating meaning according to the work, and one distinguishes among a) the place where each event unfolds, b) the nature of the event and of its participants, and c) its relation with other events, which can be anterior, posterior, or simultaneous in the time belonging to the *histoire*. In *Zadig* the relation between geographical location represented or referred to and the nature of what happens there is very loose. The Proppian coding shows that departure, transfer, and return do matter; for it is traditional to conduct the quest on a geographical scale and at the moment of resolution to return the hero to the point of departure: the oldest tale is a traveler's tale. Apart from the exotic names of persons and places,[10] it matters little, for instance, to the *nature* of the consultation whether Zadig is a slave in Egypt or in Virginia. A dropped garter was a sign in Paris and perhaps not in fact in Babylon; brigands wander everywhere; priests can be persecutors in all cultures, etc. Only "Le Bûcher" attaches itself specifically to a particular geographical region, but the narrator himself generalizes it by explaining how the custom of burning widows migrated from Scythia through India to Arabia and that it threatens the entire Orient. This genealogy of the crime ends by reducing its geographical specificity and by dwelling more on the commonplace, already used in the episode concerning Azora, according to which desolate widows are easily awakened to new erotic interest. This *topos,* the barely restrained, easily released lust of widows, exists in most European cultures. Voltaire uses it to show the fickle nature of Zadig's wife Azora, who is willing to cut off part of her dead husband's body in order to heal her new lover; and Zadig's means of stopping the oriental widow from immolating herself is to spend time with her arousing her interest in him and thus in life. While both incidents neatly oppose Eros and Thanatos, the cultural forces that bring them about in what is known as *real life* are distorted or suppressed in both cases.[11]

---

[10] In proper names there is a preference shown for *A*'s: Azora, Arimaze, Arnou, Astarté, Almona, Arbogad; for *S*'s: Sémire, Sétoc; for *M*'s: Missouf, Moabdar; and for *O*'s: Orosmade, Orcan, Ogul, Otame. Both good and bad persons exist in all three groups; Moabdar and Arbogad are almost anagrams of each other; the *Z*'s are all important: Zoroastre, le livre du Zend, Zadig. Readers surely note the exoticism and there is a comic potential in the repetitions of all kinds.

[11] Throughout history, single women, divorced and widowed, young and old have been seen by men as threatening to them. The supposedly comic topos of the widow's sexual insatiability is an attempt to contain by mockery the freedom and relative social and financial power she sometimes possesses. A fictionalized example of these fears and their result in modern times is the stoning of the widow in *Zorba the Greek.* They also make of widows fair and less guilt-producing game for seduction. The practice of burning them was not, we may be sure, due to their stubborn desire to die, as Voltaire would have it in his story; it was rather a convenience, wrapped in religion and

The relative lack of geographical specificity for the forces at work in the incidents does not, however, eliminate the signifying capacity of the oriental setting. The tale offers as its decor one-half of a traditional opposition between East and West. The ethos attributed by Christian Europe to the so-called pagan east is one that includes a concept of arbitrary violence and unjust autocratic acts committed by satraps who live and die by the sword. The setting thus seems to claim antiphrastic status — exotic and therefore unlike us. Antiphrasis is however denied; in a second reversal, this violent East is depicted as containing the same structure of power, influence, and chance that the West comports; and the superior Christian civilization instead finds similarities between itself and the lands of barbarity. The overt opposition is finally subverted and becomes deconstructive reflection.

The voyage substitutes itself for causality and for necessity in the passage from the *histoire* (represented actions, content) of one episode to that of another. The essentially contiguous nature of most of the sequences is probably counterbalanced in the reader's perception by the forward movement of the voyage, which is largely irrelevant in the ways just described; but even though not all are simply contiguous with each other, all are related in one profound way. The forces represented are the same from episode to episode and are superimposable. They all generate the same oppositions. In the *histoire* the events and the reflections recorded oppose a Zadig wise and virtuous with a Zadig punished. They contrast the undeservedness of his aggressors whom he believes evil with their successes and rewards. That this opposition is explicit in the text is clear in the recapitulations and exclamations, many of which have been quoted above. It is also manifestly concentrated in the episode of the hermit where virtue is punished in three of the four visits and where wickedness is rewarded in one. This quantification by the *récit* intensifies the presentation of the manifest oppositions. The

---

tradition, by which the male-dominated society disposed of what it feared. Similar impulses may explain the accusation, torture, and murder of witches — most of whom were unmarried or widowed females — in Europe and in North America: E. William Monter, *European Witchcraft* (New York: Wiley, 1969). For a radical presentation of this fear and its many social consequences in different cultures, see Mary Daly, *Gyn/Ecology: The Metaethics of Radical Feminism* (Boston: Beacon Press, 1978).

latter thus arise from almost all the episodes, and they are never resolved or synthesized: it is simply that they are sometimes rendered briefly invalid and that they are finally annulled since in the last chapter Zadig wise and virtuous becomes also Zadig happy and rewarded, the evil ones are tortured by regret, and those conditions are predicted for the indefinite future.

The immanent structure produced by the *récit* broadens the scope of the manifest oppositions and alters them. There is no synthesis here either. The manifest structure expressed by the hero and to which the reader is often witness expects virtue and happiness, vice and punishment to go together. Most of the episodes contradict this expectation and thus contradict any theological ethics of destiny in favor of a natural ethic, similar in spirit to those of Diderot and of Rousseau although much less elaborated than either of theirs. That the just equivalence between virtue and reward, vice and punishment do obtain at the beginning and at the end of the story is a phenomenon the symmetry of which is felt as belonging to the *récit* or signifier and not as inherent in the material events reported. One has no sense of reading a representation of the slice-of-life type according to which homogeneous incidents would reveal themselves in succession. Rather, shape is given to them by the arrangement in the signifier. Virtue, untested at the beginning, tested and triumphant at the end, does nothing to synthesize the oppositions observed in the middle by hero and reader. The initial and final stages are simply cases of the absence of evil.

This immanent opposition between virtue rewarded and vice punished is suggested by events and by the narrator. It offers itself as an existential correction of the oppositions that most events suggest and that he expresses. *Correction* here means *modification, not annihilation.* This is so because the *récit* shows the virtuous and persecuted hero being nonetheless happy at the end and nonetheless destiny for others. One lesson derivable from his final happiness is that perseverance in the game of chance or destiny can end well: if *Zadig* is the Book of Destinies, we can entertain that belief. Another lesson, which does not exclude the first, is also available: led in that direction by the events I coded above with the hero as donor, the reader can observe that Zadig at the same time undergoes evil destiny in his own mind and constitutes beneficent fate in the lives of others. In the views expressed by him wisdom brings misfortune and impotence, but the fatality of the *récit* makes of wisdom an agent of change and of power for others. The difference between the manifest structure and the immanent one is a correction by the latter of the hero's perception but without his being shown as having articulated it. This emphatic and permanent correction reflects a view held by nearly all the eighteenth-century French philosophers, that of the wise and virtuous ruler as destiny, the enlightened despot as capable of making changes for the betterment of mankind's usual fate.

This reversal resembles one I shall point out in *Candide*. In both stories the hero, who is an eiron manifesting a perplexing opposition, escapes it in the immanence of reception. The immanent structure becomes manifest in the *histoire* at the very end though Zadig is not made to articulate any realization of it as Candide does. By the subtraction of harmful fate, he is no longer an eiron; that is, his perceptions are no longer inferior to the reader's and to the narrator's. He is master of all circumstances, and he is uniquely destiny for others. The emblem of the immanent structure closes syntagmatically and semantically on itself, and thus simply replaces the other:

A   B   B   C

On bénissait Zadig et Zadig bénissait le ciel.

The repetition of the hero's name at its center, by suggesting that A is to B as B to C, puts Zadig and Providence, "le ciel," together. The hero as philosopher-king thus assures the link between A, his subjects, and C or heaven.

The *histoire* has then made Zadig's initial belief, that virtue brings happiness, come true after his passage through a series of reversals of that belief. During those episodes, a meaning superior or corrective to the simplistic oppositions of his discourse was nonetheless transmitted. It shows that even as he undergoes destiny's trials, he himself constitutes or incarnates a portion of it. The difference between the contribution made by *histoire* and by *récit* constitutes a correction by the reader of Zadig's perception of divine (in)justice; and the final beatific state reifies the perception that was available all along.

The co-existence of the two paradigms projected by the episodes of the tale is guided and completed by the archetypal presentation of character. Unlike *Micromégas,* here only one character plays the role of hero, that is, in Propp's terms, occupies the hero's sphere of action. The more the world of the character is reduced to singularity — the same thing (obstacle) happens over and over to the same person (hero) — the nearer it is to the primordial mythological type of structural organization of the text. The presence of other heroes in their briefly recounted spheres — Sétoc, Ogul, the fisherman, etc. — reinforces the archetypal plight. They are isomorphs of the principal hero, but the tale stays close to myth by the hero's solitude in his own quest. In the same way, by the infinitely repeatable episode of unmerited suffering, this tale is closer to ritual and to myth; the beginning and end truncate those episodes without claiming internal necessity, and they allow the mass of the tale, like *Candide*'s, to be seen as spilling out into eternity, without marked borders. Neither do the hero's birth and death frame the narrative, which would be a mark of "news" instead of myth, that is, the sign of proximity to modern linear plot-narrative. [12] Rather, a form of death occurs inside the tale in Zadig's disappearance after the theft of his armor. This movement is followed by his return in disguise and by his transfiguration. The schema of fall and of rebirth belongs also to myth. The voyage and the loss and gain of Astarté provide a veneer of linear construction on a narrative that retains also the cyclical nature belonging to myth. The final miracle — they lived happily ever after — belongs to linear narrative and parodies the happy endings of non-didactic stories; but the miracle begins when Zadig emerges from his tent after sleep, a gesture — "entrance into enclosed space and emergence from it" — that characterizes a middle event typical of myth (Lotman, p. 171). This parentage with myth may also be seen as parody of myth, the long-suffering Zadig recalling while trivializing Job, Sisyphus, and Prometheus. The tale is almost a parody of multiple kinds of meaning — moral, religious, anagogical — and in its imitation of myth as literary process, it has the potential to criticize and to devalue the moral force of myth itself.

[12] Lotman, pp. 169, 180.

II.4. MODAL COMMUNICATION

It seems clear that the *conte philosophique* can be described neither as character-centered nor as plot-centered. Although its narratives are anecdotal and apsychological, they cannot be seen as falling into the category of plot-centeredness in the same way as a *nouvelle* does; for the anecdotes accumulate, all having the same structure of experience and seeming to derive their broad form from factors not inherent in the events represented. The genre can be said to be theme-centered, and it offers itself as a series of parables inside a broad parabolic structure.

Among the means the didactic text employs for directing its decoding are those that I have termed *modal,* those requiring cognitive operations beyond the simple reception of sense and beyond first image-building. Direct verbal aggression requires no adjustment of sense, but it does break with the context of story-telling by a covert narrator, and it is openly manipulative of the reader's judgments and sympathies. A phrase suggesting some kind of substitution — *Paris* for *Babylon* — or reversal — *idiot* for *vénérable* — belongs in a second category of didactic modes, and more extended passages encouraging lengthier re-reading or double reading by translation form a third. In the previous chapter I further distinguished the technique of satiric dramatization, entire scenes that show characters making fools of themselves instead of the narrator's telling something about them. The directions for understanding these scenes most fully are varied: the depiction of inconsistent behavior (Sémire, Azora, Missouf), the isolation and exaggeration of a single trait (Yébor, Itobad). The lesson can be explicitly drawn by the narrator at the end of the scene, but most often it simply stands with a potential appeal to an unprovable standard of common sense (Barthes's gnomic code in *S/Z*) and lets us decide that the *mages* or the judges, for instance, exhibit behavior and beliefs that we ought to condemn by that standard. This commentary like all except the first named above, direct aggression, is implicit. These types of modal communication are mixed and are sometimes blurred in *Zadig.* I begin by describing the simplest type and then cite an entire passage in order to study the mixture of modes that is found there.

Like *Micromégas* this tale begins with a cluster of aggressions; and, as we might expect, the first chapter also bears a high density of deictics, the second-highest of the tale. The two forms of control, abuse and deixis, unite to habituate the reader to being trained and instructed. They do not seem to orient very precisely her moral values. The targets are scattered and trivial compared to the gradually constructed philosophical question posed by the episodes of the story itself. Given the variety of the early targets — *vieux derviches* in the epistle; the young and rich, typical conversation, and people's knowledge of metaphysics in Chapter One — the critic may conclude that the referential and deictic effort expended has as its principal result the establishment of the particular discourse-relation, one in which the reader shall be alert to receiving lessons and to applying them to her own existence. This kind of exercise in reference characterizes the philosophic story and makes it didactic.

In Chapter Four also, deixis and vituperation accompany each other in high density. Deictics surround especially the targets of criticism, references to specific abuses found in the cultural or referential code. They are not, however, so culture-specific that they cannot be decoded very easily by almost anyone. The greatest number of signs of *narration* accompanies the largest incidence of aggressions and of references to contemporary events and persons. In 1752, several lines were added at the head of the chapter. The twenty-two lines, in Ascoli's critical edition, are the expansion of a three-line reference made in previous versions to an unnamed person, who becomes Yébor in 1752. According to the first version, this person had written thirteen volumes on griffons and he had persecuted Zadig for his down-to-earth remarks about those creatures. The hero is saved in those lines by Cador's brother, himself a *mage* like the added Yébor; this narrow escape made the hero decide to give up the company of scholars. The new version erases all sign of the good priest and scholar and makes of the hero's salvation the occasion for yet another attack on that class, which is portrayed as subject to manipulation through its vices. The new version speaks of an *archimage,* Yébor, in whom critics have seen a reference to the archbishop Boyer; presumably this was apparent to contemporaries. Examination of deixis and of the modes of reception explains why most readers feel that it points overtly to referents

sharing the time and space of the discourse-relation that was contemporary with the publication of the story. This is true whether
or not one grasps the particular historical allusion. Intense invective
passes directly by the present tense of the indicative and by the past
of the conditional. There are no veils. The narrator abuses his
target: "le plus sot des Chaldéens; et partant le plus fanatique."
Two uses of the conditional, sign of the narrative instance, accompany two cases of citational irony; the phrases I emphasize below
recall ecclesiastical language to all readers familiar with such expressions in Christian ritual. Here they are used by an evil officer of
another religion, for which the reader is invited, by the echoes, to
substitute the Roman Catholic and its leaders, the archbishop for
instance: "Cet homme aurait fait empaler Zadig *pour la plus grande
gloire du* soleil, et en aurait *récité le bréviaire de* Zoroastre d'un
ton plus satisfait." A general rule is uttered parenthetically in the
present, "(un ami vaut mieux que cent prêtres)"; and in a brief
dramatization, words are lent to Yébor who gives reasons for killing
his victim. His speech is made ridiculous both by the controversy
itself — griffons and rabbits are sacred objects — and by the balanced form of his pronouncement, ironic by implied mention of a
typically balanced Solomonic decision: "Eh bien! dit Yébor en
branlant sa tête chauve, il faut empaler Zadig pour avoir mal pensé
des griffons, et l'autre pour avoir mal parlé des lapins." The authority of his statement is further sapped in advance by the phrase
interrupting his reported speech and describing him as bald and
shaky. The narrator hits this target two more times; but in the two
sentences that follow the attack is extended to the whole class to
which the archbishop belongs. The solution to Zadig's condemnation
is sending a woman to the "collège des mages" to promise them
sexual services in exchange for their signatures on the accused's
absolution. A criticism of the *docteurs* arises from their disappointment that no one was killed; they deplore the fact and predict
from it the decline and fall of Babylon.

In the rest of the chapter, a simple present tense signals the
connection between the description of Zadig's suppers and the society
belonging to narrator and to narratee: "... il avait su bannir l'empres-
sement de montrer de l'esprit, qui est la plus sure manière de n'en
point avoir...." This is one of six such uses of the present tense for

atemporal reflection, generalizations attaching the reader's time to that of the story by the lessons thus made available. The five others are the following:

> [The envious one] corrompait toute la joie de la société comme on dit que les harpies infectent les viandes qu'elles touchent. . . .

> Les plus implacables haines n'ont pas couvent des fondements plus importants. . . .

> L'occasion de faire du mal se trouve cent fois par jour, et celle de faire du bien, une fois dans l'année, comme dit Zoroastre. . . .

> Il savait que des vers impromptus ne sont jamais bons que pour celle en l'honneur de qui ils sont faits.

> Il aimait la poésie, et il y a toujours de la ressource avec les princes qui aiment les vers. . . .

These sentences invite and reinforce an easy decoding by substitution or by doubling. The present tense is conventional for the epigram and the proverb, and it imports them into the reader's experience. Babylon can equal Paris or Potsdam where guests at dinner try too hard to be clever, where people write bad poetry, and where jealousy rages. There, however, one might find a king who loves verse, and mercy follows as night the day. The fifteen words, "et il y a toujours de la ressource," etc. were added in 1752 when Voltaire was visiting Frederick's court.

This sensitization of the text or of the reader, already begun in the first addition to the chapter, may explain from the genetic point of view the *laisser-aller* in the direct abuse of the *envieux*. He also is painted in the most negative terms without the veil of litotes or of antiphrasis: "Personnage dont le méchante âme était peinte sur sa grossière physionomie ... rongé de fiel ... bouffi d'orgueil ... bel esprit ennuyeux" who never succeeded in anything and who has difficulty gathering even a few flatterers for dining. He is compared to the harpies mentioned above.

The bare sketch of the scenes in which Zadig is accused, imprisoned, tried, sentenced and sent to punishment approaches the mode of satiric dramatization. The targets — judges, the law, the curious who await his death, his own parents who regret not inheriting his wealth — all are rapidly evoked and demolished by the reported way of their interesting themselves in his fate. The opposites of these ways, the positive values implied by what most people would consider the unfair and tasteless behavior of the targets, are to be inferred. The *récit* then suddenly quits serious condemnation and offers a less dangerous target that is implied in Zadig's reactions to his own plight. When the hero is saved, the narrator does not repeat the lesson by moralizing, but tells instead of the hero's shame at having written poor verse. The serious though somewhat random attacks now give way to treatment of a courtly and elegant sin. The heaviness of the pejorative description of his enemies and of the multiplication of injustices done him disappears in the end of the incident where Zadig, face down before his king, begs forgiveness for being a bad poet.

The small number of remaining instances of direct verbal aggression includes two shots fired at all of mankind in Chapter Nine — "la terre ... les hommes tels qu'ils sont en effet, des insectes ..." — where the deictic *notre* and the present tense help bring these remarks out of the *récit* and into the realm of *narration*. The other instance of such destructive comment applies to another of Zadig's enemies; like Yébor and the envious one, Itobad is classified rapidly and entirely: "fort vain, peu courageux, très maladroit, et sans esprit" (Ch. 17). This creature further ridicules himself in the report of his responses to the enigmas in the last chapter; his speeches are told by the narrator who attributes gossipy simplifications to the false hero: "Il répondit qu'un homme comme lui n'entendait rien aux énigmes, et qu'il lui suffisait d'avoir vaincu à grands coups de lance"; and "Itobad disait toujours que rien n'était plus aisé, et qu'il en serait venu à bout tout aussi facilement s'il avait voulu s'en donner la peine." In the final contest his miserable character is completely destroyed as, armed to the hilt, he faces a Zadig dressed only in nightshirt and cap; and he is defeated. The last sentence about him continues the dramatic mode of criticism: "Itobad alla se faire appeler monseigneur dans sa maison."

There are both negative and positive dramatizations. Chapter Five contains a positive one, a contest to decide on the most generous person in the kingdom. The three cases plus Zadig's are treated as marvels, and the reader may understand that the reverse is usual, that is, greed and self-interest. Another staging of positive values in order to point out their absence in the world occurs in Chapter Six where after general remarks, two examples of the hero's Solomon-like decisions are recounted by use of direct dialogue. Either base or admirable individuals may thus be the center of a dramatization, and the *rieurs* must be nimble in finding out on which side they are supposed to be.

In general, dramatization of behavior to be condemned is less distinct in this tale than in *Micromégas*. Most are cases of referential opining, but the targets are scattered and traditional — bad judges and bad priests populate the oldest literatures, the *fabliaux* in France, for example — and the exposition includes here more telling than showing. This fact can be related to the exact nature of the hero's dilemma, which is only partly due to nameable, describable enemies. The latter insert themselves into a larger interrogation, the question the text poses, that is, "Why do the good suffer?" It does not easily admit a single important agent who can be blamed. The accusations are punctual, that is specific, and give the impression of being both traditional and random. The diffuse attacks on particular targets reflect the vast cultural intertext of meliorism in which the work was produced. Inside the gloomy picture it is nonetheless worthwhile to make the archbishop Boyer pay in ridicule for his cruelty and for his narrow mind. The specificity of meliorism plays itself out on the dark background all the same, and the moments in which one is led to view precise forms of behavior or of speech as dangerous or foolish are less elaborately dramatized than their parallels in *Micromégas*. They tell more of events than of individuals; what happens is inconsistent, unreasonable, illogical, and so forth. Even though people are most often the agents, their particular traits finally matter less than the act itself, its gratuitous nature and its unfortunate consequences. This helps create the consciousness of historical chance that I have mentioned. It serves as antithesis to the idea of destiny regulated by God, Providence, and it is thus anti-Leibnizian. Where chance reigns over destiny, man can act.

At the same time as each anecdote presents itself as amusing and interesting, a riddle (the basilisk), a dilemma (the debt), a joke (the nose), these fragments, the series of incidents, offer themselves as the working out of the general unhappiness predicted at the beginning of the story by various means (Section 1, above). The impression of scenes that foreground a situation rather than an individual explains itself when one realizes that the twist or paradox is everywhere present, the story-teller's favorite ploy. The anecdotes are parables of the reversal of expectations, parables of surprise. In Chapter Nine a woman cries for help but really does not want it; Chapter Ten: the valet is more valuable than his master; Chapter Eleven: a widow tries to kill herself without really wanting to; Chapter Twelve: men will value a sacred animal over human life itself; Chapter Thirteen: because they will gain no money, priests, the guardians of the highest values, regret that a woman's life is saved; and so on. The permanent mode of communication is the multiplying of cases that demand reflection upon general irony, that point to it over and over again. D. C. Muecke (p. 67), citing Kierkegaard, observes that irony used and depicted in this sense does not attack particular practices or existences (although this tale does that too), but it points to an incongruity of the whole of a time and of a situation, here of all of human nature as well. (This is not a form of textual irony; it is a concept of irony or paradox divined behind a set of circumstances, as in the banal journalistic use of the word *ironically.*)

There are thus several kinds of exposition of values: positive, requiring reversal to see the target of criticism; negative, requiring reversal to see the generalized value; scenic, showing; and discursive, telling. This creates a dynamic between a *series* of complete scenes to be read as emblems or parables of a general state and the *sum* of events that is promised as a grand unified parable having meaning. The expectation that the parts will make a whole is more acute here than in non-didactic stories, and this expectation is disappointed. The grand parable disintegrates for reasons I have often suggested above and which I shall now summarize.

II.5. DECONSTRUCTION. THE ANXIETY OF IGNORANCE

Even the casual reader feels little coherence in what is being offered as exemplary. The statements of didactic purpose found in the dedicatory epistle and the particular discourse-relation that I have already described constitute positive and continuous offers of guidance. At no given moment, however, does one feel confident of the instructions available; in many ways it constantly saps its own authority as guide. The text frustrates instead of facilitating the search for meaning; it is against interpretation. It is also *about* interpretation, and I propose to view it as an allegory of (mis)reading.

One of the deconstructive factors is the text's demolition and transformation of the idea or project of mimesis. Didactic literature offers a particular kind of reflection, that of a lesson, of a truth. In the fact of the continually renewed promise of instruction, the reader, believing a large part of the game to be the pleasurable discovery of the message, attempts to develop a strategy for its reception. The meta-reader, the subject conscious of its own and the text's fragmentation, is the site of reunion of many texts — cultural, personal, and so forth. This complexity, this plethora of texts that she is, wields a multiplicity of factors that make sense; she can thus try different strategies, juggle grids, selectively respond at each moment. In this activity, the undecidability or indeterminism of successful strategy is the primary deconstructing message of *Zadig;* and for the fragmented subject, it replaces any essentialist lesson that it is possible, fragmentedly, to derive. Before the multiplicity of potential parodies of other texts and of specific practices, the critical reader has to perform more, to try more things, to adjust grids more often; and she is frustrated in the performance because no certainty finally becomes avalaible. One might imagine that the mimetic expectation is willingly or conventionally put aside because she recognizes fairytale-form. The discourse-relation, however, constantly positions the fairytale-code in a referential code as well. The folkloric aspects thus do not prevent the expectation of some objective reflected truth. That this prospect is always denied, however, means that the text is constantly foregrounding its own loss of innocence. In multiple ways it destroys itself as representation.

Among the several zones in which deconstruction of didactic and of mimetic logic takes place is the portion of the *histoire* that contrasts the hero's feeling of being helpless before the accidents of fate ("mais quel sera le serpent?") with the readers's observation that besides being subject to destiny the hero is also destiny for others. This perception is attributed twice to Zadig himself, once negatively and still in the perspective of this own bad fortune: he says, "Je vois ... que les malheurs de ma destinée se répandent sur la tienne; " and once he sees himself as a positive instrument but complains of the lack of recompense: "O puissant Orosmade! ... vous vous servez de moi pour consoler cet homme; de qui vous servirez-vous pour me consoler?" (quoted above in another context). The numerous episodes in which Zadig acts as enabler for another character's desire gradually accumulate. They magnify an insight that he does not completely share, but they nuance his perception of his own dilemma. One episode is particularly constitutive of this insight, for it contains signs that encourage it, those emitted by the fisherman (who calls him *ange sauveur*) and by the narrator. The augmenting of the didactic complexity is also more accessible to the reader than to the hero, and indeed it is the narrator who summarizes the imbalance in the exchange between the two characters. He does so in a way that encourages the realization of the hero's place in the scheme of accidents. He pronounces the emblematic sentence, "Ils se séparèrent: le pêcheur marcha en remerciant son destin, et Zadig courut en accusant toujours le sien." Up to the very end this double situation continues to be manifest; the hero is at the same time fate's victim and its agent for others. The hermit will finally tell him this, and he thus learns for a special case what the reader could know about all of them: "Souviens-toi de ce pêcheur qui se croyait le plus malheureux de tous les hommes. Orosmade t'a envoyé pour changer sa destinée." The reader's omniscience comes from her complicity with the narrator, but it is limited to that domain and is thus only relative; she is not granted omniscience about her own destiny, and the text continually proves it. Viewed in this perspective, the title of the tale seems to suggest two truths. In *Zadig ou la destinée,* the conjunction *ou* can indicate not choice, but a double state: he is a factor in the destiny of others, but that is not the problem. In the sentence treating him and the fisherman, the hero is still an eiron, complaining of injustice; but the sign of his power is present, even though only in the reader's eventual supratextual perception of the fact that the syntactic proximity between *son destin* and *Zadig* suggests a semantic similarity as well in spite of the rigorously contrasted elements. *A* is not to *a* as *B* is not to *b,* and so on.

A	B	C	D

Le pêcheur marcha en remerciant son destin et
Zadig   courut   en   accusant   le sien.

a	b	c	d

The syntactic parallelism of the two phrases produces contrast and emphasizes the linear, fragmented state of the two events as well as insisting upon the absence of understanding and of synthesis in the story and in the *récit*. In both, the two lines can continue without ever meeting. The second possibility that the title suggests is something like "Zadig or an experience/experiment in destiny," which makes an explicit contrast between the *exemplum,* Zadig's adventures, and the general idea of providential fate. Positioned in the larger problem, the title reveals this duality by the ambiguity of *ou* and of *ou bien,* that is, the difference between *identity* and *exclusion*.

Two other codes come into play in the depiction of the protagonist, and they contribute to the destruction of the idea of hero. Logically they exclude each other, but they are both present: the tragico-mythical one and the comical eironic leading to parody. As I pointed out in the third section above, the plot-curve resembles that of myth, not that of literature or news — the hero's existence is a uniform given with an incident of loss and one of reparation demarcating the part recounted; and he undergoes symbolic death and resurrection. Further insuring his membership in the class of the admirable, he shows both physical prowess and wisdom in many episodes; for those reasons and by his exalted governmental position, that of minister, he has the culturally-given right to dramatize himself in misfortune as a tragic victim of fate. Sequence also reinforces the mythical, even god-like, resonance of his adventures, for the minister is made a slave before becoming king. This, as well as the incident in which he appears on the field of battle without his armor and is jeered, recalls the precept according to which "The humble shall be exalted"; and they support in these further ways an available view of Zadig as mythical hero. At the same time he is comical and his mythic potential mocks myth, for these very features can be reversed and cast down. The passage from minister to slave and from slave to king belongs also to the comic grotesque (bonnet and nightcap on the field of battle), to carnival, and to traditions of the reversal of roles (Cador was a more valuable slave than Zadig, at first) for certain privileged periods.[13] Added to this way of deciphering the up-and-down movement of the hero's fate are the quasi-simultaneous lamentations and their minimizing *chutes* by which Zadig is made to deflate his own rhetoric and to appear foolish even as he expresses the dilemma of mankind. The potential for the tragic and mythic reference co-exists with the comic and eironic, and both grids are offered by the same group of signs. Our interpretative strategies vacillate in this respect also. The mixed presentation of the hero as potentially both comic and tragic resonates with parody of the novel and of the epic. His destruction is both rhetorical and literary; by referring to those kinds of texts and to their heroes, Voltaire disapproves of the hero as a literary personage and indirectly undermines both the comic and the tragic figure. The implicit opposition remains the one between literature and ethical or moral analysis, questions of destiny posed in natural, not literary (religious) terms.

Another of the elements of intertextual construct is the hero's permanent wondering about generalized, global, agentless (in)justice. The status of these interrogations as serious reference to theodicy has its formal, and deconstructive, equivalent in the anecdotal schema itself, in the parabolic nature of the incidents. In the episodes ending in a *pointe,* the reader is subjected to a back-and-forth movement between the little paradoxes — revealed by attacks on specific individuals and by attacks on general traits of humanity — and the grand interrogation about fate and unhappiness in general, the cosmic paradox, general irony. In this movement, two kinds of plot-logic conflict: 1) the innocence of the text, events seen as occurring and only accidentally pointing to a theme, and 2) the impurity of the text, where the theme is seen as directing the selection of incidents. Many stories contain either surprise or paradox that gives them their point and that is primary in their being perceived as stories. The tale accumulates short stories that reiterate paradox and

---

[13] This is all well known through the books of Mikhail Bakhtin, already cited, and through Wolfgang Kayser's *Das Groteske, seine Gestaltung in Malerei und Dichtung* (Oldenburg: G. Stalling, 1957).

generate an insistent paradigm of life's quirkiness that stresses unhappy (for the hero) fortune and foregrounds the phenomenon of stories themselves. The critic detects the second, the impure logic named above. The reflection, the lesson, cannot be both *arranged* (having a beginning and an end) and *true,* especially given the existential demonstrations of Zadig's positive effect on others that go against the other demonstrations of fate's cruelty for him. An induction of truth from innocent evidence, the first logic named above, derives the lesson from real and chance happenings. The hero's displays overtly select out the lesson, and the tale's do too. Its unfolding resembles deductive process, the impurity named above, and the *conte philosophique* foregrounds it without naming the given from which all is derived. Events follow one logic; and meaning follows another, an illogic or a-logic, that requires misreading. By radically separating the two logics, *Zadig* exposes particularly clearly this paradox of any critical analysis. It typifies and thematizes the difficulty. It combines two thematizations, one, *lack of meaning* — it is absurd that the good are punished — and two, *meaning assigned* — the angel says everything means something, and he simply assigns meaning as Meaning. His act gives to the *récit* primacy over the *histoire,* for his speech says only that he *is saying* that there is meaning. This meta-assurance coincides with what any story-like signifier says to us also by the fact of its being divided into chapters and of its having words on the page. The conclusion, however, Chapter Nineteen, exhibits neither lack of meaning nor meaning assigned; the topic does not even come up, and it is not possible to choose. The good are rewarded, the evil are punished, happiness finally reigns because it is time to stop reading.

Most damaging to the claims the didactic-mimetic text makes for itself are the content and arrangement of the last three chapters. I take them up again in order to review some of the points just made. The reader probably entertains the possibility that the hero's trials and his perplexity can be considered as due to the agency of Providence. That word, associated with theodicy, belief that all is for the good, appears four times in the tale; for example, just after the theft of Zadig's armor, it occurs twice:

> Il lui échappa enfin de murmurer contre la Providence, et
> il fut tenté de croire que tout était gouverné par une des-

tinée cruelle qui opprimait les bons et qui faisait prospérer
les chevaliers verts. Dans cet équipage, il côtoyait l'Eu-
phrate, rempli de désespoir et accusant en secret la Providence, qui le persécutait toujours. (Ch. 17)

It appears again when the hero submits (Ch. 18) and when he and
the queen live happily ever after: "La reine et lui adorèrent la Providence" (Ch. 19). Before the three final chapters, references to
forces outside his control employ the words *fortune, sort, destin,
destinée* without capital letters. This means of vindicating divine
justice in the face of misfortune and of suffering was being debated
in Europe all through the eighteenth century and reflects the particular form taken at that time by the universal desire to make sense
of what is perceived as unmerited evil. (The *Théodicée* of Leibniz
appeared in 1710.) This instinct or desire is as strong in certain
readers as it appears to be in the exclamations of the hero. The
text, however, does not long allow the reader the satisfaction of this
attempt. If she has already tried to project sense onto the previous
incidents, the episode of the hermit probably puts it into question
again. All the preceding episodes led her and the hero to doubt the
good sense of Providence; now an agent appears, and a group of
events rewarding the unjust and punishing the just is concentrated
into the four supposedly exemplary and explanatory visits conducted
by the hermit. As he was before in the tales of three lives, Zadig
is only an observer in the four visits. His reactions are rage and
submission. The reader who by imagining a providential agent had
already tried to create coherence as the hermit later proposes it will
tend to be scandalized as Zadig is by the acceleration of injustice
and by its concentration. She will perhaps be obliged to reject her
own accommodation with that portion of injustice distributed
throughout the previous episodes. Another kind of reader, one who
has resisted taking the step to theodicy, will probably feel confirmed
in her suspended judgment when she follows the explanations given
by Jesrad. Zadig's "Qui te l'a dit, barbare?" and his hope for the
correction of the wicked find their echo in her.

The conversation with the hermit-angel juxtaposes those two possibilities without ever synthesizing them. It could have, for instance,
presented a materialistic or deterministic view of causality, in which
human will to change and to correct also figures as one of the forces

affecting events. [14] The passage offers no synthesis, only silence; and it thus frustrates for an indefinite period the search for meaning. The would-be interpreter's faculties are exercised in both directions without being permitted to resolve, to explain, or to erase the moral scandal that reason assigns to the kinds of injustice described. This constitutes the principal and perhaps the most memorable experience of this text; and it is a fact that renders particularly futile the search for its "right" reading. The critic can simply describe most of the forces and processes that are available and that occur in reading. Those who do not like living with uncertainty, this *and* that instead of this *or* that, will choose one way or the other, will *select* the sense that allows conclusion about meaning. It so happens that the reader who elects to retain the problem as unresolved espouses the *contiguous* or discrete nature of the last three episodes. Cause and effect between them and between the moments they record are entirely suspended and so is judgment. From the visit with the angel and the successful living out of the trials, Zadig passes to a reward, one predicted, already and in any case, by the inexorable movement of fairytale sequence and delayed only by the supernatural apparition which teaches him only submission. Since his obedience to contingency was never in question — he was buffeted about by it through the first seventeen chapters — nothing is changed except that he now graciously submits to more agreeable chance by becoming king and marrying the queen. The text thus might be said to invite a final solution anyway — that fate arranges things for the best — for agreeable chance might be thought just as fundamental to the story/life as the unpleasant sort; and there were earlier "lucky" moments recounted as well as this last triumph.

The sense of two quests is still present at the end, for the reader sees the concrete happiness attained but feels the absence of the wisdom also sought by the hero and promised by the hermit. The folk- and philosophical endings diverge because it is expected that the former give a sense of completeness as well as closure; but the latter, the quest for wisdom, is simply abandoned. Narration gives it up; it is absent from the signifier but not necessarily from the

---

[14] This more subtle effort to deal with the question of cause and effect finds novelistic presentation in Diderot's *Jacques le fataliste*: Sherman, *Diderot's Art of Dialogue*, pp. 131-45.

signified that the reader may continue to draw. The lesson she constructs for herself is not necessarily the abandonment of the question. Completeness can come only *from* closure for those readers who wish it thus. The hero's last tasks (25, 26 repeated) are indeed the direct cause of his right to reward (30, 31), but the trials (12, 13) imposed by the angel make him see only a concentrated version of what he has already lived in Chapter One through Thirteen and heard in Chapters Fourteen through Sixteen. The angel's explanation — "... tout est épreuve, ou punition, ou récompense, ou prévoyance" — assigns meaning to everything, but it adds no new information. The decoder has no reason for believing the hero changed or enlightened by it, for even as he lived through disastrous contingency he was already presented as virtuous and wise. This too prevents the reader from believing the angel's proofs have taught her anything she had not already observed.

The form of resolution without its content is one construct of the double questing paradigm of the philosophical story. The grammar is present; the rhetoric is not. Pursuing the analogy of the tale as sentence, one imagines it to resemble a long sentence the meaning of which one will see at the end when we have heard each word and identified its syntactic function. We expect that all the parts will make sense once we have seen the whole and that the whole will be meaningful once we have seen all the parts.

We are thus not satisfied that there is continuity, a relation from cause to effect and from part to whole as we pass from the combats to revelation to enigmas and to the hero's reward. Instead, their juxtaposition records the essential ambiguity of the angel's explanation. I use the term *ambiguity* not in the sense of *open-ended,* but as positively *double*; for the angel's discourse contains two discontinuous utterances: 1) everything is reward or punishment, that is, purposeful and meaningful, but 2) you cannot know which and when. It invites the leap of faith that can embrace totalitarian meaningfulness, once again a grammar without rhetoric, a form without content.

This indetermination doubles itself: it reigns both in life for the hero and in the literary experience of the reader. In anything larger than subsequences, where cause, effect, and enablers are sometimes clear to the protagonist and where a manifest satiric message is clear to the reader — that is, in the larger view promised to Zadig by the angel and promised to the reader by the fact that she approaches the end of the story, both are denied explanation and are frustrated in that part of their expectation. However, both are compensated, although not with understanding, but with the sense of an ending, that is with a form. Zadig wins everything, and the reader gets to read the expected "happily-ever-after." Life's signs fail the hero; trying to make sense of existence, he cannot know. The literary signs fail the reader: trying to make sense of this literature, she is not allowed to guess. She is constrained to accept ignorance. Like the book of destinies, this book is not blank either; it is simply unreadable and always already misread.

Wolfgang Iser has written on several occasions about the degrees of indeterminacy of different kinds of texts. [15] He speaks of utopic and of ideological novels that finish with a *tour de force,* thereby compensating their own indetermination, and he opposes this sort to the type that articulates the indeterminacy: "Which one, dear Reader . . . ?" The naïve reading of *Zadig* can see it as falling into the first category, the scene of the angel and the last beatific vision constituting this *tour de force* that wraps up all the threads in a utopic ending. Since the hero's *mais* and the position of the chapter and the absence of deixis all aid in removing determinisms, the critic can, however, just as easily see that the text is a very determined one, in both senses of the word, and that the story ends in a *tour de force* of *in*determinacy, a sudden definitive hiding or disappearance of what was to be made evident and had always been hidden. The last chapter returns to the charge of determinacy by the nature of its discourse — deixis recaptured — by its content of heavy distribution of rewards and punishments and by the announcement of eternal bliss; but its very certainty and solidity seem to sharpen the indetermined determination that it just left behind.

Satiric genres leave us with nothing. That might suffice to account for the various absences that one feels in *Zadig,* but the topic can bear elaboration. The tale announced itself as philosophical, as teaching something, a solution that turns out not to be there. It is

---

[15] Iser, *The Act,* passim.

very funny, but teaches no positive moral; and so the *conte philosophique* is essentially a *divertissement* with a negative lesson, un-
readability, like in that to the book of destinies. The constant
negative, negated moral intertext is the Christian idea of rewards
and punishments and history à la Bossuet. These are constantly
replaced by a new view of history from which God is absent. Part
of the narrator's commentary on chance occurrences (the parrot, the
letter that saves Zadig, etc.) parodies another intertext, the science
of cause and effect. If both God and science are undependable, the
only proper treatment of destiny may be *ironic,* that is, refusing to
be drawn into the metaphysical question of forces and of agents
(distance) and admitting that the concept is of no use (reversal).

Even in the absence of a positive lesson, however, the question
raised by the subtitle remains. The description of the hero's fate is
a sort of immanent theory of destiny; it can be seen as parody of
one of the *conte*'s sources, the tale that ends happily. As such it is
an immanent criticism of the concept of destiny as well. Even if
one accepts the criticism implied, one can also seize upon the outcome
and see there a form of realistic optimism, the idea that chance and
gratuitous forces can make one lucky too. *Zadig* and *Candide* are
true versions of *La Théodicée*: the optimism of both — unexpressed
in *Zadig,* explicit in *Candide* — consists of making the best of circumstances. The personage Candide will not be a caricature of
optimism, he will *be* optimism, the only kind possible.

The grammar of revelation, of solution, and of truth is present
both in the *histoire* and in the *récit*. The *histoire* includes a hermit-
angel, a book of destinies, promises, tests: both tradition and explicited content say that the long-awaited answer is due. The incident
that announces itself as the key to everything does the most damage
to that very pretension. The *récit* has its own grammar of resolution;
one approaches the end of the signifier, and that is traditional form's
promise of a chord resolving the tension and dissonance that have
gone before, but revelation is absent. A further subversion of grammar is the interruption in the crescendo of both *récit* and *histoire*:
the place and content of Chapter Eighteen constitute syntactic deviance. Instead of preceding or following the two sets of tests, it
separates them. It could either come before both and thus equip
the hero with the extra wisdom and prowess necessary to accompl-

ish the tasks — although he has already demonstrated these skills throughout the story — or it could follow his successful perform-ances and, by conferring understanding consecrate his achievements. It does neither, and the critic receives the deviance as a refusal of teleology and of providential thinking. The overt messages — "… tu étais celui … qui méritait le plus d'être éclairé" and "tout est épreu-ve" — are abolished by the twisted syntax. It lays to rest Nietzsche's fear that "we shall never get rid of God, for we still believe in grammar." The text that claimed to offer and to believe in repre-sentation and in truth subverts both Destiny's ethics and its gram-mar.

Chapter III

> L'Optimiste: celui qui croit que l'on naît dans le meilleur des mondes.
> Le Pessimiste: celui qui craint que ce ne soit vrai.
>
> Anon.

III. 1. Competence

1.a. *Initiation*

Candide is long. It is four times as long as *Micromégas* and a third again as long as *Zadig* and as *L'Ingénu*. The reader's experience of it differs from that of the others by this quantity and by what it permits and entails. Greater length brings an enrichment of the standard plot in which boy finds, loses, and finds girl; three lines of quest are clearly developed, the searches for the heroine, for freedom, and for philosophy. It also allows a considerable expansion of the didactic or ideological dimension of the action. Like the others, this tale immediately shows itself as susceptible of double reading; by coupling a proper name and an abstraction its title *Candide ou l'optimisme* claims that it bears a lesson. It thus announces the need for abstractive procedures of decoding and offers itself as a problem posed, as an interrogation on life and justice. The subtitle invites the reader to consent to the popular pretend-translation, "Traduit de l'allemand de Mr. le docteur Ralph, avec les additions qu'on a trouvées dans la poche du docteur, lorsqu'il mourut à Minden, L'an de Grâce 1759." The surname *Ralph* forms a kind of *chute* by its abruptness, a single un-French sounding syllable coming after the preliminary *Monsieur le docteur.* The explanation that was added in 1761 to the title and subtitle, "Avec les additions qu'on a trouvées dans la poche du docteur, lorsqu'il mourut à Minden, L'an de Grâce 1759," uses a solemn event and factual syntax but is made comic by the place where the papers were found, in his pocket, instead of the more dignified and more usual trunk in the attic or drawer of a desk. [1] The long title thus already offers games and intertexts reminding the reader of conventions of other novels and stories. It begins her training in decoding these kinds of meaning, in appreciating both the literary and the philosophical referents.

By their length and by their vocabulary the titles of the thirty chapters differ considerably from the nineteen of *Zadig,* the latter in their brevity corresponding to the punctual nature of the adventures linked together. Here, they resemble those typical of many novels, employing regularly the names of the characters and such words as *comment* and *ce qui* attached to verbs in the preterite — *devenir, advenir, arriver* — all stressing the fact that a story with the same characters in each episode and with continuity is unfolding: things happen *(advenir),* and here you will learn how *(comment).* The title of the first chapter is typical: "Comment Candide fut élevé dans un beau château et Comment il fut chassé d'icelui." Whether the space between chapters is considered to be a place to rest during an oral reading or to be the sign of a change to another event in a silent reading, the segmentation usually obeys certain laws of suspense, of a new action foreseen, announced but not yet developed: the storm starts at the end of Chapter Four; the inquisitioner gives a nod to his lackey at the end of Chapter Five; Candide knows he must flee and wonders where to go at the end of Thirteen. Sometimes the pause for pointing at what follows is underlined by *ainsi,* an adverb that takes on the value of a deictic: "... ils parlaient ainsi dans un cabaret" (Ch. 9), "... et le commandant parla ainsi à son cher Candide" (Ch. 14). Other kinds of pointing to the production of the tale include the simple titles

---

[1] When one considers Voltaire's almost obsessive interest in Pascal, the fact that the latter's *Mémorial* was sewn into his coat and found there at his death comes to mind as an allomorph of the doctor's relation to his text.

"Histoire de la vieille" (11) and "Suite des malheurs de la vieille" (12). The fact that the end of one chapter begins the episode elaborated in the following acts as a compensation for the lack of causal conjunction between events. The links are the sort that can be called "and then," not "therefore," and their essential disjunction would be more apparent if the spaces between chapters also marked the ends of episodes.

The familiar beginning, "Il y avait," announces a make-believe that is encouraged by the fantastic name of the baron and by the perfection of the young hero. The narrator does not delay giving a sign of his presence; *je crois* appears in the third sentence and a demonstrative adjective in the fourth, "cette demoiselle." At least three things in the first paragraph create the narrator's mischievous nature, and they do so by the kind of modal acrobatics that will actualize both the playful and the didactic aspect of the text. One is the name *Thunder-ten-tronckh* which mocks what the French heard as plosive and heavy in Prussian names of place and of families. The same kind of joke will be repeated in the second chapter where the name of a city mentions several German words for *city,* Valdberghoff-trarbk-dikdorff. [2] The next target in the first chapter is the snobbery of the baron's sister. She preferred bearing a bastard to marrying its father, her social inferior. The litotic *ne ... que* makes its first appearance in this connection: "... parce qu'il n'avait pu prouver que soixante et onze quartiers ..." requires reversal of its literal minimization of the neighbor's claims to nobility. The mockery of Westphalian culture and the implied superiority of French refinement, the value in the name of which the criticism is performed, are transmitted in the next paragraph. It begins "Monsieur le baron était un des plus puissants seigneurs de la Vestphalie, car son château avait une porte et des fenêtres." The conjunction *car* marks a presupposition and it effects the ellipsis of a playful syllogism: 1) in Westphalia, a chateau with windows and door is

---

[2] Spanish names are also targets; in Chapter Thirteen, Don Fernando d'Ibaraa, y Figueora, y Mascarenes, y Lampourdos, y Souza. A single Dutchman is mocked in another proper name, Vanderdendur, the last syllable having semantic value corresponding to the quality of the man represented: it is he who cut the leg and hand from the slave. The real publisher Van Duren has his name echoed there: Haydn Mason, *Voltaire: A Biography* (Baltimore: The Johns Hopkins University Press, 1981), p. 50.

the sign of a powerful owner, 2) the baron's has both, therefore 3) he is powerful. The single word *car* is itself often powerful in the story. It is the principal lexical attribute of the kind of reasoning performed by Pangloss and imitated by his pupil. *Car* denotes the opposite of chance, that is, logic. It belongs to philosophical discourse, not to narration; so it is not the narrator who says it, but Candide and his master. The word thus appears both as a stylistic, ironic effect and as the icon of one of the structures produced by the story. The *même* of the next sentence is the narrator's ironic — to be reversed — commentary: "Sa grande salle même était ornée d'une tapisserie." The adverb marks an ascension in the demonstration as we pass from pretended marvel to pretended marvel.[3] The baron's power is further illustrated by the fact that all the humblest animals and persons of the household double as higher functionaries when they are needed. The comic demonstration of his importance is sealed in a *chute*; they all call him *Monseigneur* and laugh when he tells jokes. This last fact is superficially insignificant by its nature and by its place in the paragraph, but it also has the potential to rebound and to be truly valorized by its inclusion in the list of items showing power.

These first two paragraphs have only very briefly, in two and one-half sentences, presented the hero; most of the phrases have made fun of his surroundings. The third paragraph of what is still introduction or stage-setting (time, place, and characters) rapidly enumerates the other players, giving to each a memorable trait: great body-weight to the baroness, and to the son, the phrase "en tout digne de son père," the precise function of which requires translation by a return to the worth of his father, that is, none. The last actor to be presented, Pangloss, receives a longer description and even direct quotation of one of his typical statements. The amount of attention paid to him signals the fact that he represents the ideological position that the entire story intends to refute. A phonic and semantic joke names his specialty; besides the obvious imitation of names of sciences, *méta-physico-théologo-cosmolonigo-*

---

[3] A similar opining through the adverb *même* takes place in the last paragraph of the story: "[Giroflée] fut un très bon menuisier et même devint honnête homme" marks with irony the astonishing rise of a low-living priest to the category of *honnête homme*.

logie contains two syllables that form the homonym of *nigaud*. In the caricature of philosophical reasoning that follows, "Il prouvait admirablement qu'il n'y a pas d'effet sans cause, et que ..." the adverb *admirablement* breaks with covert narration offering a judgment of value, as did *même* in the sentence quoted above. It can be received literally by attributing it to those characters around him, but it also invites reversal because of the joke preceding it and because of the insignificance of what follows, things neither susceptible of proof nor worthy of such lofty procedures. The teacher's relation with Candide and his importance for his pupil are figured both semantically and graphically: "Candide écoutait ses leçons..." comes just before the quotation; and "Candide écoutait attentivement," just after it. The name of the hero thus appears to embrace his master's speeches. The brief earlier description of the pupil's character is completed by an example of his capacities for reasoning. He applies Pangloss' precepts to the objects having importance for him. The account of his thought employs enumeration and the phrases *Il concluait que* and *par conséquent,* the latter echoing his master's *par conséquent.* All are attributes of logical discourse, markers in argumentative statements. Pangloss' speech was criticized by its ironic mention of logical patterns, and Candide's works out its own destruction by citing his master's already burlesqued mention of proper logic.

The initial situation thus described, the first discriminated occasion and the use of the preterite begin, as usual, with "Un jour...." They describe the heroine's introduction to cause and effect and to sufficient reason.

> Un jour, Cunégonde, en se promenant auprès du château, dans le petit bois qu'on appelait parc, vit entre des broussailles le docteur Pangloss qui donnait une leçon de physique expérimentale à la femme de chambre de sa mère, petite brune très jolie et très docile. Comme mademoiselle Cunégonde avait beaucoup de disposition pour les sciences, elle observa, sans souffler, les expériences réitérées dont elle fut témoin; elle vit clairement la raison suffisante du docteur, les effets et les causes, et s'en retourna tout agitée, toute pensive, toute remplie du désir d'être savante, songeant qu'elle pourrait bien être la raison suffisante du jeune Candide, qui pouvait aussi être la sienne.

The description of what she sees is easy to decipher; the reader and critic merely observe in addition that it is another, longer case of modal communication. It requires the substitution of gestures and of acts for four philosophical terms. This operation is embedded in another which consists of registering the exalted description of what is considered by some to be a base action. Like the epic account of Joseph Andrews' fight against the hounds pursuing Mr. Adams, the philosophical language applied to these acts attains an effect in the reader who recognizes that cultural code; such a juxtaposition can be called *burlesque.* The heroine's study of cause and effect then becomes a cause in her meeting behind the screen with the hero. Because this passage parodies the Leibnizian principle of sufficient reason, one can see in it a sign of the latter's gradual replacement in the eighteenth century by the idea of scientific causality. It uses Leibnizian metaphysical language while implying a principle of causal correction. The causal links are represented by many phrases which are separated from each other by semicolons and by commas. Four such particles form a sentence of transition: "Elle rencontra Candide en revenant au château, et rougit; Candide rougit aussi; elle lui dit bonjour d'une voix entrecoupée, et Candide lui parla sans savoir ce qu'il disait." Then a similarly formed but longer sentence tells of the breathless encounter: the longest piece sets the scene — "Le lendemain, après le diner, comme on sortait de table, Cunégonde et Candide se trouvèrent derrière un paravent ...." Rapid actions follow, each cause having its effect:

> Cunégonde laissa tomber son mouchoir, Candide le ramassa; elle lui prit innocemment la main; le jeune homme baisa innocemment la main de la jeune demoiselle avec une viva- cité, une sensibilité, une grâce toute particulière; leurs bou- ches se rencontrèrent, leurs yeux s'enflammèrent, leurs ge- noux tremblèrent, leurs mains s'égarèrent.

The second *innocemment* above is elaborated in the direction of a natural and uncontrollable impulse as a lengthy adverbial phrase — *avec* plus three nouns — modifies our reception of the hero's gesture, now become ambiguous in its intention. The feminine adjective *particulière,* besides rhyming with *trouvèrent* and *derrière* of the first phrase, begins a series of five such final sounds (the verbs in the *passé simple*), thus echoing and multiplying the intensity of the last gestures, which are now simultaneous rather than successive — *bouches, yeux, genoux, mains.* The narrator shows the baron's discovery of cause and effect and underlines both by using demonstrative adjectives: "Monsieur le baron de Thunder-ten-tronckh passa auprès du paravent, et, voyant cette cause et cet effet, chassa Candide du château à grands coups de pied dans le derrière ...." The rhyme that goes from the verbs of action to *derrière* forms another comic *chute.*

The narrator further affirms his own presence by an ironic (reversible) reference to his earlier report of Pangloss' discourse. The first time the famous construction appeared was in the fourth paragraph: "... dans ce meilleurs des mondes possibles, le château de monseigneur le baron était le plus beau des châteaux, et madame la meilleure des baronnes possibles." It is echoed by the narrator in the last phrase of the chapter, "... et tout fut consterné dans le plus beau et le plus agréable des châteaux possibles," where the narrating voice marks once again its distance from the character of Pangloss and from the pretensions of the chateau's inhabitants. This is another example of double citational irony since it is mention of another parodic mention. It shows the density of the auto-referential game being played. Once the narrator has established Pangloss' discourse as burlesquing philosophical logic, he can, by imitating it in his own voice, mock both Pangloss and the situation, making the reader an accomplice in the echo.

The competence that the narrator requires in the first chapter is both more playful and more uniform than that of the first episode of *Zadig.* The games played are more elaborate: words that caricature others, chains of reasoning that parody other discourse, the character's and the narrator's echo of each other's phrases. The referential critical activity consistently opposes both social and philosophical pretentiousness with naïveté and with naturalness. It lays the ideological base as it constructs the discourse-relation.

1.b. *Narration and Narrative*

1.b.i. *The Narrator and His Récit*

The narrator's relation to his story and to his telling of it is at the same time more consistent and more complex than the one that characterizes *Zadig.* First, there is a smaller number of deictic anchors in the *récit,* usually one or none per chapter. One reason for the paucity of these interventions may be purely a question of the kind of mass: the quantity of direct discourse, that is, dialogue and monologue, is greater than in *Zadig* where it accounts for one-third of the text as opposed to *Candide* where slightly over one-half of the signifier appears in quotation marks. Most of the story is not told by the narrator but is shown through the character's commenting on events or acting out their encounters — except for its first and last sentences, Chapter Twenty-two is entirely dialogued — or the narrator briefly tells the event — the death of the admiral, for example — and then the characters comment upon it together (Ch. 23). This relatively covert narration does not mean that the reader is unguided but that the kinds of guidance are different and that abstract expressions of the moral dilemma are less obvious than the vivid scenes and anecdotes that often occasion such expressions. The most important fact productive of the latter effect is naturally the quantity of dramatization, its regular appearance, and its being put into relief by the narrating voice. The latter employs deictics to point to events or to nested stories. "La vieille leur parla en ces termes" for example, points forward to the monologue following it; and "Après cette longue conversation" (Ch. 18), "En raisonnant ainsi, ils arrivèrent à Bordeaux" (Ch. 21), and "En causant ainsi ils abordèrent ..." (Ch. 23) point backward to the dialogues preceding them. The historical present augments the vivacity of certain incidents; the narrator uses it sparingly in the entire tale — about ten times — and usually briefly at the heart of an episode. I take two examples, one in each of the two events composing the second chapter. The change to historical present is usually accompanied by other signs of narration, in one case ironic uses of *ne ... que* and in the other the deictic *voilà.* When Candide is being enlisted by two recruiters, the narrative begins in the preterit; but as dialogue intervenes the verbs of the inserted commentary pass to the present: "On le prie d'accepter quelques écus, il les prend et veut faire son billet; on n'en veut point, on se met à table"; direct discourse and historical present alternate to the end of the paragraph where the reversible *ne ... que* appears:

... le lendemain, il fait l'exercice un peu moins mal, et il ne
reçoit que vingt coups; le surlendemain, on ne lui en donne
que dix, et il est regardé par ses camarades comme un
prodige.

In the brutal context, the *ne ... que* may be seen as accurately
measuring the relative insignificance of Candide's punishment; but
the reader may find all violence excessive, and she then receives the
minimization as abusive.[4] The second episode of the chapter begins
by returning to the imperfect and to the preterit and advances to a
deictic and to the historical present: "Il n'eut pas fait dix lieues
que voilà quatre autres héros de six pieds qui l'atteignent, qui le
lient, qui le mènent dans un cachot." The preterit returns immediately after: "On lui demanda juridiquement ce qu'il aimait le
mieux...." Fifteen lines further on the historical present returns to
describe a radical change in the hero's situation: "Le roi des Bul-
gares passe dans ce moment, s'informe du crime du patient; et
comme le roi avait un grand génie, il comprit ...." The reappearance
of the strictly historical tenses is rapid, but the narrative instance
manifests itself again two lines later in a future tense and in a value-
assigning adjective: "... et il lui accorda sa grâce avec une clémence
qui sera louée dans tous les journaux et dans tous les siècles. Un
brave chirurgien guérit Candide ...." The fact of *sera louée* instead
of *fut louée* imports into the narrative present the application of
such an act to powerful persons who exist in that same present and
who might see themselves in the model of clemency and be flattered
by the comparison or encouraged to imitate the model in order to
deserve its praise. This is another instance of the text's movement
back and forth between the historical framework of the events told
and the here and now of its narration and reception. By the present
of narration, the events are brought closer to the narrator's time and
place; his proximity to them conveys his interest in his own tale:
he seems caught up in it and seems to be living it with the characters.
The use of *brave* for the surgeon who saves Candide helps to keep

---

[4] Similar uses are "Pangloss dans la cure ne perdit qu'un œil et une oreille"
and the series by which Eldorado is described in Chapter Eighteen, "la porte
n'était que d'argent" and so on. In these cases also, the minimization suits
the context but not the reader's experience and so must be reversed to attribute
exceptional quality to the traits described.

the reader's sympathy on the hero. Those who aid him will always be praised; that is, the hero is good, and we are constantly encouraged to desire his safety. Another example of bringing the events nearer to the narrator's *locus* is the spatio-temporal details, the deictics *voilà, ce, on* and the present of narration; all occur just after Cunégonde tells her story to Candide in Chapter Eight: "Les voilà qui se mettent tous deux à table; et, après le souper, ils se replacent sur ce beau canapé dont on a déjà parlé; ils y étaient quand ...." Similar but more vivid yet is the passage to the present in the struggle between the hero and one of the heroine's lovers. Chapter Nine begins with narrator's pointing — "Cet Issachar" — and delivering information that sketches the character and discourages sympathy for him — "était le plus colérique Hébreu." Six lines later, verbs in the present and deixis — *notre* and, most extraordinarily, *vous* (even though it is contained in a ready-made expression) — combine again to place the crux of the action in the most immediate light:

> ... il se jette sur Candide; mais notre bon Vestphalien avait reçu une belle épée de la vieille avec l'habit complet. Il tire son épée, quoiqu'il eût les mœurs fort douces, et vous étend l'israélite roide mort sur le carreau, aux pieds de la belle Cunégonde. [5]

Our reception of epic or chivalrous acts is guided by the low language that conveys them and travesties their tradition.

---

[5] The pluperfect *avait reçu* shows that the verbs in the present retain their past temporal value since normally an action previous to those of verbs in the present would be transmitted by the *passé composé (discours)* or a *passé simple (histoire)*. The same is shown by the imperfect subjunctive of the next sentence. In any case some semanticists consider the historical present to mean past action as it is seen from the point of view of the time of communication. The change to the "present" is a function of the distance of the action from the narrator, not of any absolute temporal value. (Thomas Cox, "The Inchoactive Aspect in French," *French Review,* 56 [1982], 228-40.) Other such uses of the historical or narrative present occur in Chapter Twenty-two when Candide, terribly moved, visits the false Cunégonde ("... il entre ... son cœur palpite, sa voix sanglote"); in Chapter Twenty-four where, after accepting Martin's bet, he asks Giroflée and Paquette to dine ("Aussitôt il les aborde, il leur fait son compliment, et les invite à venir à son hôtellerie manger ..."); and in Chapter Twenty-six when the miracle occurs: "... il se retourne, et voit Cacambo."

The reader gains the impression of a present and active narrator also in the varieties of flashbacks, of catching-up, and in the associated lexicon of *meanwhiles* that smooth the temporal adjustments and make each one manifest at the same time. These manipulations of the order of the *histoire* show an omniscient narrator; but this one, unlike *Zadig*'s, never bothers to predict events and usually does not correct his characters' misconceptions. Once, he contradicts one of Candide's perceptions by juxtaposing the hero's assessment with his own authoritative comment, in Eldorado, where his error serves not to make him appear ridiculous but to show the distance between Eldorado and ordinary society. The hero thinks the children he sees are the king's; the narrator calls them "petits gueux." In the other case of the narrator's overtly remarking something that Candide does not know, he says the hero did not notice that Paquette and Giroflée had not thanked him for helping them. The reader probably receives this remark more as commentary on people's ungratefulness than on Candide's simplicity, although both ideas are available (Ch. 25). In most cases, the narrator lets the characters' perceptions stand. When Pangloss tells Candide that Cunégonde is dead, the narrator takes no responsibility for his mistake; our mistrust of Pangloss and our knowledge of what a story is may make us doubt that the heroine could really disappear so soon. This is another area of chaos in the story. The confusion and unpredictability of events are massive. Here the disorder is more subtly conveyed. Conventional linearity — finding the heroine and marrying her — is thwarted, for the early news of her death, a stopping point if there ever was one, turns out not to be true. Furthermore, once she is lost she is found again. There are other, similar subversions of finality, of endings to sequences: other characters are said to have died, to be gone — Pangloss was hanged until dead; the young baron was stabbed to death — but they too show up again alive and are identical with their past selves. The omniscient narrator does not help the reader at all here; he lets her remain in the error shared by the characters: Candide saw Pangloss hanged, and he ran the baron through with his sword. This forms a kind of perpetual return that is a further disruption of linear logic, that is, of any sense of cause and effect. Whether these misconceptions are related in monologues that bring us and the hero up-to-date on events, like Pangloss' recital of the sack of the chateau, or Cunégonde's tale of the same event and of its results for her, or whether it is a fact told in the usual preterit by the reliable narrating voice — Candide's running his sword through the baron after which no one says he is dead, but the hero assumes it — the reader gradually learns the limits of the narrator's guarantees.

Not all the long monologued flashbacks — Pangloss', Cunégonde's, the baron's, Paquette's, Giroflée's, the old woman's, Cacambo's — concern the past of the other characters. Paquette's, after her departure from the chateau, Giroflée's and the old woman's stand outside the plot that concerns the original family. Since the characters who request those three tales insert each of them into a challenge to find someone who is happy (Paquette and Giroflée) or to prove who is the unhappiest *(la vieille),* the reader probably grasps them as illustrative of a theme, suffering, as well as constitutive of past action.

There is another use of the present tense that is a sign of narration. As the present transmits in fact a vivid past in the cases cited above, in the generalizations for which the narrator is responsible it translates an action or a state that is not strictly present in absolute time but that has instead the universal validity of atemporal reflection. They are thus not part of the narrative but contribute to enriching the relation between narrator and reader. Deictics further emphasize these brief exits from the narrated past: "... ces angoisses inconcevables que le roulis d'un vaisseau porte dans les nerfs et dans toutes les humeurs du corps ..." (Ch. 5); "... cette alarme que tout inspire dans un pays inconnu" (Ch. 16). Even though *Candide* is longer, it contains a smaller number of these than does *Zadig,* about six as opposed to over twenty in the earlier and shorter story. This corresponds with the fact of a narrator whose guidance does not usually point explicitly either toward the hero's dilemma or toward the lessons we might draw from it. Only one use of the present tense seems to refer precisely to a Parisian present that the author and his contemporaries shared: "... dans une assez plate tragédie que l'on joue quelque fois." Compared with all the other uses of a verb in the present to signify something not simply present, it stands out almost as a slip of the consistency shown elsewhere; but it occurs in Chapter Twenty-two, which is set in

Paris and which exudes *actualité* in its referents — *le faubourg* Saint-Marceau, *le théâtre,* Fréron, Mlle. Clairon, etc. — and unease in its discourse. Many readers and critics have felt that it is the least successful chapter. The kind of dissonance I have just mentioned helps account for this impression.

Although it does not often speak of consequences, the narrator's management of temporal zones does evidence itself in the vocabularies of precedence and of coincidence. The first major disruption of the correspondence between the chronology of the *histoire* and that of the *récit* occurs in Chapter Thirteen. It uses a conjuction of simultaneity, *tandis que,* and a deictic, *voici,* to point to the recital of what preceded, put in the pluperfect tense: "Tandis que la vieille parlait ... on vit entrer dans le port un petit vaisseau; il portait un alcade et des alguazils et voici ce qui était arrivé." He tells what those pursuing the hero and the heroine had been doing up to the moment being recounted in the principal line of the plot, the one following Candide's adventures in their chronology. In the next chapter, he twice uses the pluperfect again for the past of the past he is narrating. He rushes backwards in order to bring the reader up-to-date on Cacambo: "Candide avait amené de Cadix un valet ...." In Chapter Seventeen he adds information from the past of the past, and the flippant "tout le monde sait" sounds like compensation for the lateness of the information: "on parlait péruvien; c'était sa langue maternelle; car tout le monde sait que Cacambo était né au Tucuman, dans un village où on ne connaissait que cette langue." In Chapter Twenty a simple *cependant* marks coincidence of the two ships' movement and of the conversation between Candide and Martin. In Twenty-three present participles mark simultaneity: "En disputant ... en attendant ... Candide aperçut un jeune théatin ...." The first sentence of Chapter Twenty-nine transmits another coincidence of events with *pendant que* for the co-existence of conversation and violence. Besides calling attention to the fact of the narrator's arrangement of his story and to our dependence on him, this kind of juxtaposition exemplifies one of the fundamental structures of the tale; and it sometimes permits meaning that shows cause and effect (sequence) or contradiction (simultaneity) between events. I shall take this up again in Section 3 on paradigms.

Another place in which the narrator manifests his presence and his didactic intent is the description of the auto-da-fé that constitutes the short sixth chapter. The passage exudes understatement and words demanding reversal. In the first paragraph and one-half of the sentence following, a description in the past perfect shows what decisions and preparations had been made for the ceremony before the moment when Candide and Pangloss were arrested:

> Après le tremblement de terre qui avait détruit les trois quarts de Lisbonne, les sages du pays n'avaient pas trouvé un moyen plus efficace pour prévenir une ruine totale que de donner au peuple un bel auto-da-fé; il était décidé par l'université de Coimbre que le spectacle de quelques personnes brûlées à petit feu, en grande cérémonie, est un secret infaillible pour empêcher la terre de trembler.

One sees that *sages* means something like *idiots* but also *cynical politicians,* and that the phrase "had found no better means ... than the auto-da-fé" must be read as "the best they could find was an atrocity." The adjective *bel,* coherent with their design, must be read as *ugly* or *grotesque;* the minimizing *quelques,* as *already too many; à petit feu* is a ready-made expression, of course, but the *petit* harmonizes nicely with the process of understatement, even a low fire being also already too much, and too long. There is irony inherent in the expression in any case, for *à petit feu* means a long, slow burning and is thus violent in fact. The proximity of *petit* to *grande cérémonie* devalues *grande. Grande* is consistent with the intent of the sages but must be reversed to *miserable* and *cruel,* and the *secret infallible* is neither secret nor infallible: it is public and ineffective, for it cannot prevent earthquakes. The cosmos is made to refute it brutally after the ceremony, at the end of the first paragraph: "Le même jour, la terre trembla de nouveau avec un fracas épouvantable." The lack of rigor in all these suppositions and projects is put into relief by *en conséquence,* an empty appurtenance of logical rigor in the context. Once again it recalls the problem of causality and its link with optimism. The sages are also ridiculed by their consequent but trivial choice of crimes to be punished: "... un Biscayen convaincu d'avoir épousé sa commère, et deux Portugais qui en mangeant du poulet en avaient arraché le lard." Pangloss and Candide, the next victims, are guilty of even less, apparently, "... l'un pour avoir parlé, et l'autre pour avoir écouté avec un air d'approbation." The rest of the description — their incarceration, the procession, and the punishment — uses adjectives and verbs that recall the phrase *grande cérémonie — sermon pathétique, belle musique, fessé en cadence* — and that borrow the language of elegance attached to royal ceremonial and public festivals: the prisoners are not said to be put in a cold and slimy dungeon but in "appartements d'une extrême fraîcheur"; instead of being described as plunged into darkness, they are never "incommodé du soleil"; and their heads are "decorated" with paper mitres. The reader who shares the narrator's horror of these proceedings will decode the entire passage by reversing all the laudatory epithets. This episode offers a coherent stretch of discourse in which the same operation must be continually performed in order to actualize the meaning from the simple sense.

The twentieth chapter begins with a sort of commentary that is rare in the story. The narrator shows the action by dialogue more often than by telling it; and, as I have said, he both shows and tells more than he comments or analyzes. At this moment, however, he ceases to propel the action forward. He summarizes the past and present situations of Candide and of Martin, first by stating the fact that they are similar in having seen and suffered much and then by speculating about an "even if" (expressed by *quand* and the past conditional) in order to stress the vastness of the evils of which they converse:

> L'un et l'autre avaient beaucoup vu et beaucoup souffert; et quand le vaisseau aurait dû faire voile de Surinam au Japon par le cap de Bonne-Espérance, ils auraient eu de quoi s'entretenir du mal moral et du mal physique pendant tout le voyage.

The second paragraph prolongs the comparison between the two men by analyzing what differentiates them. The narrator's authoritative voice gives hope to Candide and nothing to Martin. It twice uses the concessive *quoique* to recapitulate a part of the hero's misfortunes and to show that his hopes compensate for them. The end of the parallels and of the differences diminishes the hero and returns a comic tone to the unusually direct assessment:

... cependant, quand il songeait à ce qui lui restait dans ses
poches, et quand il parlait de Cunégonde, surtout à la fin
des repas, il penchait alors pour le système de Pangloss.

This *chute* contrasts with the four balanced phrases preceding it
— the two that begin with *quoique* and the two beginning with
quand. The first incidental clause — *surtout à la fin des repas* —
breaks the cadence and erases any seriousness one might have about
an optimism that arises from good digestion. This cause ridicules
mightily the effect that has already been invalidated many times
over, the hero's predilection for the system extolled by Pangloss.
The pause for authoritative summary and for comparison of fortunes
is rare; the *chute* that separates narrator and his hero is not, as
I shall note below.

The narrator has exposed the time and place of the represented
world as being contemporary with his own, coincident with the
earth as he and the reader know it. This is unlike the time and space
of *Micromégas* and of *Zadig*. The universe of the action is not a
fantastic one; neither are the actors impossible to imagine in life,
although only one characteristic is attributed to each. The overt
coincidence of the fictional world with something like that of Europe
in 1759 encourages the reader to make comparisons and to apply
to her world the judgments available from the narrator's relation to
events in the tale. The story thus has neither psychological nor
geographical improbabilities. It is psychologically coherent and geo-
graphically exact. The concentration of chance encounters and of
returns from the dead is the factor that comes the closest to being
fantastic; each taken separately is not especially improbable, but
the number per page certainly is, as is the number of natural and
man-made disasters. None is outside the reality in which the author
wrote, however; and none, alas, is outside present-day reality either,
as every commentator of *Candide* has remarked. Consent to the kind
of compression they receive in the story comes from the reader who
has accepted the pact implied in an overtly didactic literature and
whose attention is captured by the comic presentation of concentrated horrors and by the continuous philosophical questioning.

The narrator is omniscient and reliable, and he is fond of his
récit: he stresses its tellability both by the persistent, though par-
cimonious, creation of a discourse relation — deixis, litotes, excla-

mation ("O ciel! à quel excès porte le zèle de la religion dans les dames! ") and the historical present tense — and by the multiple services that he overtly but rapidly renders with the *meanwhiles* discussed above. Excepting Chapter Twenty-two, one has the impression of uniformity and the idea that he controls a certain art of story-telling, mostly by having it tell and show itself but also by giving gentle *coups de pouce* in the direction of a thoughtful, ideological reception.

1.b.ii. *The Narrator and the Hero*

Since the narrator gives no evidence of being unreliable, the reader's sympathy for Candide follows where he leads. How does he manipulate the reader's relation with the characters? I shall examine two of them, the hero and his faithful servant, Cacambo. The most obvious reasons for our fixing our attention upon Candide are the title and the brute fact that he is present on every page. We never lose sight of him, but modern tales and their unreliable narrators have taught us that that would not necessarily in itself be enough to guarantee our loyal interest in him. Another cause of it is the consent to didacticism, the essence of the story and its reason for being; but the subtle alternations of mockery and of approval orchestrated by the narrating voice also play their part.

In the first chapter the hero appears as a bastard child with three or four traits, "mœurs douces ... jugement assez droit ... esprit simple" and an inability to keep what he thinks from showing on his face. The accounts of his thoughts confirm this description by direct statement. The central figure is thus not entirely admirable, but the title and the repetition of his name in the chapter show that he is the hero, the one whose story will be told. Like *Zadig,* this tale offers a protagonist who will dominate the page and our attention and sympathy, but who, although he inspires sympathy, does not make us follow him in his false reasonings. Even though one can sympathize with his plight — the universality of evil is the psychological or sentimental point on which the reader's attachment to him and to Zadig rests —, and even though the reliable narrator says several times that he is good, one can rarely wholly approve the analysis the hero makes of events or of his own situation. This split in the didactic hero takes a special form in *Micromégas,* the doubling of characters in the hero's sphere of action; the more extreme versions of naiveté and of error are lodged in the Secretary and not in the eponymous hero himself. Here, however, Candide unites, as does Zadig, qualities accepted and qualities mocked. From the genetic point of view, the author's challenge or problem is to create a narrator who can guide the reader to sympathy with an eiron. From the point of view of response to the characters, the reader moves through the story consenting to combine under the proper name of the hero both moral goodness and ideological simplicity — no problem here: that is fairly common in life — the naïveté manifesting itself by mechanical assessments of his dilemmas. It must further be observed that this sweet and simple fool is a terrific swordsman and "vous étend" several people "roide mort" during the course of the story. We have to consent to squeezing this skill in under the same proper name that covers innocence and the unthinking repetition of Pangloss' ideas. It is easy to do so in an episodic narrative; and since his enemies are depicted as odious, we can enjoy his getting rid of them.

An idea of our mixed assessment of the hero can be obtained by looking at two of his earliest responses to events. Upon being helped by the good Jacques, he throws himself down before him and commits *non sequitur:*

> Maître Pangloss me l'avait bien dit que tout est au mieux dans ce monde, car je suis infiniment plus touché de votre extrême générosité que de la dureté de ce monsieur à manteau noir, et de madame son épouse. (Ch. 3)

The *car* indicates that the first phrase should follow from the second; but the second exposes two cases: one, Jacques, could confirm Pangloss' belief, but the other, the orator and his wife and chamber pot, could not. Candide selects facts that correspond to his master's argument. Unimpressed, the reader advances to her hero's next reactions to events and finds him exclaiming before the wreck that is Pangloss *redux.* The questions he asks of his master are legitimate and motivated by what he sees — "Comment cette belle cause [love] a-t-elle pu produire en vous un effet si abominable?" — but the narrator makes him say them either in fractured philosophy like that just quoted or in naïve cries and shouts: "O Pangloss! s'écria

Candide, voilà une étrange généalogie! n'est-ce pas le diable qui en fut la souche?" Once, however, he responds with good practical sense to his companion's extravagant chains of reasoning; and he thereby refuses discourse on causality: "—Voilà qui est admirable, dit Candide; mais il faut vous faire guérir." This same kind of response will be his twice again in the final chapter; and it has in both cases similar provocation: hearing Pangloss' chains of kings who were assassinated, Candide interrupts: "Je sais aussi … qu'il faut cultiver notre jardin"; and after another of his teacher's lengthy linkings of cause and of effect, he says, "Cela est bien dit … mais il faut cultiver notre jardin." It is of interest, in understanding the fluctuations applied to the reader's sympathy, that the final, famous, and approvable phrases resemble one pronounced early, a sensible remark mixed in among all those revealing an excitable child. In the first example, the one from Chapter Four, he acts to aid his teacher by begging for Jacques's help. The chapter ends with discussion between Pangloss and the Anabaptist; the child is silent.

Another way in which Candide is made both simple and right appears in Chapter Six where his exclamations follow the experiences of the auto-da-fé which have themselves been transmitted as scandalous by the narrator's heavy use of the particular kinds of irony I described above. Coming just after the two-paragraph description that the reader receives with negative bias, the hero's first cry seems perfectly motivated: "Si c'est ici le meilleur des mondes possibles, que sont donc les autres?" Besides being motivated by the scene described, this statement also traces and resists Leibniz. In the first half of Candide's statement, this is obvious to educated readers; but the second half also dialogues with ideas expressed in *La Théodicée*: "… que sont donc les autres?" invokes the infinity of other possible worlds of which ours is said to be the best and the most probable. In the next he makes a distinction between his importance and that of Pangloss and of Jacques, one with which we might not agree but one that might be received as the sign of generous spirit:

> Passe encore si je n'étais que fessé, je l'ai été chez les Bulgares; mais, ô mon cher Pangloss! le plus grand de philosophes, faut-il vous avoir vu pendre, sans que je sache pourquoi! O mon cher anabaptiste! le meilleur des hommes, faut-il que vous ayez été noyé dans le port!

However, just after those touching regrets for the suffering of his idols, the speech begins a sort of decline toward the final *chute*. Regrets that concern the heroine's fate are not *per se* less noble than those touching Jacques and Pangloss, but the text sets up the minimization of the hero's concern for her by the repetition of *faut-il*, the first two uses of which ridicule his idea of causality and the third of which — "... ô mademoiselle Cunégonde! la perles des filles, faut-il qu'on vous ait fendu le ventre! " — by the particular mention of a part of the lower body draws the picture of a fate perhaps less glamorous than hanging (Pangloss) or drowning (Jacques).

In an incident that the narrator allows to inspire more horror than his account of the Inquisition, Candide's distraught reaction is for once not tempered by a comic *chute* or by any reminder of his simplicity. After meeting the slave who lacks a leg and a hand and after questioning him, Candide's cries burst forth as usual:

> O Pangloss! ... tu n'avais pas deviné cette abomination; c'en est fait, il faudra qu'à la fin je renonce à ton optimisme. —Qu'est-ce qu'optimisme? disait Cacambo. —Hélas! dit Candide, c'est la rage de soutenir que tout est bien quand on est mal; et il versait des larmes en regardant son nègre; et en pleurant, il entra dans Surinam. (Ch. 19)

His indignation stands uncorrected, and for once *il faut* ("il faudra") seems to suit the circumstances. In other places also the narrator validates the hero's indignation by reinforcing it. After the loss of his sheep at sea, Candide says, "Hélas! ... voilà un tour digne de l'ancien monde," and the narrator relates that "Il retourne au rivage, abîmé dans la douleur: car enfin il avait perdu de quoi faire la fortune de vingt monarques" (Ch. 19). The historical present and the strong adjective *abîmé* increase the chances of sympathy; and the nearly redundant *car enfin*, familiar and associated with oral expression, stresses the obviousness of his reasons for despair. Similarly, in Chapter Twenty-four, when he is discouraged at not having news of his valet and when he performs a long recapitulation of the places he has visited since sending Cacambo to find Cunégonde, his cries remain uncorrected by the narrating voice, which tells their effect: "Il tomba dans une mélancolie noire, et ne prit aucune part à l'opéra alla moda, ni aux divertissements du carnaval;

pas une dame ne lui donna la moindre tentation." An expression
that is nearly the same, *noire mélancolie,* accompanies another description of his despair, in Chapter Nineteen; that one is not
mitigated either.

The reactions in Chapters Ten and Thirteen show one kind of
alternation between silly and approvable summary by the hero.
After the theft of Cunégonde's money and jewels, Candide says,
"Hélas! ... le bon Pangloss m'avait souvent prouvé que les biens
de la terre sont communs à tous les hommes.... Ce cordelier devait
bien, suivant ces principes, nous laisser de quoi achever notre voyage." The next time he exclaims (Ch. 13), invoking his master
as usual, he takes some distance from him, reacting to the overwhelming number of unhappy tales that the ship's passengers have
just told:

> C'est bien dommage ... que le sage Pangloss ait été pendu
> contre la coutume dans un auto-da-fé; il nous dirait des
> choses admirables sur le mal physique et sur le mal moral
> qui couvrent la terre et la mer, et je me sentirais assez de
> force pour oser lui faire respectueusement quelques objec-
> tions.

The echo of Leibniz's language and of traditional theology continues
to sound in the distinction between *mal physique* and *mal moral*
attributed to Pangloss. *Sage* and *admirables* are almost ready for
reversal in the naïve hero's discourse. Another sequence of reactions
illustrates the continuing variety of content in the rigid pattern of
recapitulation and assessment. In Chapter Fifteen, the hero invokes
his teacher again to refute the baron's refusal to allow his marriage
— "Maître Pangloss m'a toujours dit que les hommes sont égaux;
et assurément je l'épouserait" — and after running his beloved's
brother through with his sword, he makes a tally of the persons he
has killed and evaluates their importance in another comic *chute:*
"Hélas! mon Dieu ... j'ai tué mon ancien maître, mon ami, mon
beau-frère; je suis le meilleur homme du monde, et voilà déjà trois
hommes que je tue; et dans ces trois il y a deux prêtres." This
particular outcry is more intense at the start, for the classical tragedy's *hélas* is reinforced this time by *mon Dieu;* the verb *tuer* is
repeated and contributes to the comic veneer of simplicity completed
by the premature and thus Moliéresque "mon beau-frère." The *déjà*

of *voilà déjà* implies both that he is too young to have begun killing people but that it was bound to happen eventually and that there are surely more murders to come. The sudden clinical precision on the civil status of each dead man completes for the reader the comic detachment between the naïve hero and his violent acts.

In the next chapter, the narrative assigns to him an unusual number of pauses for reflection. One ridicules him by the word *jambon* and employs a *chute;* the latter is reinforced by the narrator's pointing to the contradiction between his sadness and his appetite:

> Comment veux-tu ... que je mange du jambon, quand j'ai tué le fils de monsieur le baron, et que je me vois condamné à ne revoir la belle Cunégonde de ma vie? A quoi me servira de prolonger mes misérables jours, puisque je dois les traîner loin d'elle dans les remords et dans le désespoir? Et que dira le *Journal de Trévoux?* En parlant ainsi, il ne laissa pas de manger.

The second pause for reasoning begins also with *hélas* and tries again to apply Pangloss' lessons to the spectacle of love between women and monkeys; he soberly cites his teacher's citing of examples from Antiquity. In the third reflective moment he invokes Pangloss upon awakening and finding himself a prisoner of the Oreillons. Obedient to the master — "Tout est bien; soit ..." — he objects all the same, "... mais j'avoue qu'il est bien cruel d'avoir perdu mademoiselle Cunégonde et d'être mis à la broche par les Oreillons." His naïve objection to being cooked and eaten is that it is "peu chrétien"; this would not impress persons intent upon destroying precisely that class of humans, the Christians who have invaded their lands. In his fourth intervention, having been saved from death, Candide imitates his master without naming him; like a good pupil he rapidly recapitulates his good fortune and passes with agility from cause to effect:

> Quel peuple! ... quels hommes! quelles mœurs! si je n'avais pas eu le bonheur de donner un grand coup d'épée au travers du corps du frère de mademoiselle Cunégonde, j'étais mangé sans rémission.

He again selects portions of his story, as he did in Chapter Three, choosing the part of his adventure that corresponds to Pangloss' optimism: "Mais après tout, la pure nature est bonne, puisque ces gens-ci, au lieu de me manger, m'ont fait mille honnêtetés dès qu'ils ont su que je n'étais pas jésuite." This particular speech by an unconscious eiron is of the type "out of the mouths of babes" and surely pleased the Jesuits' enemies.

Recapitulations and appeals to Pangloss continue through the next-to-last chapter and then cease completely in the last. In Twenty-seven, Candide is still wishing for his master and for his wisdom ("Ah! ... si Pangloss était ici, il le saurait, et nous l'apprendrait"). In Twenty-eight he summarizes the misfortunes of Pangloss' life in posing to him the critical question, "Eh bien! mon cher Pangloss ... quand vous avez été pendu, disséqué, roué de coups, et que vous avez ramé aux galères, avez-vous toujours pensé que tout allait le mieux du monde?" In Twenty-nine he indignantly rehearses what he has done for the baron who still opposes his marriage to Cunégonde. These last examples of Candide's cries and repetitions are by then familiar to the reader, and it is difficult to see any psychological evolution in their sequence. The protagonist is created by the reader on the site of the name, of one trait of character, and of a large number of *Ah!* and of *Hélas!* The opinions represented under his name vacillate, often in the space of a few lines. As late as the twenty-third chapter, when he is described as "étourdi et choqué" by the murder of the English admiral, it suffices that the scene change in order that the behavior attributed to the name take up again optimism's formula: "Tout est bien, tout va bien, tout va le mieux qu'il soit possible." This exercise has a name in classical rhetoric; it is the *épiphonème*. [6] Pierre Fontanier defines it thus: "... une réflexion vive et courte, ou un trait d'esprit, d'imagination, ou de sentiment, à l'occasion d'un récit ou d'un détail quelconque, mais qui s'en détache absolument par sa généralité ou par son object particulier ...." [7] The character's coherence is minimal and consists almost entirely in his passivity; once the shock of the first encounter with injustice is registered (Ch. 4: "Ah, meilleur des mondes, où

---

[6] Jean Starobinski, "Sur le style philosophique de *Candide*," *Comparative Literature*, Summer 1976, 199.

[7] *Les Figures du discours* (Paris: Flammarion, 1968), p. 386.

êtes-vous?"), and up to the last chapter, the critical reader finds no psychology, no evolution, but she supplies coherence by consenting to the proper name's uniting the two unsynthesized reactions, those of interrogating experience and of repeating optimistic formulas.

The relation between the hero and the reader can be put into sharper focus and into the perspective of a gamut of possible relations if we look at the way in which the narrating voice provides us with information about another character, Cacambo, and the way in which that voice suggests what our attitude toward the valet should be. In the section above, I mentioned the manner in which the narrator at the beginning of Chapter Fourteen prepares in two lines the appearance of the new person. He has never been mentioned before, but has presumably been with the hero since Cadiz, that is, since that Atlantic port of Spain where he passed in Chapter Ten. We are thus now to believe, if we care to reflect upon it, that he has been a member of the group in the *récit* from the middle of Chapter Ten; and in the *histoire,* he was present during the crossing, through the old woman's story, the interrogation of the other passengers, the landing in Buenos Aires, and the efforts made by the governor to obtain Cunégonde for himself. Since the old woman and the heroine find their advantage in staying under the governor's protection, and since Candide is too simple to get away by himself, the *récit* gives birth to a valet just in time to take charge of the simpleton who must flee for his life:

> Candide avait amené de Cadix un valet tel qu'on en trouve beaucoup sur les côtes d'Espagne et dans les colonies. C'était un quart d'Espagnol, né d'un métis dans le Tucuman; il avait été enfant de chœur, sacristain, matelot, moine, facteur, soldat, laquais.

In providing his hero with this helper, the narrator is at pains both to give confidence in him, for we are used by now to Candide's being taken in and deceived, and to remind us that even though the hero needs help, he is still a good fellow. He performs these orienting and reassuring functions: "Il s'appelait Cacambo, et aimait fort son maître, parce que son maître était un fort bon homme." The narrator then ceases this heavy guidance and returns to describing the action: "Il sella au plus vite les deux chevaux ...." In order that this at least remain clear in the sea of accident and deception, the narrating voice reminds us four more times of the confidence we are to have in Cacambo: "Cacambo ne perdait jamais la tete" (Ch. 16); "Cacambo, qui donnait d'aussi bons conseils que la vieille ..." (Ch. 17); and "le fidèle Cacambo" and "C'était un très bon homme que ce Cacambo" in Chapter Nineteen. As we shall see in the application of the Proppian functions, this kind of instruction about the confidence he can command in the reader corresponds to the fact that he, like the old woman, serves constantly as enabler or donor in the action. It is apparent that there are great differences between this kind of information and that derivable from the hero's discourse and actions.

III. 2. SYNTAGMATIC PROCESS

2.a. *Distribution in the Signifier*

Like most of the *contes,* this one advances according to a principle of motion in space. In the *histoire* the hero starts out at random seeking food and shelter. Since he was expelled from the castle, his quest is at first simply one for survival; his departure was involuntary, and he had to leave his love behind. Like many traditional folk- and picaresque heroes who "go off to seek their fortune," Candide moves from one accidental encounter to another, running into people and into natural disasters. The voyage has here a slightly different potential for producing meaning than in *Micromégas* and in *Zadig.* Although the impulse in *Micromégas* is less frenzied, in all three stories the fact of movement founds the impression of questing, and quest is the prime motivation for changing places. In *Candide* the hero is first motivated by the need to survive, and then he learns that Cunégonde is alive and finds her, makes his fortune, and loses the heroine again; so that the initial quest for sheer sustenance is gradually replaced by a search for Cunégonde. This pursuit is delegated to his servant when Candide gives Cacambo money and sends him to find the heroine; but the third and permanent quest, the philosophical one, continues to found his regular expressions of the alternation between wonder and despair, his ceaseless commentary and questions about what happens to him. The hero's passivity accounts for the fact that this all-pervasive interrogation does not motivate the voyage in the *histoire;* but, like in that to *Zadig,* it is a sort of *basso continuo* sounding throughout the events that are causes and effects of travel. The latter provide the raw materials and the occasion for his reflection, the testing in experience of his teacher's doctrine.

It has often been remarked that Voltaire's tales place successive episodes in various capitals and countries of the globe. In the *Princesse de Babylone* the content of the abuses denounced is often related to the country being visited by the protagonists. In *Candide* it is not always tightly attached but is more so than in *Zadig.* The pretentiousness criticized in Chapter One is portrayed as specifically Prussian. The hypocrisy in Parisian society depicted in Chapter Twenty-two might be found also in Potsdam, but the proper names are identified with Paris. The specific abuses committed by the Jesuits in the New World are more closely integrated to geographical place; but the attacks on Christianity's wars against the heathen could be considered as appropriate in many other settings; and Jesuit practices are targets in many of the places depicted, Lisbon, Paris, and Venice as well as in Paraguay. If Candide had seen Paquette and Giroflée in South America and the baron in Venice and if the former event had preceded the latter, no other part of the intervening text would have had to be changed. Such events are contiguous, not continuous; and they tend, among their other functions, to create an impression of repetition that works against a strong consciousness, thematic or structural, of a voyage. The very loose attachment of events to their setting and of events to each other (Ch. II, p. 48 above) finds a sort of compensation, however, in a certain order discernable in the geographical transpositions. One critic made a clear diagram of the movement; it goes from east to west and back again: from Germany to Holland, Portugal, the Atlantic Ocean, Argentina, Paraguay, then to the Oreillons's territory and Eldorado. Both of the latter are said to be in South America, but they are imaginary. The maneuver back east then begins: Surinam, the Atlantic again, Paris, England, Venice, then to a place near Constantinople, at sea again, and finally to the farm near the Propontis. [8] The displacements can thus offer an impression

---

[8] Pol Gaillard, *Candide* (Paris: Hatier, 1972).

of cumulative tension and of causal development to what is an essentially punctual recital of events. Furthermore, and this is the subject of Section Three below, with the exception of the chateau, Eldorado, and the final garden, all the incidents generate the same paradigmatic meaning. From that point of view they can be substituted for one another in time — the succession of the narration — and in space — the countries of the story — without changing the meaning produced by each one. At the same time, by the very fact of their being spread out over variously named places, the circumstances repeated can be understood as universal, and by the fact that those places appear to follow a geographical order, the incidents might even seem to be the causes of each other. Narrative technique might be seen as weakening the tale's opposition to a principle of causality in events, or else it can be said to compensate for the uneasiness that would be produced by the reign of chance in all areas of meaning produced by the text.

2.b. *Order in the Signified*

Candide's lack of initiative in both areas, action and thought, makes of him the type of hero that Propp calls *victim*. Because of the reader's divided sympathy for him, which I have already examined, it is more accurate to call him a parody of the victimized-hero. He probably would not be looked upon as a questing hero for the reasons I just enumerated and for those that become apparent when one attempts a Proppian coding for his adventures. At the same time, the logic of events — a heroine lost and found two times; safety and freedom lost and found many times — imitates the multiplication of a sequence the doubling of which is typical of the most banal folktale, the quest for the object that both Propp and Greimas code in their systems. In a similar way, even though the hero does not announce the project of testing Pangloss' philosophical beliefs, questions doing just that are the ones he candidly asks at each change in fortune, much as Zadig asks why the good are punished at each point of his trajectory toward Astarté. This observation and the difference from Micromégas, whose departure is involuntary but whose quest is intentional, group the two heroes, Zadig and Candide, in an eironic category and put the grammar of their adventures into the linear paradigm of quest even though the concerted and conscious impulses in that direction are not portrayed. It is known, besides, that Propp and his functions do not code motivation but only each substantive action linked to another action, and that functions are definable by their consequences, not by the intentions that might or might not be represented with their description. The two eirons are, however, different in the kinds of involvement in events: although things happen to Zadig, as they do to Candide, he is also enterprising in about seven of the episodes, the ones I coded as sub-sequences in Chapter Two above (Figure II.C).

The attempt to apply Propp's functions to *Candide* helps reveal the complexity of its composition and the variety of questing activities that surrounds the name of the hero. It is a convenient method for isolating the outlines of the traditional folkloric plot and for grasping the presence of more than one thread and the orchestration of all of them. Unlike *Zadig* the first chapter here puts into place all the problems to be solved in the other twenty-nine chapters. The most obvious and the most traditional is that of retrieving the lost heroine; the hero falls in love and loses her in the first episode. Finding her is the broadest and most explicited project of the otherwise passive hero. There he may be seen as a questor who initiates something, but in more of the episodes — Column II below — he clearly belongs to Propp's category of *héros-victime* who undergoes something. A very large number of episodes or units concerns more precisely problems of physical safety and of freedom than direct progress toward finding Cunégonde. For this reason, I have separated them from the marriage-quest itself and coded them in another column, although the broadest grammar of any traditional quest can include any kind of trial and reaction, even those not immediately advancing the acquisition of the desired object. I label this category "Freedom-Quests," for freedom continually poses itself as problematic. Hunger, persecution, imprisonment, and at the very end boredom, are all states from which the hero has often to free himself. Since he is in and out of them all, these episodes are more punctual in nature and do not form one line of plot in which events are connected to one another. The two quests just named begin in the same moment, that of the hero's expulsion from the castle; he loses both his living and his beloved. I have coded as part of the third quest (reaction to events or analysis) the moments of general discussion bearing upon the existence of evil and the moments of exclamation in which the hero invokes his teacher's or, later, Martin's lessons and tries to apply them. Although there is no formal announcement and although these incidents often appear as a sort of punctuation occuring after catastrophic events, they occupy much more space than Zadig's observations about evil rewarded. Many of them are unmotivated in action and are depicted as more or less spontaneous debate during, for example, a passage by boat from one continent or country to another. The tradition of literature's recording what travelers say to each other hardly needs comment. The quests will be coded as *grammars* of quest; the functions account for that only, without regard to motivation. Whether or not the rhetoric of quest is also present and whether it can be inferred will be discussed later.

The moments that compose and advance the search for the heroine are widely spaced in the story. After the idyll at the château and after being expelled for transgressing the implied injunction not to pretend to the heroine's social level, Candide begins his wanderings, and the action concerns his physical survival and safety until Chapter Four in which he learns that his first loss is worse than he thought: the heroine has been killed. This doubling or intensifying of the initial loss is recalled later when he finds and loses her again. The reiteration of loss and its intensification (loss by death) provide reminders, through the many picaresque episodes, that the hero does have a goal. Although no motive other than Jacques's is given for the trip by boat to Lisbon, it is effectively a "transfer of the hero" (15) continuing the movement that draws him near to his next meeting with the heroine. This occurs in the seventh chapter where his persecution, coded also in the second quest as lack of freedom, can be seen as trial and reaction (12, 13) earning him the magic object (14) — care, seclusion — provided by the old woman, the donor who leads him to the heroine. The lack, 8^{Ia}, is thus repaired, 19^{Ia}. The reparation is momentary, for in Chapter Nine he learns that she is in fact the property of two other men, not his, 8^{Ib}. He engages in combat against each (16) and is victorius (18), thereby reacquiring the right of possession (19^{Ib}). Through the succeeding episodes, until the thirteenth chapter, hero

FIGURE III.A

Chapter & Abbreviated Events	QUEST I (marriage)	QUEST II (freedom)	QUEST III (fusion of theory and experience)
1. hero, heroine in castle	0	0	0
teachings of Pangloss			2, 3
handkerchief, expulsion	2, 3, 8^{Ia}	2, 3, 8^{IIa}, 10, 11	8^{IIIa}
hero taken into army		6, 7, 8^{IIb}	
2. hero beaten for wandering, spared by Bulgarian king		8^{IIc}, 12, 13, 19^{IIc}	
3. war, hero flees		12, 13, 15, 19^{IIb}	
hero begs, is threatened		12, 13, 14neg.	
hero interrogated, chamber pot		12, 13, 14neg.	
hero helped by Jacques	8^{Iabis}	14, 19^{IIa}	12, 13, 14pos.
4. hero meets Pangloss, learns heroine is dead			
hero discusses evil with Pangloss			12, 13, 14neg.
hero has Pangloss treated by Jacques			12, 13

FIGURE III.A

Chapter & Abbreviated Events	QUEST I (marriage)	QUEST II (freedom)	QUEST III (fusion of theory and experience)
4-5. hero, J, & P on boat for Lisbon	15		
5. storm, earthquake, J. is drowned, P. reasons			12, 13
5-6. hero tied, beaten by Inquisition, P. is hanged		6, 7, 8^{IIc}	
6. hero tests P's doctrine			12, 13, 14neg.
7. hero saved by old woman hero meets heroine	12, 13, 14, 15 19^{Ia}	15, 19^{IIc} 14	12, 13
8. heroine's story			
9. hero twice risks losing heroine, kills her two lovers	(8^{Ib}, 16, 18, 19^{Ib}) repeated		
10. hero, heroine, & old woman flee, pursued	21, 22		

FIGURE III.A

Chapter & Abbreviated Events	QUEST I (marriage)	QUEST II (freedom)	QUEST III (fusion of theory and experience)
theft of heroine's jewels			
hero reasons, invokes P's teachings		8^{IIa}	12, 13, 14neg.
hero becomes captain		12, 13, 14, 19^{IIa}	
hero, heroine, old woman in flight on boat, reason together about P's system	21		12, 13
11-12. old woman's story			
13. all passengers tell their stories			12, 13
hero invokes P's system			14neg.
heroine leaves hero for governor	8^{Io}		
14. hero pursued, in flight aided by old woman & by valet	15, 21, 22		
encounter with baron, hero invokes P.			
15. baron's story			12, 13, 14pos.
baron refuses hero permission to			

FIGURE III.A

Chapter & Abbreviated Events	QUEST I (marriage)	QUEST II (freedom)	QUEST III (fusion of theory and experience)
marry heroine, hero kills baron, hero & valet flee, disguised	$[8^{Id}, 16, 18, 19^{Id}]$ 21, 22		
16. hero delivers woman from apes, gets no gratitude, but remembers P's lessons			12, 13, 14pos.
hero & valet caught and bound, hero invokes P		8^{IIe}	12, 13, 14neg.
valet finds solution		15, 19^{IIe}	
17-18. arrival in Eldorado, visits	momentary (Chapters 17-18) fusion of II & III, but 8^{I} subsists, and so 8^{II} & 8^{III} are taken on again by return to outside world:		
departure to seek heroine	10, 11		
19. loss of most sheep, i.e. of money		8^{IIf}	
encounter with crippled slave, hero invokes P			
hero exploited by Dutch shipowner	12, 13, 14		12, 13, 14neg.

FIGURE III.A

Chapter & Abbreviated Events	QUEST I (marriage)	QUEST II (freedom)	QUEST III (fusion of theory and experience)
at sea toward Venice	15		
all passengers tell their stories, hero invokes P			12, 13, 14neg.
20. at sea, hero and Martin discuss			12, 13
hero recovers sheep, draws lesson			14pos.
21. nearing France, hero & M debate		12, 13, 14, 19ltt	12, 13
22. arrival at Bordeaux. hero & M go to Paris			15
hero repeatedly robbed and tricked			(12, 13, 14neg.) repeated
hero saved by M, exclaims against evil		16, 18neg. 22	12, 13, 14neg.
23. in discussion with M, hero invokes P			12, 13, 14neg.
hero & M view execution of admiral, hero reacts			12, 13, 14neg.

FIGURE III.A

Chapter & Abbreviated Events	QUEST I (marriage)	QUEST II (freedom)	QUEST III (fusion of theory and experience)
24. arrival at Venice, hero optimistic			12, 13, 14pos.
encounter with Paquette & Giroflée, their stories, hero says M. is right			12, 13, 14neg.
25. visit with Pococurante			(12, 13, 14neg.) repeated
26. Encounter with six kings, hero says P is right			(12, 13) repeated 14pos.
27. en route to Constantinople	15		
hero in conversation with M says P is right			12, 13, 14pos.
hero meets Cacambo, learns heroine is ugly			**12, 13**
conversation with M, hero invokes P			12, 13, 14pos.
encounter with baron & P			12, 13
28. stories of baron & P, hero interrogates P			14neg.

FIGURE III.A

Chapter & Abbreviated Events	QUEST I (marriage)	QUEST II (freedom)	QUEST III (fusion of theory and experience)
29. hero rejoins heroine, frees her & old woman	19^{ic}		
baron opposes marriage	25		
30. hero sends away baron, marries heroine	26, 30, 31		
boredom		8^{IIg}	
discussion: hero, P, M			12, 13
reappearance of Paquette & Giroflée			12, 13, 14neg.
consultations:			
derviche			28
old man & children			28
P's discourse on the death of kings			24, 28
work	19^{IIg}		

(A description of the numbered functions is found on page 38 above.)

and heroine remain united; and the next peripeteia occurs at the end of that chapter when Cunégonde leaves Candide for the governor of Buenos Aires, a third loss for the hero, 8^{Ic}.

A transfer again follows the loss, the hero is pursued (21) because of the two murders (22); and help is given him, horses and directions (15), by the old woman and by his valet, who makes his first appearance here. The old woman stays with Cunégonde, whom she has been serving. The logic of the *histoire* does not allow her to be a companion for the hero in South American jungles that are the setting of the next adventures. Candide is a passive and naïve hero; and so, the same logic says, he must continue to have a helper, donor of magic auxiliaries, inventor of disguises. Cacambo appears to take over that role. The next chapter contains one episode that also advances the thread of the traditional marriage-quest: in an action parallel to the killings of his two rivals, Candide kills the baron (16, 18) who has denied him permission to marry Cunégonde. Both the 8^{Id} and the 19^{Id} (bracketed in Figure III.A) are hypothetical, for they occur inside a previous loss, 8^{Ic}, that will not be repaired until Chapter Twenty-nine. This new murder also requires flight (21), this time in disguise (22). In Chapter Nineteen, a trial and reaction with negative results relate to a specific attempt to get nearer to Cunégonde, that is, by traveling to Venice for the reunion with Cacambo who is in the meantime supposed to pick up the heroine in Buenos Aires and take her to Venice for this meeting. Another transfer of the hero follows this trial (Ch. 19), and another transfer codable in this column — the trip to Paris having been a philosophical distraction unrelated to the marriage-quest — occurs between Venice and Constantinople (Ch. 27) where he knows the heroine to be, thanks to his valet's returning to him with that news (Chapter 26). He rejoins her (19^{Ic}) in the next-to-last chapter and must perform a further difficult task (25), for the baron still opposes his marriage to his sister. After consulting his friends (26), he gives his enemy back into slavery (30, punishment of the aggressor) and marries the now ugly heroine (31, here a parody of the hero's reward). As is clear from the figure above, this most traditional of the lines of folkloric plot accounts for a very small number of episodes when one separates it from those containing various other forms of deprivation. The rectification of the latter does not lead in any particular logic from one episode to another, but most of these events are the occasion of the manifestation of evil forces — both human and natural — and the occasion for ingenious solutions brought by benevolent donors or by chance.

The series of beatings, imprisonments, punishments, extortions, and so forth has been called Quest II in the figure above. The loss of the heroine (8^{Ia}), coincides with the loss of the hero's means of living; and his accepting to act and departing (10, 11) are in fact involuntary. He loses his freedom of movement as well (8^{IIb}) by letting himself be deceived into joining the Bulgarian army (6, 7), and is then bound (8^{IIc}) and beaten (12, 13) for trying to escape. He is spared by the king (19^{IIc}). That freedom — from punishment — is regained; but 8^{IIa}, lack of sustenance, subsists. War provides another test and reaction — horror and flight (12, 13); the hero goes to another village (15). He then leaves the theater of war and of the army (19^{IIB}). The narrator reminds the reader that through all this, the hero acts without ever forgetting Cunégonde. He thus joins the two lines of endeavor, I and II, in the signifier. Two other incidents may be seen as trial and reaction, failing also to render the object permitting freedom from want (under Chapter III, Figure III.A); 8^{IIA} is still unsolved. Then the encounter with Jacques repairs the lack of the various freedoms (14, 19^{IIa}). This moment coincides with the first explicit application of Pangloss' lesson to what happens (12, 13) to the hero. He believes that Jacques's help confirms his teacher's belief in this best of worlds, so the doctrine is the key to understanding for Candide, a "magic object" (14) in that search. This has been coded as Quest III, and I shall return to it after completing the reading of II.

The next episode showing a new lack of freedom is that in which the hero is deceived (6, 7) and is imprisoned and punished (8^{IIc}). The reparation (19^{IIc}) here comes from the old woman who effects his transfer (15) to a safe place. The magic object is Cunégonde's money. In the struggle for survival, the next blow is the theft of the latter's jewels (Ch. 10), 8^{IId}, motivating the hero's using his military training in order to get a job (trial, reaction, magic object, victory, 19^{IId}). The episodes of the next four chapters do not include physical deprivation until, in Chapter Sixteen, the hero and his valet are bound and threatened (8^{IIe}). The servant finds the solution; they escape (19^{IIe}).

The accidental arrival in Eldorado brings about an end to both the quest for ease, II, and that for theory's application, III. It could thus be coded 19^{II} and 19^{III}. The events of the stay itself could be coded if one took as *lack* (8) the visitors' incomprehension and as *test* (12) and *reaction* (13) their confrontation with the various aspects of the utopian society. They gradually attain understanding, reparation, etc. The moment of their comprehension of the place is also that in which the hero remembers a lack that is not satisfied by this place; 8^{I} subsists, and so he voluntarily takes on again the risk of the others, 8^{II} and 8^{III}, by returning to the outside world in order to continue the marriage-quest. He consents to act, departs, and immediately loses part of the newly acquired magic object, the wealth carried by the sheep, 8^{IIf} (Ch. 19). He is thus again subject to evil chance. That loss is repaired in the next chapter; he finds, again by chance, one of the animals and thus recovers a part of the fortune he will use throughout the episodes remaining. The hero fails continually in the combat against the Parisian aggressors until Martin saves him from the robber-society by leading him away from it. This, the end of Chapter Twenty-two, is the last of the episodes in which his personal freedom and security are threatened. The physical wants and dangers of Quest II end here; but after seven more chapters, a new form of discomfort arises. It is boredom. It alone threatens the persons who are now safe from physical want and harm. All the characters now enter the hero's sphere of action. They share this lack (8^{IIg}), and they share in the search for its solution by the discussion coded in III. The way out of the dilemma is found by a process of elimination: a return to testing Pangloss' thesis and methods yields no results and sends them back to the purely practical remedy learned from the old man and proposed for their use by Candide.

The third quest is prepared in the first chapter by the citing of one of Pangloss' lessons. It and the hero's admiring reaction might be looked upon as two of Propp's preparatory functions, 2, injunction or order given, and 3, execution of the order, seeing things in the master's way. The hero's expulsion and the narrator's underlining the difference between lesson and fact — "et tout fut consterné

dans le plus agréable des châteaux possibles" already quoted —
manifest the lack that is still implicit for the hero. The reader is
urged to see it now, the lack of coherence between Pangloss' theory
and Candide's experience (8^{III}). In the middle of Chapter Three,
the hero is shown for the first time imitating Pangloss' language;
and he names him a few lines later when Jacques comes to his aid.
After this trial and reaction, Jacques brings the magic object,
coded 14, that delivers him from want; the hero therefore states
the positive correspondence between his teacher's doctrine and what
just happened to him (12, 13, 14pos.). When he learns from his
master of Cunégonde's death, he again uses the former's language
but implies a negative correspondence between it and the fact
that he has just learned (Ch. 4) (12, 13, 14neg). In the same
chapter, he responds to Pangloss' explanation of his own sorry state
by asking if the devil is perhaps at its source; his teacher answers
at length, and Candide turns to practical matters (12, 13).

These three manners present in the signifier — positive, negative,
and uncommitted — invoke the doctrine and confront it with experience. They alternate throughout the story from then on at fairly
regular intervals (Figure III.A, Column III). From the visit to Paris
(Ch. 22) onward the negative results accumulate; and during the
lengthy cease of events belonging to the second quest, from the end
of Twenty-two to the middle of Thirty, every episode concerns this
kind of testing, Quest III, until the hero finds the heroine and
marries her. The results are usually negative. After that moment,
the final chapter takes up again the confrontation between Pangloss'
theory and everyone else's experience. The first, the discussion among
Candide, Martin, and Pangloss, does not make a decision explicit;
the second, the return of Paquette and of Giroflée, gives the victory
to Martin and to pessimism. Then, with the two consultations, the
effort to resolve the lack of correspondence is put on another footing.
The dervish's rejection of metaphysical discussion is a denunciation
of Pangloss, now revealed as a false hero, since he pretends to
coherence but has not provided it. The second consultation denounces him again, for the old man refuses to answer Pangloss' questions
about the evils occurring around him, and he offers the example of
an agreeable self-sufficiency unconcerned with either doctrine or
events. The text and Candide give Pangloss one more chance (24):

he makes a last speech, but it offers no help toward rectifying the lack. Candide responds by interrupting him and by changing the subject (28) to work. Martin seconds the motion. The description of each character's useful work provided the happily-ever-after ending for both Quests II and III, and Candide reiterates the solution (19) that the traditional recital of rewards and of the past's future justifies.

The quest for coherence between Pangloss' doctrine and Candide's experience is complicated in Chapter Twenty by the addition of Martin. He is a pessimist; and as soon as he and Candide begin their movable conversation — their debates punctuate the incidents remaining in the tale — the encounters of optimistic theory and catastrophic experience result in more and more *14negatives* (magic object denied). When Martin wins the contest, that is, when Candide chooses him, it is specifically for the purpose of discussion: "Il faut avouer que les autres [the other contestants] étaient pour le moins aussi malheureux que lui; mais Candide espérait que le savant le désennuierait dans le voyage." The dialogues that follow present Martin's views as clear opposites of Pangloss' teachings, and the reader familiar with Voltaire's own historical language finds echoes of it in Martin's first long speech: the world as *globule,* the folly of war and of the *assassins,* "courant d'un bout de l'Europe à l'autre." This first explicit presentation of the viewpoint opposite to the one being tested is confirmed by events that follow it in the *histoire* and in the text: an "Au milieu de cette dispute" introduces a scene of war between two ships and of a hundred men drowning; it thus bears out Martin's dark view of mankind. One notes the contrast with many of Pangloss' speeches; they are also followed by catastrophic events but are contradicted by them. The next conversation (12) between Candide and his new friend contains a reminder that the hero has not forgotten his search for Cunégonde. He keeps that goal alive in the reader's mind by similar remarks (Chapters, 20, 23, 25) through the chapters (20-29) in which Quest II dominates. Martin is the witness and finally donor of Candide's safety in the long series of misfortunes imposed on the hero in Paris. The hours blackest and most dense with petty injustice pass under the disabused eye of the pessimist. After more discussion, another dark and arbitrary wrong, the murder of the admiral who lost a battle, is viewed by the hero and by his friend (Ch. 23). After Martin wins the bet about the couple in Venice (Ch. 24), the lengthy visit and interrogation of Pococurante leaves Candide amazed and Martin blasé. Martin thus has an important share in the donor's sphere of action; and he is often the donor of the magic object, the understanding that Pangloss's doctrine does not account for certain facts. These findings are coded 12, 13, 14pos.

The large number of episodes seems to distribute itself in a way that guarantees sustaining the reader's interest in the fiction while packing in a large amount of both philosophical discussion and existential demonstration of its didactic point. The thread that tradition has thought most interesting, the struggle of lovers to find each other, establishes itself immediately; but afterwards the very small number of episodes actually advancing that plot — about fifteen out of the more than seventy — is spread thinly, that is, at widely spaced intervals through all the remaining chapters. It ends at the beginning of the last chapter. The series of incidents showing physical dangers and loss of freedoms, traditionally second to the marriage-plot or serving it, begins at the end of Chapter One also and repeats itself through all six of the episodes that follow immediately. After a series of indignities, coded in II, has been committed against the hero, the testing of optimism is explicited in the *histoire* near the end of Chapter Four. From then on, the activity of testing the doctrine constitutes a fairly regular punctuation of all the incidents and accounts for thirty codable events, that is, for over forty percent of the total. The other two quests are completed before this one ends; the least compelling, II, first; the easiest next, the romantic one; and this leaves the point announced by the subtitle, "ou l'optimisme," to occupy the whole last chapter, one of the longest besides.

III. 3. PARADIGMS

3.a. *Spheres of action*

The questing perspective supposes various objects and agents of each quest. In Quests I and II of *Candide,* the designation of the member or members of each sphere seems evident; for the third it is more problematic, and the difficulty helps to pinpoint the forces at work in the narration of the didactic or ideological portion of the tale.

FIGURE III.B
Spheres of Action

	I	II	III
Object of Quest	Cunégonde	freedom from want and from constraints	fusion of optimistic theory with experience
Mandator	the baron *père*	Candide	Candide
Hero	Candide	Candide	Candide and finally the others
Aggressor	the two barons, Jewish and Catholic lovers, agents of church	baron *père*, army, church, Oreillons, chance	evils, misfortunes
Donor	old woman, Cacambo	king, Jacques, Cunégonde, sheep, Cacambo, Martin	hostile : Pangloss benevolent : Martin
Magic Auxiliary	information, transport, etc.	money, horses, disguises, etc.	optimism, pessimism
False Hero	—	—	Pangloss

The object of the hero's marriage-quest is obviously Cunégonde, and her father sends him on the search even though that is not his intention. The result of his expulsing Candide is a quest to find the heroine again. The aggressors, the ones who cause the loss or who threaten her loss and provoke the combat with the hero, are the two barons (father & son) and the two lovers whom he kills in order to regain her. Donors in this quest are the old woman and Cacambo who obtain for him magic auxiliaries such as transportation for escapes. No false hero pursues the same goal as Candide. The second quest, the one for survival and for freedom from want and from constraints, naturally has the hero as his own mandator; the baron *père* is an aggressor who causes lack (8^{IIa}). Other aggressors are the Bulgarian army (8^{IIb}), the church ($8^{IIc, d, e}$), the Oreillons (8^{IIf}), and chance (8^{IIg}) in the withdrawal of the physical threat that leaves boredom as the last misdeed or lack in Chapter 30. Donors, those giving the hero a magic object that helps him to remove the lack or want, include the Bulgarian king, who gives absolution; Cunégonde, who gives money; the sheep, who carry enough wealth for the entire second half of the adventure; Cacambo and Martin who both get the hero out of mortal danger by disguises and by guile. There is no false hero. The philosophical (III), rather than material (I), quest has as its object, one infers, the testing of optimistic theory taught to the innocent hero by Pangloss. Candide is again his own mandator; it is he who spontaneously tries to make the application to his life. The aggressor — who causes the lack, here, of cohesion between theory and events — could be seen as experience itself since experience consists of the evils and misfortunes that prevent the hero from fusing the two. Pangloss offers what he believes to be a magic auxiliary, his theory; he may be seen as a hostile donor since most of the hero's putting his lessons to the test results in a failure of the object (14neg.) needed to attain correspondence between lessons and reality. Martin can be considered a benevolent donor since his system does on occasion successfully account for events, which fact each time means failure of Pangloss' system since it is the opposite of Martin's. The views are thus the magic auxiliaries proposed for repairing the lack, 8^{IIIa}, of coherence. One can see Pangloss as a false hero since he pursues the same quest, claiming to explain everything by his system, and since his efforts give negative results; his pretensions are finally denounced, that is, ignored.

The hero's sphere in the philosophical quest has the special property of gathering new members as the tale progresses. The group sitting around Candide and discussing the problem of evil is twice expanded to include all the passengers of a ship. Although their tales in the first case are more like raw materials for the contemplations of the hero, of the old woman, and of Cunégonde, and although they can thus not be considered as questors, the mass of misfortune that they represent underlines the universal and thus fundamental nature of the question that Candide and the text are posing. This humanity represents us in the aggregate as Candide and his friends represent us in the particular. The group of protagonists ends in the last chapter by containing every named character of the story, except those who are dead and one, the baron, whom nobody wants around. The sphere of questing hero thus contains at the end eight individuals — Candide, Cunégonde, the old woman, Pangloss, Martin, Paquette, Giroflée, and Cacambo — who all participate in the first of the last two consultations, the one that declares Pangloss' questions useless. The hero and his two mentors alone visit the man who provides the example they finally follow. Then the whole group enters into Candide's solution. It offers a microcosm of humanity come to the end of its failed collective quest for answers, resolving to make do with working and with being safe.

3.b. *Theory and Experience*

The grammar of this narrative, the relation among its units, is more analogical (paradigmatic) than sequential (syntagmatic). In the forces they depict, most of the episodes exist independently, juxtaposed as though situated on a same synchronic transversal. A sequential or syntagmatic possibility would describe a relation of progressive coherence from the first unit of the text to the last. This extreme has already been eliminated by the description made in the previous section of three linear but fragmented and alternating quests. Any given narrative exhibits to different degrees analogical and sequential relations among its units, and this analytical schema can help characterize it. I have already shown the sequential nature of the episodes situated in different locations; but since geographical chance does not establish causal or syntagmatic links between units, these may be examined in themselves and their common structures described.

Each of the events of Chapters Two through Sixteen and of Chapters Nineteen through Twenty-nine serves as an illustration of the anti-optimistic thesis, and for each the demonstration is logically complete. The reader, observing catastrophe and suffering accompanied by the commentary "Tout est au mieux," understands that the formula is being ridiculed. This accumulation of examples of such juxtaposition makes the reader follow the empiricist method praised by Bacon and by Locke; it is as though Lockean epistemology dictates the narrative type and as though the reader discovers the thesis by induction. [9] One example of this procedure should suffice to remind us of its permanence in the story:

> Le lendemain, ayant trouvé quelques provisions de bouche en se glissant à travers des décombres, ils réparèrent un peu leurs forces. Ensuite ils travaillèrent comme les autres à soulager les habitants échappés à la mort. Quelques citoyens, secourus par eux, leur donnèrent un aussi bon dîner qu'on le pouvait dans un tel désastre: il est vrai que le repas était triste; les convives arrosaient leur pain de leurs larmes; mais Pangloss les consola, en les assurant que les choses ne pouvaient être autrement: "Car, dit-il, tout ceci est ce qu'il y a de mieux; car s'il y a un volcan à Lisbonne, il ne pouvait être ailleurs; car il est impossible que les choses ne soient pas où elles sont; car tout est bien."
> (Ch. 5)

The passage from experience to theory is made inside one sentence — "... larmes; mais Pangloss les consola ..." — and it quotes the master's pseudo-deductive syntax, the transitions of which are assured by four uses of the conjunction *car*.

Each episode produces at least two kinds of meaning: the opposition just described, and another that is understood in addition to it. The manifest meaning or sense is polemical; it comes from the duality between optimistic theory and catastrophic experience. The poles of the contrast are explicited in the content or story;

---

[9] Jean Starobinski notes this parallel with the style of Voltaire in "La doppietta."

and, by their repetition in each episode, they are shown to be contradictory, that is irreducible. The other opposition is immanent to the text; it is produced without being manifest in the content. The horror of life contrasts with the search and need for happiness; and in this opposition, conciliation of the two poles is effected by the reader. The manifest structure replies to Leibnizian theodicy by juxtaposing it with its irreconcilable opposite, experience. However, the immanent contrast in Voltaire's story, that is, the *meaning* derivable, offers more than a destruction of theodicy; for, suscitating the correction of the problem posed by the manifest opposition, it permits a positive response in the conciliation of horrifying experience and the enduring search for happiness. The conciliation can be effected by the reader; that is, she can resign herself to their coexistence.

The presence of the irreducible opposition (theory and experience) makes itself felt (manifest) in all the aspects of the text. Pangloss' comments on the earthquake were exemplary. The juxtaposition is even more explicit when the doctrine is named and defined: "Qu'est-ce qu'optimisme? disait Cacambo. — Hélas! dit Candide, c'est la rage de soutenir que tout est bien quand on est mal ..." (Ch. 19). A philosophical development also contains the dichotomy at all moments: Pangloss traces the genealogy of his venereal disease. Its origins in chance and in pleasure and its finality as a necessary evil are simultaneously declaimed:

> Paquette tenait ce présent d'un cordelier très savant qui avait remonté à la source, car il l'avait eu d'une vieille comtesse, qui l'avait reçu d'un capitaine de cavalerie, qui le devait à une marquise, qui le tenait d'un page, qui l'avait reçu d'un jésuite qui, étant novice, l'avait eu en droite ligne d'un des compagnons de Christophe Colomb. (Ch. 4)

The polarity reveals itself also in the various behaviors attributed to Candide, who is a site on which the synthesis of opposites struggles to be achieved. The psychology we imagine for him or attribute to him is torn between the two poles; and the alternations between 14pos. and 14neg. in the Proppian coding of Quest III represent his efforts, alternately satisfactory to him and failed, to conciliate the irreconcilable. The mixture of his reactions has already been mentioned above (Section I.b.ii.).

The syntax of the sentences themselves sometimes underlines the dichotomy. The conjunction *tandis que* twice signals the simultaneity of contrary facts:

> 'Tout cela était indispensable, répliquait le docteur borgne, et les malheurs particuliers font le bien général: de sorte que plus il y a de malheurs particuliers, et plus tout est bien.' Tandis qu'il raisonnait, l'air s'obscurcit, les vents soufflèrent des quatre coins du monde, et le vaisseau fut assailli de la plus horrible tempête, à la vue du port de Lisbonne! (Ch. 4)

The designation of the doctor as *borgne* also points to the foolishness of his discourse. The other use of the conjunction follows in the next chapter:

> [Candide] veut se jeter après [Jacques] dans la mer: le philosophe Pangloss l'en empêche, en lui prouvant que la rade de Lisbonne avait été formée exprès pour que cet anabaptiste s'y noyât. Tandis qu'il le prouvait *a priori*, le vaisseau s'entr'ouvre; tout périt, à la réserve de Pangloss, de Candide, et de ce brutal de matelot qui avait noyé le vertueux anabaptiste ...." (Ch. 5)

In these instances, the conjunction suggests both its senses; it means also *au lieu que, whereas* or *instead of which*. It thus signifies *opposition* as well as *coexistence*.

The presence of optimistic theory in the company of catastrophic experience also informs the destructive irony of circumstance in "Rien n'était si beau, si leste, si brillant, si bien ordonné que les deux armées ...!" of Chapter Three and the devastating antiphrasis of Chapter Six, the "bel auto-da-fé." [10] Here the reader grasps at once the coexistence of evil *(auto-da-fé)* and optimism *(bel).* Calling an armed spectacle *beau, leste,* and *brillant* is equivalent to thinking like Pangloss, combining admiring adjectives and the name of an organism made to spread death. The reader distinguishes the narrative voice from that of the characters, and she knows in each case how to understand the opposites. In so doing, she performs the corrective about-face that irony commands; she thus experiences by enacting it the polemical impasse explicited elsewhere in the text.

---

[10] Both cited by Jean Starobinski in "Sur le style ...," p. 197.

These examples of ironic juxtaposition are reflected in the irony of the protagonist's situation, the one he lives when he faces suffering while affirming optimistic doctrine. To the extent that the reader applies or tests the situation against her own experience, it is again corrected or refused in its inability to coalesce with her sense of existential or general situational irony. The latter dictates rather the immanent structure of the episodes — the horror of life endured and the continuous striving for happiness. This process constitutes yet another condemnation of philosophical optimism. In tropological terms, one can speak of *oxymoron* as the guiding figure of the *conte;* manifested in the story, it operates also in the reader's reception of the text.

The reader's rejection of the manifest opposition results in acceptance of one that is immanent as corresponding to her experience:

FIGURE III.C

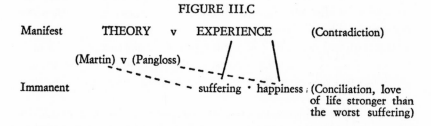

Manifest   THEORY   v   EXPERIENCE   (Contradiction)

(Martin) v (Pangloss)

Immanent   suffering · happiness   (Conciliation, love of life stronger than the worst suffering)

Endurance and its cause, the need (desire) for happiness, do not coincide with theory, the positive pole of the manifest opposition, that is, with dogmatic optimism. Suffering while going on living is not the same as espousing the doctrine that all is for the best. Instead endurance along with suffering falls under the sign of experience, and theory is simply left out of the conciliation. The immanent opposition is a logical one — for why should one go on living if life is nothing but suffering? — but the logic of experience is stronger: at no given moment can it be inferred that one will continue to suffer or that one will never be happy. By this logic, hope never dies; and one continues to pursue happiness. The difference between the manifest and immanent messages is that between a metaphysical solution and the necessity of a practical one. A further replication and correction of structures may be seen in the fact that each of the coexisting immanent opposites is incarnated in an extreme theoretical, manifest position: Martin, who sees only evil everywhere, represent "All is for the worst"; Pangloss, "All is for the best." That Candide is the site of this conflict and that he reflects first one and then the other of the two views is emphasized in the last chapter where the names *Martin, Pangloss,* and *Candide* are printed together six times in its first half. Both propositions, the pessimist's and the optimist's, are excluded from the immanent reconciliation; and this exclusion corresponds to the Enlightenment's and Voltaire's condemnation of all metaphysics.

The old woman's story is emblematic of the immanent opposition. It accumulates around a single individual a series of overwhelming misfortunes, revealing them in concentration while constituting a pause in the evils befalling Candide. The ubiquity of catastrophe that geographic or spatial displacement affirmed has temporal extension as well in the telescoping of an entire life of suffering into a retrospective tale. At the end of the recital, the resolution of disaster and the desire for happiness find emblematic expression: like all the other characters, she refuses, even in immense distress, to end her life: "Je voulus cent fois me tuer, mais j'aimais encore la vie" (Ch. 12). In the rest of the paragraph, the old woman continues to insist upon the coexistence of these same two opposites:

> Cette faiblesse ridicule est peut-être un de nos penchants les plus funestes: car y a-t-il rien de plus sot que de vouloir porter continuellement un fardeau qu'on veut toujours jeter par terre? d'avoir son être en horreur, et de tenir à son être? Enfin de caresser le serpent qui nous dévore, jusqu'à ce qu'il nous ait mangé le cœur?

The simultaneity of the two contrary impulses is further stressed by the old woman's use of the same word in the expression of opposite impulses: *vouloir porter* and *veut jeter* share the same verb and mutually exclusive meanings; *avoir son être en horreur* and *tenir à son être* share the same noun and show how it is tossed from one impulse to its opposite.

Both pairs of contrasting elements are present in all the episodes with the exception of the three gardens: optimistic theory and later pessimism confront devastating experience, and the suffering that results from it contrasts with the desire to go on seeking happiness. Analysis of the two oppositions, manifest and immanent, shows that they are superimposable and that, for the reasons just described, the reader is led to reject one in favor of the other. She is thus witness and judge in the defeat of philosophical optimism, and the defeat is double because of its double aspect: in the diachronic perspective, the contradiction is reiterated by the manifest opposition; and in the synchronic perspective, the reader exercises constant refusal of that paradigm by the preference she gives to its immanent and reconcilable version, "I can't go on, I must go on."

3.c. *Closure*

The problem of closure is paradoxical or problematic in the case of paradigmatic or analogical narrative sequence. How does such a text motivate the arrest of its potentially infinite repetition of the same structures and stop before the reader is bored? In the case of strongly sequential, syntagmatic narrative, the text closes itself since the succession of textual units is both justified and irreversible in its linearity even when it is not chronological; and it tends toward an ultimate unity that absorbs all the others. The analogical may be seen as an additive or disjunctive series, $a + b + c \ldots + n$; and the sequential, as multiplicative or conjunctive, $[\{(a \times b) \times c\} \times d] \times n$. The paradigmatic has no internal reason for coming to an end. This kind of composition is typical of a polemical work since the first tool of didacticism is repetition. It is also typical of a didactic age the narratives of which imitate both in their genesis and in their reception the epistemological method, induction from experiment, by which its authors preferred to view their world. This is anti-classical, against traditional logic and syllogism; it parallels the resistance to old principles of causality that are being undermined in the tale. The reader normally expects that the end of a novel or story be the ultimate result of what has preceded it. She feels a series as an irreversible succession of events, the first of which are the causes of those following, until the end, which is the resolution of the sequence. Furthermore, resolution of the sequence should also be solution of the problem. Instead, in the *conte,* the narrative structure is transformed into a problematic structure, one that poses a question and is thus *scientific* in the modern sense of the term. However, in the present case, precisely because of the discontinuous nature of the units, the final scene cannot be the logical and necessary conclusion of the narrative sequence. [11]

There are three gardens in the story. Consideration of all three permits description of the last one, the one that closes the series of episodes. The first, life at the chateau, can be seen as Edenic (Ch. 1); the second, Eldorado, as utopian (Ch. 17-18); and the last, the *métairie,* as real, inviting the heroes to work (Ch. 30). It is remarkable that none of the three includes both the oppositions I have identified as being generated by all the episodes. The German castle and Eldorado bear witness to only one-half of the manifest duality. Optimistic theory has its origin in Chapter One, and it has a temporary justification in Chapters Seventeen and Eighteen. In those two places, the doctrine seems vindicated since optimism reigns alone. Neither catastrophe nor suffering is present. The usual explicited polarity between theory and experience renounces the functioning of one of its halves. In the final garden, the misfortunes of the protagonists are again suddenly and arbitrarily absent. The component of experience no longer overwhelms them. The subtraction of externally caused pain leaves boredom as its residue, and the solution to it is quickly found. The disappearance of suffering is unmotivated in the *histoire,* in the content of the action itself. Evil continues to exert itself in the represented world, but it acts at a distance from the heroes:

> On voyait souvent passer sous les fenêtres de la métairie des bateaux chargés d'effendis, de bachas, de cadis, qu'on envoyait en exil à Lemnos, à Mytilène, à Erzeroum .... On voyait des têtes proprement empaillées qu'on allait présenter à la Sublime-Porte.

By some magical cause — the author-experimenter's pen in the *récit,* creating lucky chance in the *histoire* — these horrors no longer touch Candide and his companions. The positive half of the immanent opposition alone acts upon them: they work, they strive. Each of the gardens is thus an exception to the rule of the double paradigm. The castle and Eldorado translate into temporary experience the

---

[11] I have borrowed distinctions like continuous and contiguous from David H. Richter, *Fable's End: Completeness and Closure in Rhetorical Fiction* (Chicago: U. of Chicago Press, 1974). He treats Candide at length.

positive half of the manifest opposition; both are transitory, for in both cases, involuntarily (Ch. 1) or voluntarily (Ch. 18), the real hero departs, leaving Eden and Utopia. The vegetable garden is also a scientific and moral garden; and at the end, it puts the search for happiness, the positive half of the immanent opposition, in the foreground. It does not, however, give up the conciliation with misfortune of which the impaled heads in the background remind heroes and reader. This evil parade confirms the idea of the arbitrary removal from catastrophe of Candide and of his friends and links it to the feeling of chance and thus of paradigmatic narrative. These three episodes invite a synchronic perception of the episodes in linear sequence. The confrontation of these three moments engenders in yet another way Voltaire's moral: the concretization of theoretical optimism gives utopia; while its experiential counterpart, the need for happiness, finds unified expression in the famous garden. The repeated experiment produces its moral by offering at every turn homologies of its fundamental opposition and of its corrected version. It thus leaves almost no interpretive flexibility.

Seen in this perspective, the units of the tale are repetitive and cumulative, but not progressive. The double play of the opposition, with its absence of emphasis on linear and discursive continuity, leads the reader to draw a lesson that is perfectly clear, the simultaneous rejection of fatalism and of finalism, that is, of any theodicy or justification of evil. Such is the thesis demonstrated by the experiments; but it is not pure allegory, for the immanent dichotomy is conciliated by the reader's resignation to the coexistence of opposites, by her accepting as non-contradictory the coexistence of opposites. Everyone knows that these are the meanings the tale usually produces: the critical reader sees how she arrives at them and why she cannot deviate from them.

The philosophical tale thus borrows one of the compositional attributes of myth: on the horizontal plane, a temporal succession of events, and on the vertical, packages of relations the sense of which is independent of the horizontal succession.[12] If we add to this the fact that the packages are here all the same and that there

---

[12] E. Meletinskii, "L'Etude structurale et typologique du conte," trans. by Claude Kahn, in V. Propp, *Morphologie,* p. 212.

is no necessity at work in the succession, we may arrive at a constant or law of the *conte philosophique*.

III.4. Modes

Candide communicates modally in a large number of ways; indeed, it seems to be the most complex of Voltaire's stories when it is looked at from this point of view. In Chapters One and Two above I cited typical occurrences of four types of modal communication, but in this case it will be necessary to expand the scope of the devaluative schemes employed. While there are as usual many words, sentences, and scenes inviting operations beyond the reception of simple sense and attacking precise traits and abuses, there are also targets large and permanent enough to be felt or inferred from virtually every scene of the tale, including those in which concrete referents are invoked and decried. The latter are easy to see and include both natural evils (earthquake) and unnatural ones (priests and war), but they also serve as agents of the wider target, that of the general presence of evil and of suffering in the world, the moral scandal which is one-half of the modal reading one is constantly summoned to perform. The other half of it is the widest target, Pangloss' optimism, implied and defeated in nearly every scene. The impact of this double necessity, the emotional climate encouraged by it, is a violent one — hatred of injustice, anger before suffering — and perhaps all the more so as the scandal is replicated by a seemingly perverse (inappropriate) comic vision of some of the worst catastrophes imaginable. By presenting these in acceleration and in concentration — for example, by multiplying the number of maimed creatures, deprived of some part of their bodies — the narrator produces a troubled reception in his interlocutors, who are forced to struggle with the tragic content and the comic manner. For instance, the matter-of-fact tone in which the old woman describes her mutilation, or the narrator's description of the diseased Pangloss "crachant une dent à chaque effort" mitigate in reception the horror of the events. (This is not always the case: there is nothing comic in the presentation of the slave's damaged body in Chapter Nineteen.)

The little evils make the big, doctrinal evil seem worse; and the receptive operation is twice modal, for the optimistic doctrine is itself an interpretation against which the text (events) constantly exerts itself. Certain scenes and many monologues also inspire double reception since they are the parody or caricature and thus the denigration of other forms of cultural communication — the heroic novel, philosophical reasoning, etc. As I remarked in the case of *Zadig* and as students of satire have often observed, except in the case of specific abuses where a positive value (tolerance) is implied to replace an evil decried (intolerance), constant invitations both to inference and to the destruction of targets leave almost nothing in their place. In his position as every(suffering)man, Zadig perhaps gains more sympathy, in spite of the simplistic conclusions he sometimes draws. Candide has a tool, what Montaigne sought as an *instrument judicatoire,* by which to measure events; he is testing an interpretation to determine its explanatory powers. The foregrounding of the doctrine and of its failure gives to this tale a greater internal cohesion and diminishes even further than in *Zadig* the idea of the hero since Candide the disciple constantly fails in *interpretation;* he is perhaps more pitied than admired because he has chosen a manifestly inadequate hermeneutic implement and because he persists in trying to use it. It is not really explanatory; it turns out to be an article of faith, and as such it is either taken (by Pangloss and sometimes by his disciple) or left (by everybody else).

Keeping in mind the imperfect manifestations of mode, the essential ambiguity of its reception, and the fact that any given stretch of discourse usually comports doses of several types of such communication, we may look at a few examples of the way in which these many sorts combine to the same end. In Section 1.a., I enumerated the types of operations in which the reader is trained at the beginning of the story; and in the paragraphs treating the third quest (end of Section 2.b.) and in Section 3.b., I discussed the many complementary ways in which the presence of doctrine and of its defeat is constantly actualized by the reader.

The largest amount of direct aggression appears in the long and boring Chapter Twenty-Two. Whether the criticisms are spoken by the narrator ("Le souper fut comme la plupart des soupers de Paris; d'abord du silence, ensuite un bruit de paroles qu'on ne distingue point, puis des plaisanteries dont la plupart sont insipides, de fausses nouvelles, de mauvais raisonnements, un peu de politique, et beaucoup de médisance; on parla même de livres nouveaux ...") or put into the cynical comments of Martin ("... combien y en a-t-il de bonnes [plays]? —Quinze ou seize, répliqua l'autre. —C'est beaucoup," dit Martin,") or the naïve questions and comments of Candide ("Des reines [actresses] à la voirie! " or "Cela est bien impoli," or "Qui est ce gros cochon [literary critic] ...?"), the reader finds little amusement and even less challenge, so much is the surliness expressed without veils. It is known that Voltaire struggled a great deal with this chapter, adding and subtracting episodes; he was its first critic. [13]

Another vituperative moment is more amusing. The description of Buenos Aires' governor concerned the author less directly and permitted him to exert his condemnations in a portrait that could be that of any haughty person and in which the content and rhythm of the five sentences reveal his flaws without seeming to reflect hatred of a particular being. After listing all his names, the narrator describes his behavior in general terms. After the superlative of the first trait — "le dédain le plus noble" — he creates suspense by four uses of *si, [so]*, each with an adjective. When one arrives at the *que, [that]*, one is exasperated in a way similar to that of those who know him. Their violent desire to beat him up contrasts with his pretentiousness:

> Il parlait aux hommes avec le dédain le plus noble, portant
> le nez si haut, élevant si impitoyablement la voix, prenant
> un ton si imposant, affectant une démarche si altière, que
> tous ceux qui le saluaient étaient tentés de le battre. (Ch. 13)

That lengthy sentence contrasts with the short one immediately following, and the short one is the first step in a syllogistic sequence elegantly applied to the impulses of the proud governor: (1) "Il aimait les femmes à la fureur"; (2) "Cunégonde lui parut ce qu'il avait jamais vu de plus beau"; therefore (3) "La première chose qu'il fit fut de demander si elle n'était point la femme du capitaine." This impeccable logic leads of course to action: getting rid of Can-

---

[13] *Candide,* ed. René Pomeau (Paris: Nizet, 1959).

dide and making an offer to Cunégonde. The latter asks for a full
fifteen minutes to decide. This request ridicules the woman making
it (modal communication of the fourth type, dramatization); and
it contributes to the steady presentation of Cunégonde as much less
wonderful than Candide imagines her. It is also, however, typical
of the mixture of comic ridicule and tragic necessity; for the content
of the situation makes clear that unless she wishes to die, the choice
is not whether or not she will accept the offer, but only by what
means she will be possessed: "Il lui déclara sa passion, lui protesta
que le lendemain il l'épouserait à la face de l'Eglise, ou autrement,
ainsi qu'il plairait à ses charmes."

There are many descriptions made by the narrator or by characters and in which the reader is led to make an adjustment of the
simple sense. She must substitute other language for that offered,
entirely reversing the values declared by a literal reading. The most
extended discourse which sometimes contains this sort of change is
the old woman's speech. She tells the story of her life, and the occasion or purpose is to demonstrate to Cunégonde that the young
woman has not really suffered at all by comparison — "Vous vous
plaignez, leur dit la vieille, hélas! vous n'avez pas éprouvé des infortunes telles que les miennes." The intent is therefore hyperbolic,
but the commentary on catastrophe often employs litotes. In counterpoint to the horrors described, the old lady uses minimizing *chutes*
to mark the conclusion of certain adventures. Some of her under-
statements and preteritions are the following:

> Il mourut en moins de deux heures avec des convulsions
> épouvantables. Mais ce n'est qu'une bagatelle.
>
> Mais ce qui me surprit davantage, c'est qu'ils nous mirent
> à tous le doigt dans un endroit . . . . Cette cérémonie me
> paraissait bien étrange: voilà comme on juge de tout quand
> on n'est pas sorti de son pays.
>
> Je ne vous dirai point combien il est dur pour une jeune
> princess d'être menée esclave à Maroc avec sa mère. [Details
> follow.] Mais, passons; ce sont des choses si communes
> qu'elles ne valent pas la peine qu'on en parle.

A painful hilarity is provoked in the reader by the wild contrast
between the terrors the woman has lived and her weary view that

they are finally quite ordinary. The almost monstrous digestion of violent experience and her acceptance of its inevitability contrast brilliantly with the two naïve children who listen to her: Candide, who wants to think that all is well, and Cunégonde, who wants to be acknowledged as the pre-eminent sufferer.

Another speech that encourages the reader to reverse and resist the values expressed is that of Cacambo when he describes the marvels of the Jesuits' organization and of their Latin-American war-machinery:

> ... j'ai été cuistre dans le collège de l'Assomption, et je connais le gouvernement de Los Padres comme je connais les rues de Cadix. C'est une chose admirable que ce gouvernement. Le royaume a déjà plus de trois cent lieues de diamètre; il est divisé en trente provinces. Los Padres y ont tout, et les peuples rien; c'est le chef-d'œuvre de la raison et de la justice. Pour moi, je ne vois rien de si divin que Los Padres, qui font ici la guerre au roi d'Espagne et au roi de Portugal, et qui en Europe confessent les rois; qui tuent ici des Espagnols, et qui à Madrid les envoient au ciel: cela me ravit .... (Ch. 14)

Whether the rather heavy ironic mode should be attributed to the speaker or only to the narrator's and reader's grasp of an innocent admiration matters little to the meaning available. The interpreter knows well that she should replace admiration by a severe condemnation of the practices and of the hypocrisies described.

The world's violence presents itself elsewhere in a mode that is often, as I suggested earlier, oxymoronic. The narrator's description of Candide's first war, from which *bel auto-da-fé* and beautiful armies have already been cited, has to be received through several terms that are juxtaposed with their own semantic opposites: the phrase "une harmonie telle qu'il n'y en eut jamais en enfer" requires return to the word *harmony* and its revision downward; the last expression of the paragraph, "boucherie héroïque" condenses the association of opposites. In the middle of the description, the narrator uses other minimizing terms — *à peu près, environ, coquins, quelques,* and *une trentaine:*

> Les canons renversèrent d'abord à peu près six mille hommes de chaque côté; ensuite la mousqueterie ôta du meilleur des mondes environ neuf à dix mille coquins qui en

infectaient la surface. La baïonnette fut aussi la raison suffisante de la mort de quelques milliers d'hommes. Le tout
pouvait bien se monter à une trentaine de mille âmes. Candide, qui tremblait comme un philosophe, se cacha du mieux
qu'il put pendant cette boucherie héroïque. (Ch. 3)

The approximations used to express the numbers of the dead deliberately minimize the importance of human life by this reversed
echo of Rabelaisian precision. Instead of rendering admirable and
astonishing quantities, the magnitude of its object is sapped by all
the terms meaning something like "give or take a few thousand, it
doesn't really matter." The reader may not seek the semantic opposite of the words, but may react by reversing the values implied.
The interlarded echoes of Pangloss' discourse — *meilleur des mondes, raison suffisante* — plus the direct assignment of cowardice to
philosophers conspire to attribute the casual reckonings of human
loss to the optimistic tutor who thus seems to have dictated this
offhand view of war. The juxtaposition of his doctrine and of murder
is subtly accomplished, for he is absent and unnamed while his little
clone cowers in a corner.

The scene that follows the war, the Te Deum that both kings
order sung, illustrates the fourth type of mode, the expansion of
a practice into a dramatization in which the distance from right-
thinking is perceptible to the receiver. The ironic potential of *tandis
que,* which I explained in the previous section, is exploitable here
also; for the action that follows the Te Deums belies their importance. After this — "tandis que les deux rois faisaient chanter des
Te Deum, chacun dans son camp, il [Candide] prit le parti d'aller
raisonner ailleurs des effets et des causes..." — we see that the
elsewhere Candide finds is also filled with horror. The results of the
war are laid out in lengthy, precise anatomical detail by the narrator
while God's praises are being sung in the background: for example,
"Des cervelles étaient répandues sur la terre à côté de bras et de
jambes coupés." This portion of the description has nothing ironic
in its expression; the attack it conveys comes from its proximity to
the kings' praise of God. From ironic presentation of the battle
to the Te Deums and to the cadavers, all are arranged so that the
reader notes the uncaring collusion of church and kings in the center
of the horrors their wars have visited on the people.

Another dramatization also satirizes rulers. The hero finds himself at table with six strangers who all turn out to be kings of something or other. Their speeches make it plain that they are without power or money and that Candide has more of both than they: "Quel est donc ... ce simple particulier qui est en état de donner cent fois autant que chacun de nous, et qui le donne?" The framework resembles that of Candide's consultation, a medieval genre repeated in comic mode by Rabelais, as I remarked about portions of *Zadig*. The other consultations are those with Pococuranté, with the sage of Eldorado, and with the dervish and the old man in Constantinople. In this case, however, the hero does not actually seek the kings' wisdom; but finding himself in their presence, he poses the question that permits six repetitive speeches: "Messieurs ... voilà une singulière plaisanterie. Pourquoi êtes-vous tous rois?" The application of all this to the hero's own quests is minimal; and the scene seems designed to go over his head and in to the reader's, especially if the latter is one of those members of royal families who float about Europe — then and now — powerless or penniless or both.

The visit to Eldorado and the consultation of its wisest person serve as further examples of didactic modes. The entire episode combines the third and fourth types; it is a dramatization, the fourth mode, though not of what is wrong but of something so excellent that it is itself the opposite of normal life. [14] Each detail thus puts in relief its own difference from European states and its distance from anything the reader is likely to have experienced. Consequently, the target is not designated by the content but by its negative reflection in reality, the third mode. Within this vastly ironic (reversible) tableau, one finds also many small signs of that mode — litotic *ne ... que* abounds ("les lambris des appartements n'étaient que d'or") as do phrases that must be understood as their opposite: "cette extrême simplicité." The length of this section and the sameness of its expression make it ponderously pedantic. The old man's answers to Candide's questions can be read as a sermon

---

[14] Instances of such prolonged irony showing a situation opposed to a real one are named *anticatastase* by Henri Morier in his article "Ironie," *Dictionnaire de poétique et de rhétorique* (Paris: Presses Universitaires de France, 1975).

on right religion much as can the answers of the Quaker in the *Lettres philosophiques*. It may be, as common wisdom has it, that positive didacticism is inherently boring and that only the critical and mordant type stimulates most readers. Inferring positive values from negative portraits may be a more pleasant activity than being made to feel the inadequacy of our measure before the picture of a utopian state. In any case it is with relief that one returns to the depiction of evil.

III.5. THE DEFEAT OF PHILOSOPHY AND OF LITERATURE

Although the story offers little interpretive flexibility to the reader who consents to the pact of didacticism and to the initiation described above, a thoughtful attempt to observe the representation as well as to follow what is represented leads the critic to seeing the ways in which the tale undoes the assumptions on which it founds its existence. The grammar of quest has been elaborately analyzed above, but examination of its rhetoric reveals a certain confusion of the ideals it represents as *histoire* and of the processes it supposes in its existence as *récit* and especially as *narration*. As I said of *Zadig,* the philosophical tale presents itself as both truth and fiction, and this paradox ends by exposing itself in *Candide* as well. The *conte* puts on stage two of the processes that it lives by, didacticism and diversion or amusement; certain scenes are thus so many *mises-en-abyme* of the tale itself.

The expository claims of the story are reflected by the didacticism represented in the action itself. Pangloss the teacher starts it all, and Martin is taken on by Candide as a conversational companion who has much lived and with whom he will consult constantly thereafter. Lesson-giving, lesson-testing, and lesson-seeking are time-consuming activities represented; and the reader is trained to try to fit every event into those schemes. Induced by this means and by sympathy with the candid hero into looking for an answer to the problem of evil and into finding an antidote to Pangloss' brand of optimism, the reader looks carefully at each of the successive consultations where lessons are explicitly sought, whether the meeting be with a wise person or with experience. What does the balance-sheet finally show? As I demonstrated in the section on paradigms (3, above), the largest portion of evidence puts Pangloss' optimism in a ridiculous light. Martin's pessimism is better treated both because of the respect shown his person by the narrator and because of the fact that his advice, his predictions, and his interpretations are so often justified by events. The chapter (24) where he makes an error — saying that Candide is crazy to expect Cacambo to return and to bring back his money and his mistress — is the chapter in which he is also twice permitted to say "I told you so" about Paquette's and Giroflée's unhappy use of Candide's generosity. The ideas of Martin are alternately exposed, confirmed, and refuted in one sequence that thus proposes various judgments of his wisdom. Chapter Twenty follows the contest in which the hero chose Martin to accompany him; therefore, it gives the savant a lengthy opportunity to explain his view of the world. Manicheism as it was understood and used in the eighteenth century (Bayle, *Dictionnaire,* 1695-1697) does not seem to touch Martin's single and permanent expectation of disaster. For this reason I call his position simply *pessimism.* Excepting only Eldorado, he summarizes his own experience and mentions greed, theft, murder, and jealousy in ways that recall Candide's own adventures with governments and with religions. Martin's mind is made up: far from wishing to test optimism as Candide does, he decrees: "En un mot, j'en ai tant vu et tant éprouvé que je suis manichéen."

Once again the narrator juxtaposes events with discourse and marks the simultaneity, this time with *Au milieu de:* "Au milieu de cette dispute, on entendit un bruit de canon." The event is another horror, a sea-battle in which everyone dies and which seems to confirm Martin's pessimism. As soon as Martin has said "Eh bien! " and Candide has almost decided to agree with him, they see one of the lost sheep floating in the water. A further, contradictory — because lucky and joyful — event is thus aligned with the larger panorama confirming pessimism. The joyful view is advanced by the travelers' learning that one of the drowned persons was the very man who had robbed Candide. The narrator insists on the justice of chance, on the irony of circumstance that for once worked to punish the wicked: "Les richesses immenses dont ce scélérat s'était emparé furent ensevelies avec lui dans la mer, et il n'y eut qu'un mouton de sauvé." The hero then insists in his own words on the same point: "Vous voyez ... que le crime est puni quelquefois; ce coquin de patron hollandais a eu le sort qu'il méritait." However, the long alternation of proofs for the differing points of view continues when Martin has the last word. He exercises a reversal of all the reasoning cited above; the faithful reader must again revise the ideas presented: "Oui ... mais fallait-il que les passagers qui étaient sur son vaisseau périssent aussi? Dieu a puni ce fripon, le diable a noyé les autres." That there are more justifications of Martin's pessimism than of Pangloss' optimism is clear; however, the single error — Cacambo will betray his master — seriously incriminates the Manichean's conclusions. The reader who counts the points for each realizes that the single example of the servant's return with the woman and the money is a powerful refutation of Martin's absolutism in the *histoire,* but she is also conscious of Cacambo's role as facilitator in the plot and is once again witness to the curious manner in which truth — one good man disproves pessimism — and fiction — the story needs a donor of the magic object — contradict and weaken each other in this kind of assessment.

These experiences of *le pour et le contre* can only be overcome or synthesized by a naïve leap to the same kind of chance, an agreeable one, that marked the ending of *Zadig.* Fiction offers a lesson entirely removed from the ideological interest of the previous chapters. In the same way that Zadig's "If I had slept less, I would be king" is both simple-minded and perfectly possible, so Candide's final statement of this zigzagging chapter marks him as naïve and as possessing a simple wisdom: "Candide caressait son mouton. 'Puisque je t'ai retrouvé, dit-il, je pourrai bien retrouver Cunégonde.' " Even Pangloss is finally allowed to be right when in the last chapter he traces the cause-and-effect links leading the hero to the garden:

> Tous les événements sont enchaînés dans le meilleur des mondes possibles: car enfin si vous n'aviez pas été chassé d'un beau château à grands coups de pied dans le derrière pour l'amour de mademoiselle Cunégonde, si vous n'aviez pas été mis à l'Inquisition, si vous n'aviez pas couru l'Amérique à pied, si vous n'aviez pas perdu tous vos moutons du bon pays d'Eldorado, vous ne mangeriez pas ici des cédrats confits et des pistaches.

His simplistic statement, made by a fool, also has some probability; however, it is not the proof of optimism, but a naïve view of causality nourished by hindsight. The condition and the deduction of all three statements just quoted arise from observation of the workings of chance, and not from consideration of any doctrine — optimistic or pessimistic — for none has the power to predict future events or to explain past ones other than by stating their sequentiality. Another of the hero's uses of *puisque* is not so sage since from a lucky chance he makes a deduction unwarranted by logic — that pure nature is good: the cannibals learned that he was not a Jesuit and so they did not eat him: "Mais, après tout, la pure nature est bonne, puisque ces gens-ci au lieu de me manger, m'ont fait mille honnêtetés dès qu'ils ont su que je n'étais pas jésuite" (Ch. 26). The phrase transmits to the reader, however, the same truth about chance's sometimes working for the hero, and about chance's being a name for cause and effect not perceived. Paquette emits the same kind of truth — luck is needed to second goodness — but she shows a greater understanding of it than the hero when she says, "... mon innocence ne m'aurait pas sauvée si je n'avais été un peu jolie." Both interpretations are made after the fact and neither has anything to do with doctrine. This kind of reasoning imitates by parody, simplification, and incongruity the derivation of a moral from events.

These are lessons that Zadig never articulates even though he is their beneficiary. These fragments of realistic optimism find echo in Candide's final decision to profit, like Zadig, from the bit of agreeable chance offered him by evil's cease. He takes steps, however, that are not included in Zadig's tale. His efforts to understand stop also after the visit with the dervish; and the final consultation has a purpose that is utilitarian: living by work instead of by argument. Although it is the principal activity of the tale and one of the external processes by which it offers itself as evidence, argument *(raisonner)* is finally abandoned; and the tale undoes one of the assumptions on which it founds its existence.

Tale-telling as amusement is the other process on which the philosophical tale depends, and it too is represented in the *conte*. Like the intercalated stories in *Zadig,* the accounts given to Candide and recorded in the *récit* could themselves undergo a Proppian coding having their tellers as heroes and heroines. They can also be regarded in their entirely as episodes in Quest III, although the only one explicitly attached to it by the hero is the group told by the passengers of the ship bearing him and the old woman (Ch. 13). Some of the tales catch the hero up on the past of the people he keeps losing and running into again: Cunégonde, Pangloss, the baron, and Paquette. These are not labeled as being pertinent to the didactic point, but they serve to augment the reader's store of examples going against optimism; and the fact that they all belong to former inhabitants of the best of all possible chateaux does not escape her. Other stories are offered or solicited specifically under a heading that the reader attaches to the philosophical quest. The scene in which Paquette and Giroflée are discovered combines and multiplies many of the techniques that disrupt the linear plot and thereby call attention to its ideological aspects and resonances. Similar to the other episodes containing contests to determine the unhappiest person, one part of Chapter Twenty-four begins with a bet. Catching sight of a young couple, Candide hopes to refute Martin's pessimism by betting that they are happy; Martin bets that they are not. One member of the couple is Paquette, alumna of Thunder-ten-tronckh; and one is a new character. (Their tales thus combine flashback, like those of Pangloss, Cunégonde, and the baron, with evils befalling a newcomer, like those of the old woman, the passengers, and Martin.) Both stories are told by their protagonists in direct discourse. Paquette's is longer, one page, and begins at the chateau. It makes Candide give up on one-half of his bet with Martin. Giroflée tells his in one paragraph, and Martin declares himself winner of the entire wager. Candide decides to make the two storytellers happy by giving them a lot of money; he thereby shows his continued adherence to optimism. Martin predicts the failure of this effort, and the next encounter with the two is thus prepared, as is its outcome, new unhappiness and the triumph of Martin's prediction (Ch. 30).

Another story offers itself as proof of something. Launching the challenge that she has most suffered, the old woman tells the story of her life to her fellow passengers (Ch. 11-12). The group then invites all the travelers to prove that they are not happy (Ch. 13). The passengers' stories are not recorded in the *récit*. They take a great deal of time in the *histoire* — indeed, that is one of their purposes, to make time pass — but they are not reported word for word in the signifier. The narrator foregoes these further occasions of relating adventures that could be as extravagant as those of the old woman. He puts all his eggs into one basket, the eleventh and twelfth chapters, and refers to the others only as events, their imagined mass compensating for the absence of reported matter. They point at their own thematic or didactic function — suffering is universal and constant — rather than giving the reader the simple pleasure of more kinds of detailed adventures.

At the end of her tales the old woman justifies them in two ways that account also for all the stories told in the course of the story and that are *mises-en-abyme* of the *conte* itself. One recalls the initial invitation or challenge, the occasional nature of her account: "... je ne vous aurai même jamais parlé de mes malheurs si vous ne m'aviez pas un peu piquée." The other points to the convention of story-telling among travelers — "... et s'il n'était d'usage, dans un vaisseau, de conter des histoires pour se désennuyer." Her tales and the others are both demonstration and *divertissement,* and they thus have the same purpose as the entire *conte philosophique* that contains them even as it is contained in being reflected by them.

All the tales, as well as the visits and consultations made by the hero, constitute kinds of pauses in the linear progress of the obvious action taking place in the narrative present (Quest I and II). Each occasions a certain temporal distortion of the traditional lines of action. The stories told go backwards in time and summarize long periods, and the consultations imitate time's passage by recounting word-for-word large portions of conversation. In the reader's own quest these trials give rise to reactions that put the examples into the category of the lesson applied, where they accumulate. Their exceptional temporal status and the signs that the characters themselves place before and after some of them mark their didactic purpose. This kind of reference backward and forward resists the linear movement of the main actions and gives an impression of density and of repetition or sameness. Circumstances are not only similar from one episode to the next, but the actors in them are sometimes people the hero already knows. By this contiguity, the text as story and as voyage weakens its own pretension to progress and to change, and it contributes to its own defeat as an ascension to perfect circumstances or to perfect resolution. Such an ascension would be reflected in a perfectly sequential or syntagmatic narrative. It is in part for this reason that the last chapter separates itself so radically from the fragile causal links shared by the other chapters. Both textual and ideological progress are denied.

A further thematization of the story's undoing occurs in the consultation with Pococuranté (Ch. 25). The entire *conte* represents failed didacticism in the ways I have shown, and it also exhibits the paradox of tale-telling as both proof and diversion. Confidence in philosophy is weakened in the first instance, and the flaw of literature is exposed in the second. In his conversation with Candide and with Martin, the Venetian nobleman minimizes the arte-facts surrounding him. These include painting, sculpture, music, architecture, and science as well as literature; and suspicion spreads to all artistic objects, all the production done in the name of beauty as well as of truth. Even though his attitude is condemned at the end by Martin, the length of the visit leaves an impression that corresponds to the deep realism conveyed by the entire story's survey of life's horrors and of philosophy's inability to account for them. Now, even in the absence of catastrophe and thus without the need for philosophy, all of culture is declared inadequate even to relief from boredom, let alone to the desire for happiness. This scene provides an early negative answer to the protagonists' *ennui* in the last chapter; they will not bother to relieve it by contemplation of culture's artefacts, but will go directly to work.

The vanity of literature and the inadequacy of philosophy are thus proclaimed in several ways, and they shake the foundations of the story. Declaring war by satire on philosophies, on governments, and on churches of all kinds and on all sides, the text disdains everything; and by thematizing the criticism of great books and by imitating and mocking literary fictions, literature itself arrives at its end. [15] Paradigmatic, didactic narrative is *arranged;* so it cannot be true. The quasi-refusal of syntagmatic, artful and amusing narrative obliges a like refusal of the diverting *romanesque* and of its illusions. It seems, however, that *Candide* rises out of its own deconstructive ashes, for it is a new literature. Its internal economy

---

15 Starobinski, "Sur le style ...," p. 195.

prevents us from falling prey to teleological illusion — literature with a lesson — as well as to the *romanesque* — literature as fantasy. Optimism is untenable, but the evils of life's accidents are unbearable. Carefully guiding us through the homologies among its various signifiers, the *récit* shows that its end is as arbitrary as misfortune's conclusion. If we seek to establish relation of cause and effect between its parts, we shall resemble Pangloss, the theoretician of finalism, with his pitiful reasonings and his teleological recapitulations. In the succession of the thirty chapters forming the external structure of *Candide ou l'optimisme,* the first twenty-nine cannot be the progressive causes of the thirtieth. The best of all philosophical tales is not the best of all linear narratives. It is in fact just the opposite, and in the manner of its narration as in what is said and what is meant, it imitates life and its accidents. It proposes a solution to events and to itself that is one made entirely of science and of experience, that is, of immanence endlessly renewed.

Chapter IV

L'INGÉNU

Il faut armer Clio du poignard, comme Melpomène.

L'Ingénu, Ch. 10

IV.1. Competence

1.a. *Initiation*

Although it was conventional for eighteenth-century fictions to
claim to be true, *L'Ingénu* is the only one of Voltaire's tales to
make explicit this pretension. Its subtitle announces a "Histoire
véritable" taken from manuscripts of a reverend father, who surely
guarantees veracity in the game of reassurance. It has often been
remarked that this story is set in a France that was indeed recognizable
to contemporary readers even if it was not specifically lodged within
their memory. Most of the picture of intrigues at court and of the
abusive Jesuit influence under Louis XIV was transferable to their
own time, in spite of the expulsion of the Jesuit order that had
taken place meanwhile. The *lettres de cachet* were still being used.
Visits to Europe made by so-called savages had also been known
for two centuries. The only bit of blatant fantasy occurs immediately
after the assurances of truth: the title of the first chapter summarizes
its action — the Huron's arrival on French soil — but its first two
paragraphs explain the presence of a priory and its name by telling
a fable on the model of Aesop's "Why the Bear Has a Short Tail"
or Rabelais's "How Beauce Got Its Name"; furthermore, its content

parodies two kinds of history, the voyages of Celtic saints and Mohammed's trip to the mountain. These references relativize at the outset any right to seriousness that this saint's endeavor might have. At the same time, they join the venerable traditions of beginnings that explain beginnings. The book of *Genesis* is an obvious example as are some of the oldest tales known, which are about beginnings. These are frequently of the chronicle-type.[1] The short anecdote thus supplies the origins of the setting and puts into conventional perspective the truth-claims of the subtitle.

The text then makes an abrupt turn into another kind of historicity, precise and supposedly objective: "En l'année 1689, le 15 juillet au soir ...." These words take the reader away from parodic fiction and back to the truth promised in the title. It records exact names — l'abbé de Kerkabon, prieur de Notre Dame de la Montagne, and mademoiselle de Kerkabon — and gives a short sketch of the character of each, another convention, presentation of their person and of their past.

The reader thus gets two messages, one for fantasy and one for truth, and is prepared once again to receive a lesson through a fiction, although in this case the mixture is sensibly different from that proposed by the other stories we have examined. The setting of *Micromégas* was astral; Zadig's, oriental. The French staging and the constant reference to events familiar to eighteenth-century readers link the story to historical reporting. At the same time Saint Dunstan's and the Huron's adventures are paradigmatic fictional narratives. The proximity and mixing of these two strains is notable in an era where history itself had been recounted on a heroic model.[2] Voltaire prolonged the *faits-et-gestes* paradigm in his *Histoire de Charles XII* (1731) and contributed to its transformation by his *Siècle de Louis XIV* (1751) and *Essai sur les mœurs* (1756). By naming date and time, *L'Ingénu* begins like a chronicle — a list of precisely located sequential occurences — and undergoes transfor-

[1] Lotman (p. 170) cites *The Tales of Bygone Years,* the earliest Russian compilation of chronicles (early twelfth century) that contains such tales.

[2] Frank Kermode, *The Sense of an Ending* (New York: Oxford University Press, 1967), p. 43. Hayden White, *Metahistory: The Historical Imagination in Nineteenth-Century Europe* (Baltimore: The Johns Hopkins University Press, 1973).

mation into a story, that is, into a series of events to which a beginning and an end are assigned. The idea of an *histoire véritable* contains in the word *histoire* the often-remarked ambiguity of this transformation. History is a chaos, a plethora of events, from which the author-historian makes a story upon which he or she imposes form. In this way, materials of *histoire* are emplotted and are revealed as a *récit*. A nod to the *faits-et-gestes* scheme is given in the hero's victory against the English, and it is promised for his future as a warrior at the end of the tale; but love, religion, and politics occupy more of the text than the hero's exploits, so that scheme eventually fades into the background until the very end.

In the course of the story, events are explained as comedy in the first third, as factual record in the second, and as tragedy in the last. Most critics divide the story into two halves, presumably on the basis of the setting in the provinces and in Paris, but an appreciation of the various kinds of performance required from the reader reveals three distinct discourse-relations. The "true story" is carved out of the infinite flow of supposed history, and it receives three different types of emplotment even as it refers to others not realized, the fables and histories I just mentioned. The three discourse-relations serve to define three genres created in its course.

1.b. *Instructions for Reading: Specific Competences*

In the third paragraph of Chapter One the presentation of the prior tells the reader not to take him seriously and permits her to attach the remarks made about him to a tradition of anti-clericalism. Each of the three sentences describing him endows him with a quality allowing a humorous reflection:

> Le prieur, déjà un peu sur l'âge, était un très bon ecclésiastique, aimé de ses voisins, après l'avoir été de ses voisines.

> Ce qui lui avant donné surtout une grande considération, c'est qu'il était le seul bénéficier du pays qu'on ne fût pas obligé de porter dans son lit quand il avait soupé avec ses confrères.

> Il savait assez honnêtement de théologie; et quand il était las de lire St. Augustin, il s'amusait avec Rabelais; aussi tout le monde disait du bien de lui.

This is straight-forward description sympathetic to its object while making reference to the faults of his class. The first statement places the prior in the company of clergy satirized since the *fabliaux* as breaking the vow of celibacy. The second attributes to the priestly class another of its traditional vices, drunkenness; the prior is exempt from it. The third shows that he is not a dull boy and enjoys a ribald author. In addition, he is on the right side of a serious opposition between a certain theology and the naturalism represented by Rabelais, one of the rare Renaissance authors appreciated by Voltaire. The *aussi* may presumably englobe all three qualities, all welcome; two are sympathetic weaknesses, and one is a strength. Other kinds of revelation make his sister similarly charming in mild vices: having failed to marry, she now contents herself with loving pleasure and with being *dévote,* a piquant paradox also belonging to the list of types satirized for centuries. The individuals described are thus agreeably recognizable as associated with several *topoi* of anti-clericalism, but they are likeable for those reasons. The reader continues to enjoy simple exposition and the depiction of sympathetic weaknesses and naïvetés in the characters. After the recognition-scene the rest of the section passes in dialogue between the Huron and his Breton interlocutors. His literal interpretations of the Holy Scripture embarrass the civilized Christians, and the eironic formula according to which innocence confounds science is fully and amusingly exploited.

In this comic section, the hero plays the role of *eiron* as do Zadig and Candide; however, his percussive simplicity is transformed in the course of the tale, and this is one reason for the varying modes. At first, though, neither life nor liberty is threatened as they are in the two groups of episodes following; the stakes are simply salvation by baptism. The Huron is resolutely ignorant of European and Christian customs and so participates in dialogue by which he repeatedly confounds his educators. Another large part of the comedy arises from the travesty of some qualities of the epic, for instance, in the hero's struggle for France against the English, an incident worthy of elevated treatment. The battle is begun and finished in two sentences composed of short phrases the verbs of which are in the present tense, transmitting the vigor and excitement of the encounter ("... il se joint [...] les Anglais se rembarquent"). At the end, however, it receives the deflation of a minimizing *chute,* a trivial reflection irrelevant to war:

> L'Ingénu, piqué, ne songea plus qu'à se bien battre contre ses anciens amis, pour ses compatriotes et pour monsieur le prieur. Les gentilshommes du voisinage accouraient de toutes parts; il se joint à eux: on avait quelques canons; il les charge, il les pointe, il les tire l'un après l'autre. Les Anglais débarquent; il court à eux, il en tue trois de sa main, il blesse meme l'amiral, qui s'était moqué de lui. Sa valeur anime le courage de toute la milice; les Anglais se rembarquent, et toute la côte retentissait des cris de victoire: Vive le roi, vive l'Ingénu! Chacun l'embrassait, chacun s'empressait d'étancher le sang de quelques blessures légères qu'il avait reçues. "Ah! disait-il, si mademoiselle de St. Yves était là, elle me mettrait une compresse." (Ch. 7)

The titles of Chapters Five and Six, "L'Ingénu amoureux" and "L'Ingénu court chez sa maîtresse et devient furieux," may remind the reader also of a modern epic, Ariosto's *Orlando furioso,* known and often illustrated in the eighteenth century.

Another appeal to the reader's knowledge of epic heroes and to her appreciation of parody is the reiterated comparison between the hero and Hercules. He receives this name at baptism, an additional travesty composed of a high or sacred event and low language. In the chapters following that event (4-7), his new name appears seven times. The parallel lives of the mythical hero and of his namesake are also once joined in a double epic comparison: "... il devint aussi furieux que le fut son patron Hercule lorsque Euryte refusa la belle Iole sa fille, non moins belle que la soeur de l'abbé." Since it is improbable that the Ingénu possesses this sort of information, the comparison stands out as mock epic originating in the author's playfulness and in the reader's culture, her literary competence. The name and the comparison vanish as soon as the hero is imprisoned; that is, as soon as experience becomes a dark force, the comic mode also disappears.

The second form of emplotment begins with Chapter Ten when the hero goes to prison. The presentation of the new character, Gordon, is directly descriptive; no games are played. He seems in the first lines entirely good, and the welcome he gives to his cell-mate has nothing ridiculous about it. It is neither voluntarily nor involuntarily satiric. He is presented neither as naïve nor as being of inferior intelligence. We have nothing to do but to believe and admire:

> M. Gordon était un vieillard frais et serein, qui savait deux grandes choses: supporter l'adversité, et consoler les malheureux. Il s'avança d'un air ouvert et compatissant vers son compagnon, et lui dit en l'embrassant: "Qui que vous soyez, qui venez partager mon tombeau, voyez sûr que je m'oublierai toujours moi-même pour adoucir vos tourments dans l'abîme infernal où nous sommes plongés. Adorons la Providence qui nous y a conduits, souffrons en paix, et espérons." Ces paroles firent sur l'âme de L'Ingénu l'effet des gouttes d'Angleterre, qui rappellent un mourant à la vie, et lui font entr'ouvrir des yeux étonnés. (Ch. 10)

To the experienced reader of Voltaire's prose, the multiplication of admiring adjectives — *frais, serein, ouvert, compatissant* — might seem suspect for a moment, and she might await an ironic reversal of their sense. The critical amount of time, one sentence, passes however with no such signals appearing; and the reader accepts the univocity of the description and speech of Gordon. There was one rare gloomy moment in the previous comic ambience. In Chapter Four the narrator twice delivers a flash-forward, warning the reader of doom to come. St. Yves persuaded the Huron to be baptized: "Elle sentit son triomphe; mais elle n'en sentait pas encore toute l'étendue." Four lines later, the baptism is done, "Mademoiselle de St. Yves rayonnait de joie de se voir marraine. Elle ne savait pas à quoi se grand titre l'asservissait; elle accepta cet honneur sans en connaître les fatales conséquences."

The relation between narrator and reader is thus simpler in the second section. The information delivered continues in the manner just shown, and it is rare that any re-reading or transformation of sense is necessary. In these chapters (10, 11, 12, 14), the number of signs of the narrator's presence is similar to that in the first section; but here, after reminding us of his own permanence — "comme nous l'avons dit plusieurs fois" (Ch. 10) — he multiplies the use of monstrative deixis *(ce, voici)* and indulges in a long passage using verbs in the present tense to transmit his opinion ("En effet") about history as a science and to emit maxims such as "La lecture agrandit l'âme et un ami éclairé la console." (Ch. 11) and "L'absence augmente toujours l'amour." (Ch. 14). By reporting dialogues between the prisoners and by citing extracts from the hero's journals in which he reflects on ancient history, the narrator varies the voices through which Voltaire's opinions on philosophy and religion (Ch. 10), on history and astronomy (Ch. 11), on theater (12) and on the sciences and the novel (14) are transmitted. In the first scene he points to the fact that the action consists of dialogue: "... la conversation roula sur la Providence, sur les lettres de cachet, et sur l'art de ne pas succomber aux disgrâces auxquelles tout homme est exposé dans ce monde," "chaque jour la conversation devenait plus intéressante et plus instructive," "Après leurs lectures, après leurs raisonnements, ils parlaient encore de leurs aventures" (Ch. 10). From time to time he passes to invective, not bothering to borrow another voice, and employs the present tense, deictics, and references to French literary life:

> Le bonhomme avait quelques-uns de ces petits livres de critique, de ces brochures périodiques où des hommes incapables de rien produire dénigrent les productions des autres, où les Visé insultent aux Racine, et les Faydit aux Fénelon.

Damning critics further, he has the Ingénu compare them to "certains moucherons qui vont déposer leurs œufs dans le derrière des plus beaux chevaux: cela ne les empêche pas de courir." Then, linking his own metaphor to the tone of the previous remark, the narrating voice calls these people the "excréments de la littérature." The violence of this direct abuse breaks the general tenor less in this section than its type does in *Zadig* or *Candide,* for the action in prison is manifestly a pretext for the concentrated transmission of a number of strongly-held opinions. The reader has little required of her in actualizing their meaning and becomes accustomed to simple reception of abstract ideas. [3]

The pretext nonetheless includes a change in the hero that also serves a didactic purpose even though it rarely functions in subsequent events. In addition to providing the various forums just described, the scenes from prison dramatize the transformation from ignorant though talented savage to a person of refinement. This is

---

[3] There are abundant biographical reasons for this loosening of control. Mason (1981), among others, details Voltaire's dislike for certain journalists, especially his well-known hatred of Fréron, pp. 94-96.

explicit in one of the narrator's statements, heavy with deixis and thus with application to the existence the reader has in common with him:

> La cause du développement rapide de son esprit était due à son éducation sauvage presque autant qu'à la trempe de son âme: car, n'ayant rien appris dans son enfance, il n'avait point appris de préjugés. Son entendement, n'ayant point été courbé par l'erreur, était demeuré dans toute sa rectitude. Il voyait les choses comme elles sont, au lieu que les idées qu'on nous donne dans l'enfance nous le font voir toute notre vie comme elles ne sont point. (Ch. 14)

This registers itself as a position taken on the ideal relation between nature and culture, but it has little to do with subsequent events since the hero remains passive both in his own liberation and in the death of his liberator. The change in the hero is nonetheless stressed many times by the narrator, and once by a simile he points to the paradox of a prison's being the site of such a flowering: [4]

> Le jeune Ingénu ressemblait à un de ces arbres vigoureux qui, nés dans un sol ingrat, étendent en peu de temps leurs racines et leurs branches quand ils sont transplantés dans un terrain favorable; et il était bien extraordinaire qu'une prison fût ce terrain. (Ch. 12)

The third sort of emplotment begins with the return to the plight of St. Yves, in the middle of Chapter Thirteen:

> Cependant le maudit bailli pressait le mariage de son grand benêt de fils avec la belle St. Yves, qu'on avait fait sortir exprès du couvent. Elle aimait toujours son cher filleul autant qu'elle détestait le mari qu'on lui présentait. L'affront d'avoir été mise dans un couvent augmentait sa passion; l'ordre d'épouser le fils du bailli y mettait le comble. Les regrets, la tendresse, et l'horreur bouleversaient son âme. L'amour, comme on sait, est bien plus ingénieux et plus hardi dans une jeune fille que l'amitié ne l'est dans un vieux prieur et dans une tante de quarante-cinq ans passés. De plus, elle s'était bien formée dans son couvent par les romans qu'elle avait lus à la dérobée.

---

[4] The quality of autobiographical revenge in this idea is undeniable. Many critics have pointed to its genesis in Voltaire's own stay at the Bastille; van den Heuvel, pp. 298-99.

The last sentence implies a criticism of conventual hypocrisy, but it and the rest of the passage focus upon the heroine's dilemma and upon her feelings about it. It intensifies the distress to be imagined by using fixed epithets — *le maudit bailli, la belle St. Yves* — that overtly orient the sympathy of the reader and elevate the tone to one recalling that of classical — be it tragic or epic — literature to which belong appelations like *grey-eyed Athena*. In addition to the obvious potential for tragedy in the events recounted, the narrator's presence makes itself felt in dictating the sentiments we should have about the heroine's predicament. Besides attaching epithets to proper names, he multiplies the words relaying emotion — *regrets, tendresse, horreur* — and makes a general statement in the present tense, "L'amour ... est bien plus ingénieux ... dans une jeune fille," and gives it universal validity by "comme on sait." In the paragraph that follows he speaks in his own voice — "Je ne sais quoi l'avertissait secrètement qu'à la cour on ne refuse rien à une jolie fille" — associating himself thus with her situation and then emitting a dire prediction for her future: "... mais elle ne savait pas ce qu'il en coûtait."

The intrusion of the narrative instance progresses as the tale advances; the number increases considerably in the last chapters, the ones concerning St. Yves' activities in Paris. The nature and intensity of the effects of this section have several causes, but for the moment I shall treat only the deictics. The great number of them and the omniscient opinions emitted compose rigid guidelines for the reader's reactions, herding her rapidly and narrowly into a recognition of the pathetic plight of the heroine and into miming the sympathetic response suggested by the deixis. There are always, however, a few readers who find the ending bathetic and not at all moving; one can imagine that the reason for the substitution of bathos for pathos is that the constraints are so tight and so dictatorial that certain readers rebel, *reversing* the emotion by receiving it as a parody of true feeling. The indications can nonetheless inspire pity.

The number of signs of the narrative instance varies between one and eight in the first eighteen chapters, but arrives at more than twenty in Chapter Nineteen and at more than thirty in the last. Figure IV.A that follows presents most of these traces of narrative and places them in categories. (The page numbers refer to the Garnier-Flammarion edition of the *Romans et contes.*) As I have mentioned before, deictics are often found in clusters, so some of the examples include more than one type.

The orchestration of enunciation's presence attains its maximum in the last two chapters. One can appreciate the effect by noting the very small amount of such signs in *Candide* where the largest number in any chapter is three and by noting their even distribution throughout. At least an equal quantity of misfortunes is recounted therein, but it is clear that a similar content can be made to give a very different experience of the text. The regular but rare appearance of deictics in *Candide* corresponds to the characterization I made for other reasons: a series of essentially discontinuous episodes, conveying a single generic tone. The greater density of deictics in *L'Ingénu* and their multiplication in the last two chapters coincides with the differences in genre as I have described them. In this part of *L'Ingénu* frank attack and commentary by the narrative voice accompany a greater interdependence of units. The syntagmatic nature of the episodes (Section 2, below) tends to sweep the reader up in a continuity, a chain of cause and effect; and narration constantly breaks into the *récit,* guiding and amplifying her reaction. The comparative rarity of personal deictics compared to the monstrative ones is noteworthy. It works toward a more subtle referential anchorage of the discourse, the varieties of *ce* being perhaps less obvious than would be the more overtly presuppositive *on, nous,* and *vous.* The increase in value-assigning adjectives is particularly remarkable in later chapters. In these ways the narrative instance fuses with the receptive instance, and their union tends to involve the reader in a wave of sympathy, the servant of persuasive rhetoric. [5]

A second contribution to the creation of pathetic feeling, especially for the eighteenth-century reader or listener, whose principal distraction was the theater, is made by the scenic conception of the last act, Chapters Nineteen and Twenty. The emplotment is clearly

---

[5] David E. Highman also finds that the melodramatic tone is not there for its own sake but as a means of deepening the impact of the author's indignation: "*L'Ingénu:* Flawed Masterpiece of Masterful Innovation?" *Studies on Voltaire and the Eighteenth Century,* 143 (1975), 71-83.

FIGURE IV.A

Chapter	No. of pp.	Personal Deixis	Monstrative Deixis	Verb Tenses of Discourse p., p. c., f., cond.	Value-assigning Adjectives	Comparisons	Atemporal Reflections
I	5						La raison fait
II	3			qu'on appelle en Angleterre et en Hurone la trompette 328 la bonne compagnie, qui languit ... qui ne peut ... qui perd ... qui se plaît 328		il n'était pas comme la bonne compagnie qui 328	
III	2 1/2	qui accablent la nôtre 332 flatté comme on peut le croire 333	ces mots qui font tant de peine 333				ce qui est assez 333
IV	2		ce grand titre cet honneur 335	comme il n'y a jamais eu de cérémonie qui ne fût suivie 336 ne sachant pas combien l'allégorie est familière au Canada 336			vint lui-même lui parler, ce qui est beaucoup 335
V	2 1/2			Il faut avouer 336 On peut juger que 337			il n'y a aucun pays ... où 337

FIGURE IV.A

Chapter	No. of pp.	Personal Deixis	Monstrative Deixis	Verb Tenses of Discourse p., p. c., f., cond.	Value-assigning Adjectives	Comparisons	Atemporal Reflections
VI	2	on a déjà remarqué 340		toute l'honnêteté d'une personne qui a de l'éducation 339	la belle SY 340 la pauvre fille 340	aussi furieux que 341 non moins belle que 341	
				ce sont les deux pièges où les hommes ... se prennent 340			
				une indifférente qu'on mettrait en couvent 340-41	La belle SY 342		
VII	2			(epic structure in historical present tense)			
VIII	2					les flots de la Manche ne sont pas plus agités que 341-42	

FIGURE IV.A

Chapter	No. of pp.	Personal Deixis	Monstrative Deixis	Verb Tenses of Discourse p., p. c., f., cond.	Value-assigning Adjectives	Comparisons	Atemporal Reflections
IX	2 1/2	je vous le laisse à penser 348					
X	4	comme nous l'avons dit plusieurs fois	Cette question tenait évidemment 351 Ce roman de l'âme 351	Il serait … allé… si 351 En effet, l'histoire n'est que … ne plaise … languit …: Il faut … que l'histoire de France soit remplie … 351-52 Il se serait cru heureux si 352			
XI	2 1/2	Notre captif 352	Voici ce qu'il écrivit 352 Ces linostoles 354 ces brochures 354				La lecture agrandit l'âme et un ami éclairé la console 352
XII	1		ressemblait à ces arbres 355 qu'une prison fût ce terrain 355				

FIGURE IV.A

Chapter	No. of pp.	Personal Deixis	Monstrative Deixis	Verb Tenses of Discourse p., p. c., f., cond.	Value-assigning Adjectives	Comparisons	Atemporal Reflections
XIII	4	notre infortuné 356 je ne sais quoi l'avertissait 358 (In this phrase, je ne sais quoi is nominative and may not have the force of a deictic.)			la belle SY 356 la belle SY 358 la belle SY 359 la belle SY 360		L'amour, comme on sait, est bien plus ingénieux 358 car il faut avouer que Dieu n'a créé les femmes que pour apprivoiser les hommes 359
XIV	2	au lieu que les idées qu'on nous donne 360			sa juste colère 361		L'absence augmente 361
XV	2		cet étrange entretien 363	aurait pu ne pas effaroucher 363	la belle SY 362		Pour peu qu'on encourage une amante passionnée 362
XVI	2		Cet amant infortuné 366		la belle et désolée SY 364 la belle SY 366 la pauvre fille 364 son bon confesseur 364 (antiphrasis) infortunée 366		

FIGURE IV.A

	Personal Deixis	Monstrative Deixis	Verb Tenses of Discourse p., p. c., f., cond.	Value-assigning Adjectives	Comparisons	Atemporal Reflections
XVII 1 1/2	notre confidente 367	cette femme 366		la belle SY 366 souper fatal 367 le cruel 367 sa bonne amie 367 (antiph) cette brave personne 367 (antiph)		
XVIII 2 1/2			ce qu'un autre que l'Ingénu aurait deviné facilement 369	la belle SY 368 la belle SY 369 la belle SY 369 la belle SY 369 l'heureuse et désolée SY 370	comme celui de quelques honorables geôliers 368	
XIX 5 1/2	on voit bien à qui appartenait 372	cette scène touchante 370 de ce respect qu'on sent malgré soi 371 de cette tristesse qui fournit 371 Voilà que 372 à toutes ces espérances que la moindre lueur de	les hommes qui se font de nouveaux maux 373 Comment se trouve-t-il avec quelle indifférence 374 parce qu'il avait remarqué que cette belle humeur est incompatible avec la cruauté 375 M. de Louvois	touchante 370 la belle SY 370 la génereuse et respectable infidèle 370 le bon prieur 370 le vilain bailli et son insupportable fils 370 la charmante SY 371	comme des enfants 371 comme des hommes qui 371	

FIGURE IV.A

	Personal Deixis	Monstrative Deixis	Verb Tenses of Discourse p., p. c., f., cond.	Value-assigning Adjectives	Comparisons	Atemporal Reflections
		félicité fait naître si aisément 374 cette fille malheureuse 375 cette manie était trop commune à Paris 376	n'aurait peut-être pas été satisfait des souhaits de L'Ingénu 375 un de ceux qui visitent 375 De la mode jusque dans la médecine! 375-76	la belle SY 371 la belle SY 372 la fatale amie 372 la bonne amie 377 (antiph) la tendre SY 374 la triste SY 376		
XX 5		il n'était pas de ces malheureux philosophes qui s'efforcent 376 C'était là ce que disait 376 dans un de ces intervalles 377 ce calme affreux qui n'a plus la force 378	qu'on croit dit-on Quelle mécanique Comment Et comment Quel est Mais qui pourrait peindre 376 Nulle langue n'a des expressions qui 377 qui l'aurait condamnée 377 Qui peut perdre 378 Que d'autres cherchent ... (whole paragraph) 379	le bon Gordon 376 la belle SY 377 la belle et infortunée SY 378 le bon Gordon 379 horrible catastrophe le morne et terrible silence 379 la belle SY 380 le bon Gordon 380 le tendre SY 381 le bon Gordon 381	comme un père qui voit 376	que rarement font les hommes 376 qui endurcit d'ordinaire le cœur des ministres 380 Le temps adoucit tout. 381

FIGURE IV.A

Personal Deixis	Monstrative Deixis	Verb Tenses of Discourse p., p. c., f., cond.	Value-assigning Adjectives	Comparisons	Atemporal Reflections
	cette misérable gloire 378 ces lieux communs 379	qu'il n'aurait peut-être voulu revoir 380			
	ce mélange de compassion qui enchaîne ... qui exclut ... qui se manifeste 379 ce simple dégoût 380 cette horrible catastrophe 380 cet empire que donnent la douleur et la vertu 380	l'I., qui a paru sous un autre nom à Paris ... et qui a été ... 381 combien d'honnêtes gens ... ont pu dire 381			

tragic, and there is a very general theatrical intertext or inter-
space.[6] The characters gather, are enumerated and described in the
first paragraph of Chapter Nineteen. They are called "quatre person-
nages" in the second paragraph and are seen as being part of a
"scène touchante" and a "scène" which "devint plus neuve et intéressante" at the arrival of the hero from prison. Two times, once
in each chapter, the persons assembled are interrupted by an arrival
and departure: "Au milieu de cette conversation, L'Ingénu arrive"
(19); "Au milieu de ce spectacle de la mort ... le St. Pouange
arrive" (20). A useful prop is introduced in Chapter Seventeen
when St. Pouange sends diamond earrings to St. Yves as a persuasive
gift. Her friend brings them to her thinking she forgot them; and
the whole company catches sight of their magnificence. A few words
of the *aparté* between St. Yves and the *bonne amie* are overheard
by the hero. He catches sight of the diamonds; that is a *coup de
théâtre,* and he begins to reflect on their meaning. A courier arrives
bearing a letter, another frequent theatrical device. There are also
two monologues, Gordon's on persecution and the Ingénu's on the
bon ministre. The denouement takes place as meta-theater; a spectacle
forms itself within the spectacle: all gather around. St. Yves' death-
bed. The place and pose of each is described, and the meta-public's
Aristotelian reactions to the scene are recorded: "Chaque mot [pro-
nounced by the heroine] fit frémir d'étonnement, de douleur et de
pitié, tous les assistants." The word *assistants* is repeated and their
reactions recorded when, several paragraphs later, the innocent expires: "Lorsque le moment fatal fut arrivé, tous les assistants jetè-
rent des larmes et des cris." The body is exposed at the door of the
house, priests indifferently recite prayers over it, and a second scene
within the scene occurs. St. Pouange arrives and passes by, but
then — new *coup de théâtre* — learns who the dead person is and
is converted to goodness by the spectacle. An entire *drame bourgeois*
could not have been more efficient in effecting change.[7]

---

6 Haydn Mason compares Voltaire's concept of tragedy with these chap-
ters: "The Unity of Voltaire's *L'Ingénu,*" in *The Age of Enlightenment:
Studies Presented to Theodore Besterman* (Edinburg and London: Oliver and
Boyd, 1967), pp. 93-106.

7 Highman, p. 78.

The three kinds of deciphering activity thus associate themselves with three forms of emplotment employing differing intensities of deixis, and exhibiting various degrees of reference to texts and to events. The relations between episodes also vary in the three genres deployed.

IV.2. SYNTAGMATIC PROCESS

2.a. *Distribution*

There are one, two, or three episodes composing each chapter; and the last two chapters end the series of short units by describing a lengthy tableau, static in decor and dynamic with conversation, arrivals and departures. Changes in setting are frequently the marks of episodic transition; and in the three *contes* above we have examined the changes which come about by frequent geographical displacement that provides exotic interest and demarcation between events and between didactic messages. In *L'Ingénu* geographical movement does not offer the service performed in *Candide,* for example, that of giving an impression of linearity to units that all reveal the same paradigm. The number of displacements is considerably smaller; it is reduced to one only by each of the two protagonists, the Huron and St. Yves. Both go from province to capital one time. Here the place of an event has some relation to its nature whereas in *Candide,* it usually does not. The hero's education could perhaps have been transmitted in settings other than the prison although the paradox would have been lost; but the particular views both of provincial Christianity and of court intrigue are closely attached to their location. Some critics use indifferently the words *structure* or *theme* to describe the movement between country and city, but the effect produced by both series of episodes seems in that regard the same: the provinces and their religion are ridiculed, though by different methods, as much as the city-dwellers and theirs. Both have a culture that the reader is led to deplore. Narrative syntax and genre are different in all three of the groups I have defined, but the opposition between city and country belongs to the story and does not generate the structures of meaning transmitted. It might be said to generate or at least to influence genre, given that the country is comic; the city, tragic; and the prison, a limbo in between; but these are *topoi* without much novelty or excitement in themselves.

There is parallel movement by the protagonists. It goes from province to capital, and it constitutes nonetheless a signifying factor of the narrative. It is not the places between which the trips are taken that produce meaning, for the city harbors improvement and life for the hero while bringing disillusion and death to the heroine. Meaning arises, rather, from the fact of the movement and from its repetition. The voyage the Ingénu makes to Paris is repeated by St. Yves; the parallelism has a potential for signifying since a same or similar story is told twice. The double narrative begins in identity between the two, and it ends in their sharp separation. New meaning is produced at the very moment when the fortunes of the two no longer resemble each other.

The double principle is also transmitted by the quantitative arrangement of the story. The protagonists together occupy the first seven chapters; then the savage goes to Paris (Ch. 8) and is thrown into his adventures (9-12). In Chapter Thirteen St. Yves makes her trip to Paris, and Fourteen takes up again in a sort of *meanwhile* the activities of the Ingénu, thereby entwining on the level of the narrative, though not of the story, his tale and that of the young woman. Her Parisian adventures continue in the next four chapters (15-18), and the two lovers are reunited in the last two (19-20). The voyage of each protagonist (8 and 13) and the trials that each undergoes (9-12 and 15-18) thus put them in qualitative *(histoire)* and quantitative *(récit)* parallel. Leaving aside for the moment the last two chapters, one can see from another perspective that the episodic ones, the first eighteen, divide themselves into three blocks having differents sorts of relations between the units that compose them: the provincial group where the heroes are together and where the episodes are in paradigmatic relation and coded either as repeated 2, 3 (injunction, transgression) or as repeated 12, 13 (test, reaction), both pairs belonging to the Proppian system; the prison-episodes, coded a static 19 (reparation of lack) over four chapters; and the adventures of the heroine at court in syntagmatic relation with each other, continuous with no repeated functions. Examination of the narrative syntax and mode of the component episodes confirms this division.

2.b. *Order in the Signified*

The application of Propp's folkloric paradigm reveals again this double coincidence of story and of functions, and it describes the exact nature of the parallel between the protagonists: they occupy the spheres of hero and false hero in the quest for marriage and in that for knowledge or formation. The scheme is especially interesting in this most *actuel* of Voltaire's stories, for the transfer of setting causes no deviation from a traditional compositional scheme.

The division of the tale into episodes appears at the left of Figure IV.B below; the Proppian function to which each corresponds, at the right, Column I being the reading of the marriage-quest and Column II, the quest for formation or learning. [8]

Readings I and II are complete and they complement each other. Ia and IIa are partial and are offered as experiments and for comparison: each takes the Ingénu as victim as well as questor, Ia in search of an object, IIa in quest of formation. Ia is a purely sentimental coding, the object being the heroine; it ignores the formative quest of II. IIa considers the hero as a victim of society; the critical tone invites this reading at the beginning, but the truncation at 8 corresponds to the fact that society is not condemned in its entirety and that St. Yves takes over the role of victim of its abuses. IIa also corresponds to the comic portion of the tale, and its repetition of 2, 3 (injunction, transgression) shows that the opposition implicit in natural man seen as victim of culture is also truncated: those episodes are repeated as 12, 13 (test and reaction) in complete reading II.

Two complete narrative threads are superposed; that of the marriage quest (I) permits a strict application of Propp's functions. In the episodes preparatory to the misdeed, the linked functions 2

---

[8] The key to the numerals was given in Chapter One above, p. 17. An earlier version of this appeared as an article by Carol Sherman, Katherine Stephenson, Keith Davis, "Folkloric Intertexts in Voltaire's *Ingénu*," *Romance Notes*, 21 (1980), 193-99. An attempt to find material for every one of Propp's functions is recorded in Eglal Henein, "Hercule ou le pessimisme. Analyse de *L'Ingénu*," *Romanic Review*, 72 (1981), 149-65.

FIGURE IV.B

Episode	Chapter	I. Marriage	(Ia)	II. Formation	(IIa)
Priory	I	0	0	0	0
Arrival in France	I	1	1	1	1
Encounter with Kerkabons	I			9, 8¹	
Adoption	II	2, 3	2, 3	10	2, 3
a) Bible		2, 3	2, 3	12, 13, 14neg.	2, 3
b) circumcision		2, 3	2, 3	12, 13, 14neg.	2, 3
Conversion	III-IV				
c) confession		2, 3	2, 3	12, 13, 14neg.	2, 3
d) baptism		2, 3	2, 3	12, 13, 14neg.	2, 3
Attempt at "marriage"	V-VI	2, 3	2, 3	12, 13, 14neg.	2, 3
SY put in convent	VI	8¹	2, 3	12, 13, 14neg.	2, 3
Battle against the English	VII	9, 10	2, 3	12, 13, 14neg.	2, 3
Ingénu to court	VIII	11			
Dinner with Huguenots	VIII			5	
Reception at court	IX	12, 13	7	12, 13	6
Ingénu imprisoned	IX	14neg. = 8² (for SY)	8		7
Encounter with Gordon	X			14	
Education	X-XII, XIV			19¹	8
SY exits from convent	XIII	19¹	14	1	
SY learns that Ingénu is in prison	XIII	9, 8²		9, 8²	

(A description of the numbered functions is found on page 38 above.)

FIGURE IV.B

SY flees to Versailles, outwitting the bailli	XIII	10, 11 and 16, 17		10, 11
Proposition to St. Pouange	XV	12, 13		16
Persuasion by Father Tout-à-tous	XVI	12, 13		16
Persuasion by la bonne amie	XVII	12, 13		16
SY seduced and obtains documents	XVII	14		
Liberation of Ingénu	XVIII	19²	19	17, 18neg., 19²
Reunion	XIX	20	20	
Pursuit of SY	XIX	21		
Praise of SY	XIX	24		
Revelation of SY's virtuous weakness: diamonds, confession, letter	XIX-XX	28, 28, 28		I: 25, 26; 25, 26
Illness and death of SY	XX	30	31neg	
Arrival of St. Pouange	XX	30		
Recompense of hero	XX	31neg.		31/31neg.

and 3, order or prohibition and execution or transgression, are repeated five times. In the last episode of this type the Ingénu's attempt to "marry" St. Yves, seen as transgression by the aggressors, the Breton Christians, causes the first misdeed (8^1), the sequestering of his beloved in a convent. This is the second *nœud,* the obstacle to the marriage that starts the action, the changes of the story. The hero learns of the misdeed (9), acts (10) in a way that could give him the credit he needs at court (11) for permission to marry St. Yves; but his effort to obtain it from the king, the potential donor, results instead in his own imprisonment (14neg.). The consequence of his absence, not of his efforts, is the release of St. Yves from the convent, reparation of the first misdeed (19^1). Repetition of a group of functions occurring between 8 and 19 begins, with St. Yves as its hero. The goal of marriage remains; and its questor takes on a second form, repeating the functions of the first but as the false hero, according to her own perception. The imprisonment of her fiancé (14neg.) was for her a misdeed (8^2); she learns of it (9) through news of the guard's letter, accepts to act (10), departs (11), undergoes combat with St. Pouange (16), wins (the papers) and loses (her honor) (18), liberating the prisoner (19^2) and thus repairing the second misdeed of the story. Although in the action her measures have a positive result, when she and the Ingénu are reunited (20), she sees herself as having been unfaithful to him and as having false pretensions (24) before him and her family. Thus, in the remaining functions, the couple is reunited as hero and false hero. The false hero is praised (24), her defect is revealed (28), and she is punished by illness and death (30). The reward of the hero (31), now the Ingénu alone, takes the form not of marriage but of an important position in society, a place for which he was prepared in the other thread of the story, the quest for education.

Folktales do not usually treat the kind of deficiency that the Ingénu discovers in himself; Propp's discoveries can nonetheless be applied to this story, in part because it was created by an eighteenth-century *philosophe* for whom absence of culture is a grievous lack. Coding II is thus an extended application, but a complete account of the meanings produced by the tale requires both I and II. The identification of I shows that there is a complete

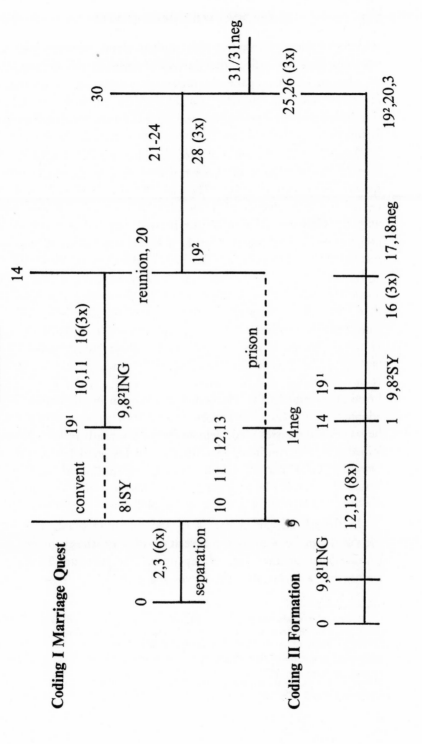

FIGURE IV.C

traditional tale present, but this reading alone, purely action and reaction, does not reflect the internal changes in the heroes; coding II does, and it prepares the reward of position that is substituted for the traditional marriage sought in I. This figure shows the simultaneity of the two codings and their common terminal function. It illustrates in I the division between hero and false hero.

In coding II, the encounter of the Huron with Europe can be seen as the revelation of deficiency that creates the *nœud* of the second, simultaneous action. The lack (8) of culture and revelation (9) of the lack give another meaning to the series of encounters with the Christian religion (2, 3 repeated); instead of being merely preparatory to the misdeed in I, they are also repeated test and reaction (12, 13) beginning the hero's education in European life and ending in his confrontation with Gordon whose culture is the magic element (14) repairing the lack in this quest. The education that takes place in chapters Ten, Eleven, Twelve, and Fourteen constitutes reparation (19) of the deficiency. These episodes with Gordon also mark the change of the quest from immanent to manifest: the Ingénu becomes his own mandator, his search becomes voluntary, and he makes it explicit: "... j'ai été changé de brute en homme" (XI). He finds himself again in the bosom of his adopted family (20), undergoes several difficult tests (25), which he successfully passes (26), demonstrating the result of his education joined with the continued manifestation of his good instincts.[9] The reward (31) in this quest is his subsequent earning of the "approbation de tous les honnêtes gens" and his becoming an "excellent officier," "à la fois un guerrier et un philosophe intrépide."

In the second half of coding II, the encounter of St. Yves with the court can be seen as the revelation of a deficiency in her, and it constitutes another sort of repetition. She may also be seen as undergoing a formation: she leaves the convent (1), observes that

---

[9] I code as trials and reactions (25, 26) his overhearing and seeing without overt reaction the evidence of St. Yves' "crime", and his forgiveness of her at the moment of confession. The mark of his change and of his admirable reaction is given more than once: "... mais il avait déjà appris à se posséder" (at the sight of the earrings), and "... mais il avait déjà appris à joindre la discrétion à tous les dons heureux que la nature lui avait prodigués" (St. Yves' worsening state) (Ch. 19).

she lacks the power to release the Ingénu (9, 8^2), goes to Versailles (10, 11) where education at the hands of three aggressors awaits her (16); she learns what life at court has to teach her (18neg.); the lack of education is thus repaired (19^2). She returns (20) to her beloved and to her family, is pursued by her aggressor-educators (21), submits to what she believes to be ill-founded praise of the use she has made of her new understanding, and is punished. The parallelism of the quests is confirmed by the sentence, "Le sentiment avait fait autant de progrès en elle que la raison en avait fait dans l'esprit de son amant infortuné" (XVIII).

Identification of the functions belonging to the traditional tale, coding I, puts in relief the strictly referential aspects of the satire and reveals the presence of a second coding that enriches the traditional framework by integrating a psychological thesis, a negative (first part) and a positive (second part) presentation of a certain culture's effects on innocent minds. The first part of II permits satire of Christianity's injunctions (2, 3) and condemnation of its representatives — the aggressors, the bailiff (8) and St. Pouange (21), and the hostile donors, La Chaise and Louvois (12, 13, 14). The second part of II transmits the process of perfecting a creature who retains his natural values while acquiring the benefit of a European education. At the same time, by the sentimental education of the female protagonist, the third part of the second coding condemns the society that effects her negative formation since common sense rebels at seeing her as false hero even though the nature and sequence of events indicate it. Here the events produce the positive and negative messages, and the lacks are not of objects but of reason and sentiment, which makes them specifically Voltairian.

The presence of a traditional intertext is not in itself surprising. However, we might have expected to see the essence of the tale in the elements remaining after separation of the folkloric constants; instead, we learn that we can also code a part of the philosophic message itself. It is clear that variable techniques of satire and irony and their historical targets participate in the tale's production of meaning (Section 4, below), but it may be that the nature of the *in*variables I and II is a fundamental characteristic of the genre and that their co-presence is one of its signs; they are not just two ways of coding the same events; each transmits a different portion of the meaning. Furthermore, by revealing the repetition of certain early functions, the codings suggest the paradigmatic nature of the first third of the episodes, the static nature of the second, the continuous nature of the last, and the double nature of the compositional principle. Far from being the occasion of a subtraction, the primary coded narratives are themselves richly productive of sense, and they found the meanings of the tale.

IV.3. PARADIGMS

3.a. *Spheres of Action*

Figure IV.D shows the population of the spheres named by Propp. In certain instances it lists the functions associated with each agent and to which of the two characters in the hero's sphere of action it belongs.

Both the Huron and the Breton woman occupy the hero's sphere in the quest for marriage; each has the same object, and each takes a separate initiative and undergoes trials in attempting to reach that end. The aggressors are those who commit the misdeed — the bailiff and the *abbé* put St. Yves in a convent (8^1), and the Père de La Chaise and M. de Louvois put the Ingénu in prison (8^2) — and the one who pursues the hero after his or her defeat — St. Pouange. What is test and reaction for obtaining the magic auxiliary in I can be coded as combat and defeat in II, the defeat of St. Yves' virtue being also a sacrificial response to the occasion for knowledge of the world, knowledge needed to rectify the lack (8^2) of power to free him. In his quest, the Huron encounters in Paris hostile donors, who fail to aid him and who imprison him instead. St. Yves' donor, St. Pouange, gives her the magic auxiliary, the documents allowing her to free him. Even though strict Proppian coding does not consider motivation or feeling, it is possible to consider the heroine's presence in the sphere of action belonging to the false hero, for the praise of her (24) that she believes undeserved is followed by successive revelations of her "sin" (28, repeated). The latter cause her death, surely a punishment of her

FIGURE IV.D

	QUEST I	QUEST II
Hero	Ingénu / St. Yves	Ingénu / St. Yves
Object	marriage	formation
Mandator	I / SY	I / SY
Aggressor	Père de La Chaise / bailli, abbé, 8[1] M. de Louvois St. Pouange, 21	———
Donor	Père de La Chaise, / St Pouange, M. de Louvois, 12, 14 12, 14neg.	Breton Christians, 14neg. / Tout-à-tous, English army la bonne amie 14 French court St. Pouange
Magic Auxiliary	/ documents 14	———
False hero	/ SY 24, 28, 30	———

8[2]

"pretensions." The psychological understanding we may exercise in this series has concrete representation in events conforming to the sequential paradigm.

The second quest is involuntary as an encounter with knowledge of the world, but each member of the hero's sphere makes a conscious decision to act in ways that end by being formative: French culture forms the Ingénu, and the hypocrisy of government and religion changes both him and St. Yves. The donors of this information are the Breton Christians, who offer instruction that the male hero does not accept; the army and the court, who educate him by leading him to prison; and Gordon, who there gives him knowledge that he prizes. *La bonne amie, le père Tout-à-tous,* and St. Pouange are the educators of St. Yves.

As we saw in *Micromégas* and in *Candide,* one character can participate in more than one sphere; and here, in addition to the heroes' acting as their own mandators, that possibility is exemplified by St. Yves' passing from the hero's sphere to the role of false hero. This change corresponds to meaning generated by her and by society's condemnation of her act. She and her friends accept to look only at her sin instead of damning the hypocrisy of a social system that made it so. The step to a higher judgment is taken by the reader and by the narrator at the end of the story, so the actions of the characters in the *histoire* remain enmeshed in the mentality that transforms the heroine into an impostor. This climate of tragic opprobrium creates in the reader instructive resistance to condemning the heroine.

3.b. *Oppositions*

Three factors mark the comic distance between the reader and the incidents of the first sequence: exoticism, both provincial and savage; the travestied epic qualities; and paratactic repetition of a single opposition. The absence or gradual reduction of all three elements in the groups that follow allows the reader to recognize the heroes as increasingly pathetic and to be caught up little by little in the sequential nature of the episodes. The changing versions of the thematic oppositions are finally lived alone by St. Yves in the last third of the story, and they plunge the reader into full pathos and into an integral *romanesque.* [10]

What structures are generated by the narrative, and what is responsible for the feeling of change in the passage from one unit to another? The opposition manifesting itself across all the episodes is that between ignorance and knowledge. Each unit of the first, the provincial, group confronts the Huron's ignorance with knowledge of French customs and of Christian dogma possessed by the Bretons. In the story a struggle takes place between the two halves of the opposition, and incidents multiply in the *histoire* at the expense of the savage; but the text produces a meaning that condemns the customs and dogma in favor of the savage's ignorance, and the literal sense is thus reversed. How does this happen? During the first supper with the strangers, his calm contrasts with the noisy questions of his civilized hosts. His slight astonishment at their gallo-centric assumptions — "Je suis de ma religion, dit-il, comme vous de la vôtre" — his literal obedience to instructions given by the Bible — thinking he should be circumcised, preparing for baptism by standing in a river — and the many clues given by the narrator — "La raison fait toujours rentrer les hommes en eux-mêmes... il se fit un grand silence" — all serve to produce the savage's superiority over his interlocutors. As he does in *Candide,* the narrator also makes eloquent use of *tandis que* to transmit his preference for the pagan hero: "On alla rendre grâce à Dieu dans l'église de Notre-Dame de la Montagne, tandis que le Huron, d'un air indifférent, s'amusait à boire dans la maison" (Ch. 2).

The second group of incidents, those concerning the Huron's trip to Paris and his imprisonment, manifests the same opposition between knowledge and its absence: the ignorant but curious savage contrasts with the learned men he encounters on the road to Paris, with the courtiers in the capital, and with the Jansenist in prison. Once again ignorance is defeated in the story — the Ingénu is arrested and put in prison — but once again the narrative also makes virtuous ignorance win out over evil sophistication in the meaning

---

[10] Vivienne Mylne remarks that this tale "progresses" from the standards of the *conte* to the mood and conventions of the *nouvelle:* "Literary Techniques and Methods in Voltaire's *contes philosophiques,*" *Studies on Voltaire and the Eighteenth Century,* 57 (1967), 1063.

grasped by the reader. The encounter with Gordon is the occasion
of a sentence emblematic of the whole section: "Le vieillard savait
beaucoup et le jeune homme voulait beaucoup apprendre" (Ch. 10).
It is the pivot of a double reversal. Life with Gordon transforms
one aspect of the savage; this can happen because the Jansenist is
the only one of the adversaries possessing knowledge who is virtuous
as well as learned. From then on the new incidents, the conversation
between the two men, continue to be situated inside the opposition
between knowledge and ignorance; but, sign of an important change,
both halves of it now apply to *each* of the two characters: "[Gor-
don] était changé en homme ainsi que le Huron" (Ch. 19). Each
gives to the other what he lacked: the savage gains acquaintance
with science and literature, and the Jansenist becomes more tolerant
and learns not to scorn human love.

   This reciprocal contribution makes it difficult to see how the text
could be said to produce a thematization of the opposition between
nature and culture or how it could be seen as bearing an intertext
of the banal view of a so-called Rousseauist return to nature. [11] This
simplification, found in the critical literature, could be the result
of a sort of projection onto the text of the pseudo-Rousseauist
injunction, but it cannot be said to arise from the rich presentation
of the ideal man in the story. The common antithesis between nature
and society does not appear as such except in as much as prejudice
is one of the facts of a certain culture, that of religious sects, and
is thus a fault. It is never shown as eliminated by a return to nature,
however, that is by the victory of one of the two terms. [12] It is
certain from the kind of synthesis of ignorance and knowledge that
the two prisoners achieve that nature and culture are not mutually
exclusive here. The Ingénu himself says what he can offer to civilized
man: "J'ai parlé d'après la nature; il se peut que chez moi la nature
soit très imparfaite; mais il se peut aussi qu'elle soit quelquefois
peu consultée par la plupart des hommes" (Ch. 12);   and he

---

11 William R. Jones summarizes these opinions in the introduction to this
critical edition (Geneva: Droz, 1957), pp. 20-23.

12 The concept of *culture* does not exist as such in the eighteenth century.
At that place in the *Encyclopédie* one finds only "Culture des terres" (Tome
IV). The idea takes form in the nineteenth century along with that of *civilization,* apparently resulting in part from the study of the relativity of *societies,*
which was the way the Enlightenment understood the relativity of cultures.

recognizes the value of certain aspects of civilization that are offered to him. At the very beginning of the tale, this later fusion of nature and refinement is suggested, for the *abbé* and his sister are impressed by the politeness and gallantry of the nearly naked stranger who appears before them. His actions contrast with those of the civilized English who "sautèrent à terre, sans regarder ni monsieur le prieur ni mademoiselle sa sœur, qui fut très choquée du peu d'attention qu'on avait pour elle." In the context of his superiority over the English, the young man's "Je suis Huron" initiates the reader in the co-existence of opposites.

In this section the surface-opposition is resolved; each, the Ingénu, representing cultural ignorance but knowledge of natural law, and Gordon, incarnating cultural knowledge but ignorance of natural law, transforms the negative part of the other's virtue. By his naïve questions about Gordon's god, the Ingénu cures his friend of prejudice and fanaticism:

> "Quoi! dit [Gordon] en lui-même, j'ai consumé cinquante ans à m'instruire, et je crains de ne pouvoir atteindre au bon sens naturel de cet enfant presque sauvage! je tremble d'avoir laborieusement fortifié des préjugés; il n'écoute que la simple nature" (Ch. 11); "Serait-il bien vrai, s'écria-t-il, que je me fusse rendu malheureux pour les chimères? Je suis bien plus sûr de mon malheur que de la grâce efficace. J'ai consumé mes jours à raisonner sur la liberté de Dieu et du genre humain; mais j'ai perdu la mienne." (Ch. 14)

For his part, Gordon brings to the savage the benefits of his culture, which refine what nature had left in the rough but without erasing his natural goodness. Thus, "ce jeune ignorant, instruit par la nature" transmits his natural way of thinking, and "Enfin, pour dernier prodige, un Huron convertissait un janséniste" (Ch. 14). The transformation will be permanent; the savage eventually becomes a warrior and dauntless *philosophe,* and Gordon forgets forever *la grâce efficace* and *le concours concomitant* (Ch. 20).

It may be noted in passing that critics' remarking an opposition between the Jansenist and Jesuit sects in the tale is probably another example of projection of a learned cultural unit onto a literary text. If we recall that the tale is set in 1689 when the conflict was still unresolved, we might expect that the two camps would appear as opposing each other in some way in the story as they did in fact in 1689. It is interesting to note the virtual absence of that neat opposition, a sign that, not surprisingly, its structures do not correspond to those exerting themselves in society in that year but instead to Voltaire's situation and preoccupation in 1767 while the tale was being written, after the expulsion of the Jesuits in 1764. The struggle for power between the sects being settled at least officially, although it continued in other ways even into the nineteenth century, the author uses them differently. Although historical fact is observed in the Jesuits' power to imprison a Jansenist, their place in the meaning produced is not that of symmetrical opposition. Jesuits incarnate a special political evil in the contrast between innocence and experience, and the Jansenist is faulted for his sectarian prejudice which differs from the innocent religion of the savage. It is interesting that even though Pascal is for Voltaire a major enemy, the *philosophe* finds much to admire in the Jansenist ethic; for the purposes of this story at least, he portrays in Gordon a moral foundation that he refuses to see in the Jesuits. [13]

If the central block of episodes contrasts with the first by the reciprocal transformation of the two halves of its opposition, it differs also from the third group, which recounts St. Yves' adventures in Paris. The same binarity arises from each unit; at each step of the way, ignorant purity clashes with powerful and knowledgeable evil. As in the first group of events, no synthesis of opposites occurs in the *story*. Victory belongs to a single side. In the provinces, dogma assimilated to knowledge triumphs: the Ingénu and his ignorance are converted and baptized. In Paris, learning and its cleverness overcome ignorant purity: St. Yves is seduced. This analysis of the superficial opposition proposed by the text brings into relief in another way the parallelism and equivalence of the protagonists' two threads of action. It reveals the manner in which

---

13 J. Nivat ["*L'Ingénu* de Voltaire, les Jesuites et l'affaire La Chalotais," *Revues des Sciences Humaines,* 66 (1952), 97-108] believes the only adversary to be the Jesuits. Francis Pruner [*Recherches sur la création romanesque dans "L'Ingénu" de Voltaire* (Paris: Archives des Lettres Modernes, 1960)] opposes this thesis, maintaining that an equal dose of criticism is applied to both sects.

the evil winners and their knowledge are doubly condemned: the reader can infer the assimilation of *conversion* with *seduction.*

What form does the resolution of the parallel and of separation take? The second paragraph of Chapter XIX, the reunion, reiterates the changes wrought in the protagonists; and the statements are part of the *histoire* since the characters make them. First, St. Yves warns the family waiting for the Ingénu that he is no longer the same, "son maintien, son ton, ses idées, son esprit, tout est changé. Il est devenu aussi respectable qu'il était naïf et étranger à tout." The prior then says to her, "Vous n'êtes point non plus la même; que vous est-il donc arrivé qui ait fait en vous un si grand change-ment?" The hero arrives, and the narrative voice confirms St.-Yves' statement about him: "... l'Ingénu, qui n'était plus l'*Ingénu*." The observation of the heroine's transformation is surrounded by two remarks on the hero's changed aspect. They are made in two dif-ferent voices. The similarity or union of the parallel is in this way accomplished once again in the *récit* and in the story; but even while it is emitted, the divergence of the two also appears: "On voyait éclater la satisfaction, la reconnaissance, sur le front de l'un; l'embarras était peint dans les yeux tendres et un peu égarés de l'autre. On était étonné qu'elle melât de la douleur à tant de joie," this last sentence being emblematic of the break in their union, of St. Yves' quitting the hero's sphere. The divergence emphasizes the ironic lesson of the general type "They no sooner find each other than they are separated! " and it helps create the pathos of the last scenes. However, the developing radical asymmetry — one lives, the other dies — is arrested and compensated for in the first sentence of the last paragraph of the tale: "Il ne parlait jamais de cette aventure sans gémir; et cependant sa consolation était d'en parler." In the signifier the asymmetry is controlled and restrained by the chiasma *parlait*: *gémir*: : *consolation*: *parler.* It signifies the difficult equilibrium attained by the hero. Surviving experience incorporates sacrificed innocence into its life and maintains the attachment by telling its story. We learn that the Ingénu takes over the role of narrator, incarnating a constantly renewed synthesis of his life and St. Yves'. For him narration replaces the tragic solution.

Each of the three groups generates the same structure: their constituent parts reveal the same opposition. However, the nature of the relation between the episodes, the passage from one to the other, changes. This is different from *Candide* where the units are in parataxic relation, each tending to suffice unto itself, and where the end of the tale is therefore an arbitrary closure, virtually un-motivated in the story and without profound syntactical relation with what precedes it. In *L'Ingénu* the units of the third group are less substitutive and less contiguous, more combinatory and more continuous, than those of the first and second groups. They also present the same opposition, that of ignorance against knowledge; but the causal and linear link between them grows more and more important as the end approaches. The contiguity in the first two sections was not strict, it is true. While the conversations about dogma are more or less interchangeable, once the savage is baptized, he cannot marry his godmother; the fight with the English and St. Yves' imprisonment are causes of the trip to Paris, and so on. In the second group, the talks with Gordon are purely contiguous and static, veritable pamphlets on history, theater, and religion, cap-able of appearing in any order. In the third section, each unit contains an element motivating the next, each visit to an official leads to the next and brings the provincial visitor nearer her fatal decision. The episodes are no longer interchangeable. Thus, while the first two groups repeat a nearly static opposition, in the third, even as it maintains the same contrast, events unfold more and more in function of each other; and a strong syntagmatic cohesion is added to the vertical structure of the episodes. Furthermore, the echo of the Ingénu's activities in prison (9-12) as it is heard in the chapters (15-18) showing St. Yves' torment invites the reader to retrospective comparison and to an enriched perception of sameness and of difference. She may extract from this a significance regard-ing the kinds of power enjoyed by the two sexes in that society and the different fates they might undergo.

This recognition of repetition at the level of an entire sequence adds itself to that of the analogical nature of the units composing each sequence and constantly mitigates the reader's simpler impres-sion of pure succession. The sequential appearance of these two adventures in the *récit* is mediated by their confrontation in the reader. At the beginning of Chapter Eighteen, the sentence already quoted says that sentiment progresses in St. Yves and reason in the

Ingénu; difference etches itself into the resemblance: the male virtue, reason, underwent its fate, while the virtue accorded to femininity, feeling, lived out its own: "Les filles apprennent à sentir plus aisément que les hommes n'apprennent à penser," the passage continues. The crossing of the two narrative threads in Chapter Fourteen also invites the comparison while its content still participates in a linear and progressive structure and while it is made of units which are still repetitive. The linear or sequential property of the text characterizes its novelistic *(romanesque)* function while the repetition at both levels, similarly structured episodes and superposable plot threads, is one mark of *didacticism*. The appellation *roman philosophique* accounts for both these aspects of the narrative, its progress and its redundancy.

We have already seen that the ignorant characters are not condemned by the reader and that the manifest oppositions are reversed in reception. This is done in the name of a broader opposition, immanent to the story, which can be expressed as innocence against experience. It surrounds and includes the superficial dialectic between ignorance and knowledge, each of the latter being a manifest, special, sub-case of one pole of the broader opposition: innocence of information is ignorance, learning is one of the results of experience, etc. Though not expressed in the signifier, this meaning is constructed by the reader who witnesses the total victory of innocence in the exemplary heroes.

This rectification of the imbalance in the superficial opposition (ig/kn) by the profound (in/exp) is brought about in part by the mode of the narration itself. Science wins in all the encounters against ignorance, but innocence triumphs in the eyes of the reader, for victorious experience — dogmatism and fanaticism (first and second groups), then hypocrisy and cruelty (third) — is condemned successively in comic, denotative, and pathetic modes. Identification of the double opposition common to all three sections permits the reader to identify by difference or subtraction the various tonalities nuancing the three groups of episodes. They are the causes of the feeling of disjointedness or lack of unity that reading this text gives. [14] If we enter for a moment into the spirit of the normative

---

[14] It is this feeling that has given rise to such titles and remarks as H. T. Mason's "The Unity of Voltaire's *Ingénu*," already cited; William R. Jones'

controversy about whether this tale possesses artistic unity, we can say that those searching for its unity are "right" because they sense the ubiquity of the fundamental oppositions that inform each scene and that those who criticize the disparateness of its parts are "right" because they are disturbed by shifts in genre.

L'Ingénu pretends to be history, and the claim is conventional, it is true. That pretension does not, however, free it from a folkloric paradigm; and the appeal to that intertextual competence is made two times, once for each of two heroes. Furthermore, as we have seen, it emphasizes their symmetry even as the asymmetry of true and false hero inscribes itself in the equilibrium. [15]

A single structure arises from each of the units of the tale; the opposition between knowledge and ignorance allows the victory of knowledge in the first and third parts of the *story* and its synthesis in the central portion:

FIGURE IV.E

Section	1 (Ch. 1-9)	2 (Ch. 10-12, 14)		3 (Ch. 13, 15-18)	
Opposition:	knowledge/ignorance	kn/ig	ig/kn	knowledge/ignorance	
Representatives:	Bretons Ingénu	Ingénu	Gordon	Jesuits	St. Yves

The immanent opposition between experience and innocence both repeats and reverses the manifest one. In this way it also conforms to the paradigm of symmetry that incorporates an asymmetrical tension, for the correction of $a:b::A:B$ is a chiasma, $c:d \neq D:C$, that represents reversal to the triumph of innocence.

FIGURE IV.F

Manifest (Sense)		Immanent (Meaning)	
a	b	A	B
knowledge/ignorance		experience/inocence	
c	d	D	C
victory	defeat	defeat	victory

---

comment, "Découvrir l'idée centrale de *L'Ingénu* n'est pas chose facile," in his edition of this work (Genève: Droz, 1957); and the subtitle of a section, "The Meaning of *L'Ingénu*," in the Introduction of J. H. Brumfitt and M. I. Gerard Davis' edition (Oxford: Blackwell, 1970).

[15] Compensated asymmetry is one of the stylistic traits discovered by Jean Starobinski in his brilliant examination of the first three paragraphs of Chapter Seven of *L'Ingénu*: "La doppietta di Voltaire," cited above, Chapter 2, note 7.

The dissolution of contiguity in the third part contributes to the transmission of a culturally derived pathetic mode, which is maintained by massive use of deixis and by a particular kind of dramatization. This characterization of the parts of the tale permits projection of various generic terms onto the groups of episodes:

FIGURE IV.G

	1	2	3
Syntax	analogical/sequential	analogical	sequential
Actualization	comic	denotative	pathetic
Genre	*conte*	treatise in dialogued form	*roman*

If my description is adequate, the question of knowing whether *L'Ingénu* "is" a *conte* or a *roman* is moot, unless last is best and the novelistic ending has the most importance by being the strongest impression remaining. The first section dramatized the difference between the Huron and the Bretons by dialogued scenes in which customs and dogma were discussed and by reporting the extravagant actions of the visitor — standing in the river, sleeping on the floor, "marrying" St. Yves. In these dramatized confrontations the reader understands ideas not explicited, and she concludes that the newcomer's naïveté reveals inconsistencies and cruelties in the Breton beliefs. The second section dramatizes the Ingénu's education by recording dialogues between him and Gordon, his own comments, and the Jansenist's cries of amazement. There is no schematic complication, for every drop of instruction is explicit. The last part not only dramatizes the reunion of all the characters, it sets them on a stage and makes of the double climax two scenes within scenes. The introduction of nested spaces and the careful placing of each character associates the event with painting also, with the *scènes de genre*. The well-known belief in physical attitude and in gesture as revelatory of sentiment is employed abundantly in the theatrical and the painted aspects of the final scenes. This generic enrichment, the succession of events, and the use of value-charged language all conspire to form a final *romanesque,* the novel being an uncodified genre that obtains its effects from all the others.

3.c. *Closure*

By these means the end of the adventure offers the possibility of feeling completeness as well as closure, the last incidents having conformed to our expectation of cause-and-effect's function, that of creating a final event that is solution or resolution in the story. It could not continue by the infinite repetition of its paradigms once causal linkages were formed in the story.

Pathos is not the final word, however. The last paragraph plus the two sentences preceding it oblige further shifts of attitude:

> J'ai fait votre malheur, lui dit le sous-ministre, j'emploierai ma vie à le réparer. La première idée qui vint à l'Ingénu fut de le tuer, et de se tuer lui-même après. Rien n'était plus à sa place; mais il était sans armes et veillé de près. St. Pouange ne se rebuta point des refus accompagnés du reproche, du mépris, et de l'horreur qu'il avait mérités, et qu'on lui prodigua. Le temps adoucit tout. Mons de Louvois vint enfin à bout de faire un excellent officier de l'Ingénu, qui a paru sous un autre nom à Paris et dans les armées, avec l'approbation de tous les honnêtes gens, et qui a été à la fois un guerrier et un philosophe intrépide.

> Il ne parlait jamais de cette aventure sans gémir; et cependant sa consolation était d'en parler. Il chérit la mémoire de la tendre St. Yves jusqu'au dernier moment de sa vie. L'abbé de St. Yves et le prieur eurent chacun un bon bénéfice; la bonne Kerkabon aima mieux voir son neveu dans les honneurs militaires que dans le sous-diaconat. La dévote de Versailles garda les boucles de diamants, et reçut encore un beau présent. La père *Tout-à-tous* eut des boîtes de chocolat, de café, de sucre candi, de citrons confits, avec les *Méditations du révérend père Croiset,* et la *Fleur des saints,* reliées en maroquin. Le bon Gordon vécut avec l'Ingénu jusqu'à sa mort dans la plus intime amitié; il eut un bénéfice aussi; et oublia pour jamais la grâce efficace et le concours concomitant. Il prit pour sa devise: *malheur est bon à quelque chose.* Combien d'honnêtes gens dans le monde ont pu dire *malheur n'est bon à rien!*

In the beginning, the fantastic recital of Saint Dunstan's founding of the priory was annulled by introduction of the "true story" of the Ingénu; now, at the end, the story, while remaining "true," takes on again the aspect of fairytale by sketching out the long and uniform future of the enduring characters. The second closure is of the type "If they have not died, they are still alive," "They

lived happily ever after," [16] or that of which Henry James com-
plained, "a distribution at the last of prizes, pensions, husbands,
wives, babies, millions, appended paragraphs, and cheerful remarks." [17] The flash-forward traditional in folktales takes place in
the verbal tenses of pure *history* in Benveniste's sense, and *discourse*
retreats: "Il ne parlait .... Il chérit .... L'abbé ... et le prieur
eurent ... la bonne Kerkabon aima .... La dévote garda .... Le père ...
eut .... Gordon vécut ... il eut ...." The fact of telescoping the future
and the presence of historic tenses make symmetrical the beginning and end of the tale, but asymmetry once again etches itself into
the chiasmatic equilibrium: St. Yves is dead, and all do not live
happily ever after; and discourse appears briefly once more to attach
the story again to the narrator-reader's present. By foregrounding
enunciation, that is, by underlining the discourse-situation, it denies
to the interpreter the satisfaction of distant history's fading away:
"... l'Ingénu, qui a paru sous un autre nom à Paris et dans les
armées ... et qui a été à la fois un guerrier et un philosophe intrépide." The two *passés composés (a paru, a été)* give information
on the eponymous hero's pseudonymous presence in the recent past
and immediate space of narration. In its general return to historic
tenses in order to recount a future in the past, the last paragraph
functions first as a sort of opening even as it marks a second closure.
Consequently, it offers a double sense of completeness: a certain
interpretant expects *apocalypse,* and the first closing provides it in
the death of St. Yves; but that interpretant also seeks *reassurance,*
and the second closure satisfies this by the happy static future it
describes.

Nonetheless, discourse and narration will not release the reader;
the *passé composé* returns in a final exclamation, emitting a moral
by an epiphoneme: "Combien d'honnêtes gens dans le monde ont
pu dire *malheur n'est bon à rien.*" The alternation between apocalypse and reassurance proffers a happy resolution, but it is abruptly
withdrawn, and the "cheerful remarks" are cancelled by the exclamation. An account of the semiotic potential of the ending cannot
declare it tragic, as if the event or story — instead of manner and

---

[16] Bruno Bettelheim, *The Uses of Enchantment: the Meaning and Importance of Fairytales* (New York: Random House, 1977), p. 10.

[17] Quoted by Kermode, p. 22.

récit — were all that mattered and as if the last paragraph were not present. Neither can it, after seeing the whole as *comédie larmoyante,* call it "flawed." [18] The *story*'s end in pathos is far from being the final word of the *récit,* and the last lines are dense with potential for the constitution of new meaning, commentary on the bitter general irony of the fates described.

IV.4. DIDACTIC PROCEDURES

In the previous chapters I have described the types of modal communication available in the three stories examined. They all contain invective against specific targets; they often invite substitution or reversal of terms and of values expressed; and they sometimes exhibit the target in a dramatized scene. In all these respects, *L'Ingénu* once again distinguishes itself from the others. It is very rarely necessary to reverse authoritative narrative statements in order to actualize their meaning. Invective is rarer also, and in one case has a new function. Directly denunciatory and overtly approving descriptions are much more frequent, and most of the devaluative judgments depend upon a broad and relatively lengthy dramatization of a circumstance, of a conversation, and of its actors. Most of the messages thus pass without necessitating cognitive operations more complex than simple reception of sense and comparison of the aggressors with their equivalents in the reader's life.

There are cases of simple inference; they welcome a tiny leap to an extra-diegetic referent. In a passage cited and discussed above, one describing the traits of the Kerkabons, the reader can attach comments made on the two to stereotypes of the anticlerical tradition. Reference to a similar satiric usage occurs in the depiction of Mesdemoiselles de Kerkabon and St. Yves as intensely interested

---

[18] Mason calls it *tragic* ("The Unity of Voltaire's *L'Ingénu*:"); and R. S. Ridgway calls it *larmoyante* and *flawed* in *Voltaire and Sensibility* (Montreal: McGill-Queens University Press, 1973), pp. 243, 246, 247. Highman ("*L'Ingénu*: Flawed Masterpiece or Masterful Innovation?") does not find the ending tragic but thinks it sweeps the reader again into the perspective of history, into a supremely ironic mode (p. 80), a cosmic one surpassing both the mechanization of the beginning and the *comédie larmoyante* of what he calls the *second part.*

in the Huron's body and in the eventual use of it. Neither of these appeals to tradition requires reversing anything, and the incarnations are all comic and sympathetic.

One of the most violent cases of invective has already been cited, that against critics, authors of periodical brochures. The other is milder, though longer-lived; and unlike the first, it has a function in the plot. The bailiff is one of the aggressors: he wants his son to marry St. Yves, and he helps imprison her in the convent when she refuses his son by showing that she loves the Huron. In the first view of him the narrator says that he "s'emparait toujours des étrangers ... et qui était le plus grand questionneur de la province." He speaks "en ouvrant la bouche d'un demi-pied" (Ch. 1). This trait is isolated and repeated often. Since it is not universally attached to the profession of bailiff, it seems to exist as a mild defect characterizing the aggressor although not dangerous in itself and therefore comic; but it is negative and thus can continue to mark his person as ridiculous and as potentially evil. Chapter Three contains three more remarks on this trait, and in Chapter Five it is repeated in mild form — "qui selon sa coutume lui demanda où il allait" — but it becomes invective as his son, destined for St. Yves, is associated with the negative opinion we learned to have of his father: "... et ce fils était encore plus sot et plus insupportable que son père." These defects are recalled and augmented in the non-comic portions of the tale, for the two characters' importance as agents in the plot persists. The simply "interrogant bailli" of the first chapter becomes in Chapter Thirteen the "maudit bailli;" in Fifteen, the "perfide bailli," and in Nineteen, the narrator mentions "le vilain bailli et son insupportable fils."

Among the direct assessments, both positive and negative, are short descriptive comments that contrast aspects of the hero with their French opposites; the Ingénu is always admirable. His quality as an early riser is admired over the

> bonne compagnie, qui languit dans un lit oiseux jusqu'à ce que le soleil ait fait la moitié de son tour, qui ne peut ni dormir ni se lever, qui perd tant d'heures précieuses dans cet état mitoyen entre la vie et la mort, et qui se plaint encore que la vie est trop courte. (Ch. 2)

The criticism hurts no one, but it serves to insist upon the hero's vigor. The positive portrait of his childhood contrasts with the "inutilités et ... sottises qui accablent la nôtre" (Ch. 3), and it adds elements to the constant comparison between natural man and certain of the critically unnatural.

Four other targets receive direct treatment from the narrator. He tells us exactly what to think of people who prove the obvious — Monsieur de St. Yves "fit très habilement remarquer" that the Huron resembles both his parents — wherein a reversal is for once required, that of *très habilement*. He slaps metaphysics with a phrase that appears elsewhere under Voltaire's pen, "ce roman de l'âme" (Ch. 10). The two doctors' ministrations to the dying woman occasion the expected criticism of members of their trade: the first is "un de ceux qui visitent leurs malades en courant," and after making further destructive comment the narrator exclaims, "De la mode jusque dans la médecine! Cette manie était trop commune dans Paris" (Ch. 19). The next chapter begins with the arrival of the second doctor. He fares no better: "... celui-ci, au lieu d'aider ... ne fut occupé que de contrecarrer son confrère. La maladie devint mortelle en deux jours." None of the targets above seems intimately related to the main action; the remarks are incidental barbs of the sort found so abundantly in the other three tales.

Explaining St. Yves' dilemma upon her arrival in Paris, the narrator makes a direct evaluation of the Jesuit hierarchy (Ch. 13). He poses two questions for the heroine — "Mais comment se conduire à Versailles? Jeune, belle, sans conseil, sans appui, inconnue, exposée à tout, comment oser chercher un garde du roi?" — and then attributes to the Jesuits themselves ("disaient-ils") an unflattering comparison between them and different sorts of food:

> Elle s'imagine de s'adresser à un jésuite de bas étage; il y en avait pour toutes les conditions de la vie, comme Dieu, disaient-ils, a donné différentes nourritures aux diverses espèces d'animaux.

He then enumerates the categories and assigns their design to God himself:

> Il avait donné au roi son confesseur, que tous les solliciteurs de bénéfices appelaient *le chef de l'Eglise gallicane*; ensuite,

venaient les confesseurs des princesses; les ministres n'en avaient point: ils n'étaient pas si sots. Il y avait les jésuites du grand commun, surtout les jésuites des femmes de chambre par lesquelles on savait les secrets des maîtresses; et ce n'était pas un petit emploi.

By the time the reader has grasped the intimate corruption of these arrangements, she is presumably horrified to see. St. Yves throw herself on the mercy of one of the lowest classes of confessors:

La belle St. Yves s'adressa à un de ces derniers, qui s'appelait le père Tout-à-tous. Elle se confessa à lui, lui exposa ses aventures, son état, son danger, et le conjura de la loger chez quelque bonne dévote qui la mît à l'abri des tentations.

The reader conscious of the tradition critical of the *dévotes* and aware of the reference to it in the first chapter will probably receive the expression *bonne dévote* as oxymoron and dread seeing the heroine in such hands. Mademoiselle de St. Yves asks to be sheltered from temptation by a type that cultivates temptation, and she does not see the dangers predicted by the narrator and reader. This kind of dramatic irony function for both members of the hero's sphere; and since they have been described as good and as beautiful, the result contributes to their pathetic relation with events.

The last and a lengthy example of direct criticism opposes St. Yves' manner of dying with the standard injunctions to fortitude and to courage, the stiff-upper-lip approach that the narrator explicitly deplores. It is here that some readers see a negative reference to the heroine's death in *La Nouvelle Héloise*. The association is inevitable, but those ignorant then or now of Julie's agony can read the vehement refusal to admire resignation in death as making St. Yves' passing all the more pathetic. Two full paragraphs oppose the death of St. Yves with two other sorts of dying, the courageous method and that insensitized by ceremony:

Elle ne se parait pas d'une vaine fermeté; elle ne concevait pas cette misérable gloire de faire dire à quelques voisins: "Elle est morte avec courage." Qui peut perdre à vingt ans son amant, sa vie, et ce qu'on appelle l'*honneur,* sans regrets et sans déchirements?

> Que d'autres cherchent à louer les morts fastueuses de
> ceux qui entrent dans la destruction avec insensibilité: c'est
> le sort de tous les animaux. Nous ne mourons comme eux
> avec indifférence que quand l'âge ou la maladie nous rend
> semblables à eux par la stupidité de nos organes. Quiconque
> fait une grande perte a de grands regrets; s'il les étouffe,
> c'est qu'il porte la vanité jusque dans les bras de la mort.

The passage begins by opposing a certain concept of death, but that
view is found in many places besides that in Rousseau's novel, and
it has received many other incarnations. The negative criticism of
a manner to be rejected takes up much less space than the positive
portrait of St. Yves, omitted in the quotation above, and the final
injunction to acknowledge a great loss when it occurs. The spectator
of this death may compare it to any sacred painting depicting the
death of a saint. It conforms to the classical ideal of a non-violent
and lengthy departure from existence and to the type of the *Grand
Cérémonial,* although the attendants are here only friends and members of the family. The traditional exemplarity offered to the col-
lectivity living out the death with the central personage is, however,
refused by the explicit contrast between. St. Yves' and her friends'
distress and the lesson-giving and revelation that is supposed to
attend a good Christian's death. Furthermore, although two priests
later stand outside reciting prayers over the body, and although
passers-by throw holy water on it, the reader may notice another
opposition to the tradition: there is no mention either of confession
or of extreme unction. [19]

Instead of admiring the dying person's calm, by the narrator's
reversal of one part of the ceremonial of death we are made to
reflect on the uselessness and on the prematurity of the event instead
of finding it exemplary and comforting. There are several other
moments of reflection upon death in the story. The death that is
dramatized opposes itself clearly to eighteenth-century common-

---

[19] Moreau le Jeune prepared an engraving of St. Yves' death with the
spectators gathered in various attitudes around her bed. Philippe Ariès has
studied the history of dying; his most recent book on the subject is *L'Homme
devant la mort* (Paris: Le Seuil, 1977). Michel Vovelle has collected accounts
of various kinds of death for the period that concerns us: *Mourir autrefois:
attitudes collectives devant la mort au XVIIe et XVIIIe siècles* (Paris: Gallimard, 1974).

places, and the other mentions of the subject also have more than perfunctory value. At different moments, the heroine and the hero consider suicide as a solution to a particular difficulty. St. Yves hesitates between death and the loss of her virtue; indeed both finally happen to her since one is the cause of the other (Ch. 17). The Ingénu's friends make it impossible for him to kill himself, but Gordon does not bother preaching the sinfulness of suicide, and the narrator's account of that fact is a short defense of it, an argument familiar to readers of the philosophes:

> Gordon se garda bien de lui étaler ces lieux communs fastidieux par lesquels on essaye de prouver qu'il n'est pas permis d'user de sa liberté pour cesser d'être quand on est horriblement mal, qu'il ne faut pas sortir de sa maison quand on ne peut plus y demeurer, que l'homme est sur la terre comme un soldat à son poste: comme s'il importait à l'Etre des êtres que l'assemblage de quelques parties de matière fût dans un lieu ou dans un autre; raisons impuissantes qu'un désespoir ferme et réfléchi dédaigne d'écouter, et auxquelles Caton ne répondit que par un coup de poignard. (Ch. 20)

Melpomene's knife makes an appearance here and again, figuratively, in Chapter Seventeen during the explanation of St. Yves' dilemma that I just mentioned:

> Tandis que cette brave personne augmentait ainsi les perplexités de cette âme désespérée, et enfonçait le poignard dans son cœur, arrive un exprès de monsieur de St. Pouange avec une lettre et deux beaux pendants d'oreilles.

This passage also makes use of the *tandis que* that is often the instrument of bitter juxtapositions. It serves again on the same page at the moment of seduction: "Elle n'eut d'autre ressource que de se promettre de ne penser qu'à l'Ingénu, tandis que le cruel jouirait impitoyablement de la nécessité où elle était réduite." The conjunction has both its meanings, *pendant que* and *au lieu que*. The list of direct interventions by the criticizing narrator has led us to those surrounding discussion of suicide, seduction, and death. It is notable that forms of verbal irony are absent in these passages: there is no safe distance.

254 READING VOLTAIRE'S *CONTES*

The most permanent targets are the agents who cause the tragedy, and they are represented and devalued in dramatizations. The
first encounters of the Huron with the Bretons give rise to conversation revealing their gallocentrism and intolerance (Ch. 1). The
hero's literal interpretations of the Scriptural view of circumcision
and of confession make him act in ways that shock his friends and
reveal the inconsistencies in Christian doctrine (Ch. 3). He makes
the same point in his discussion with the bishop (Ch. 4) and attempts
to imitate the baptisms reported in the Bible, thus embarrassing
again his indoctrinators. In another scene the hero disputes the laws
of the church (he cannot marry his godmother) and is astonished
that the Pope provides dispensation from the laws (Ch. 5). In the
next chapter the dramatization makes a point slightly more abstract,
opposing the Church's ignorance of natural law. The next scenes
criticize the Revocation of the Edict of Nantes (Ch. 8) and the practices of court politics (Ch. 7 and 9). They are punctuated by the
hero's expressions of astonishment, begun in Chapter Five, where
"l'Ingénu fut encore plus étonné qu'auparavant" upon learning that
he has to go to Rome to get permission to marry. The naïveté of
his thinking the king will reward him devalues the corrupt system
that he does not imagine (Ch. 7), and the surprise of a natural man
puts into question the procedures that amaze him. His naïve as-
sumption that he can fix everything by telling his story to the King
also condemns the royal inaccessibility to its citizens and to truth
(Ch. 8). The hero, "tout étonné," spends time in the waiting room
of a lowly *commis,* and then is amazed to learn that he has the
latter's generous permission to purchase a commission:

> Moi! que je donne de l'argent pour avoir repoussé les
> Anglais? que je paye le droit de me faire tuer pour vous,
> pendant que vous donnez ici vos audiences tranquillement?
> Je crois que vous voulez rire. (Ch. 9)

Direct discourse bears criticism of the target. The last surprise is
his arrest. Then, when he is thrown into prison he himself begins
astonishing his cell-mate, "aussi étonné qui lui-même" by his arrest
(Ch. 10) and then "étonné qu'un jeune ignorant fit cette réflexion"
on Malebranche. The esthetic of amazement that we see functioning
in *Micromégas* and elsewhere in eighteenth-century literature takes

on its familiar moral force when practised by the victims of abuse. They state their judgments clearly. The criticism of Malebranche, and thus of metaphysics, is made by the Ingénu's surprise and by his words: "Votre Malebranche ... me paraît avoir écrit la moitié de son livre avec sa raison, et l'autre avec son imagination et ses préjugés" (Ch. 10). Similarly, his comment on the Protestants' exile, although put in the form of a question, enunciates the common practical objection to the Revocation: "D'où vient donc ... qu'un si grand roi, dont la gloire s'étend jusque chez les Hurons, se prive ainsi de tant de cœurs qui l'auraient aimé, et de tant de bras qui l'auraient servi?" In the dramatic dialogue of Jansenism, the Ingénu silences Gordon with the comment: "... votre grâce efficace ferait Dieu auteur du péché aussi: car il est certain que tous ceux à qui cette grâce serait refusée pécheraient; et qui nous livre au mal n'est-il pas l'auteur du mal?" (Ch. 10). The phrase attacks the Jansenist *grâce efficace* but without turning to the Jesuits for its answer. Instead it seems to accept a certain determinism of evil; this is still criticism of theodicy. The last dialogue with Gordon has as its topic religious sects. This target receives double destruction. In the name of unity and tolerance, the Ingénu criticizes sectarianism, indirectly by his naïve questions — "Dites-moi s'il y a des sectes en géométrie" — and directly: "Voulez-vous que je vous parle avec une confiance hardie? Ceux qui se font persécuter pour ces vaines disputes de l'école me semblent peu sages; ceux qui persécutent me paraissent des monstres" (Ch. 14). After a single sentence of transition, the narrator makes the Huron launch a recapitulation of his misfortune. This technique of repetition is frequent in the other tales; here it is given only once to each of the two actors in the hero's sphere. The heroine performs her recapitulation in Chapter Seventeen, providing another parallel between the actions attributed to the two heroes. After the Ingénu's recital of his suffering, the narrator uses elevated language to approve his sentiment: "Ainsi sa philosophie naissante ne pouvait dompter la nature outragée dans le premier de ses droits, et laissait un libre cours à sa juste colère" (Ch. 14).

The tale also dramatizes a positive presentation. When the hero describes the ideal minister of war, all the bad ones are criticized by the same mechanism that made of Eldorado the condemnation of French society in *Candide*. The speech is not modal except by its

being diegetic and thus not directly authoritative, but the protagonist's credit is such and his transformation so clearly underlined
that the reader attributes authority to him. The narrator makes the
comparison explicit by adding in his own words, "Mons de Louvois
n'aurait peut-être pas été satisfait des souhaits de l'Ingénu; il avait
une autre sorte de mérite." *Mérite* requires reversal, and the aggressor Louvois is fully condemned. The placement of this heavily didactic discourse augments its force since it precedes St. Yves' sharp
turn for the worse at the end of Chapter Nineteen.

The lengthy dramatization of the reunion in Paris and the heroine's death includes an extended use of dramatic irony. This is
another reason why the last two chapters seem close to a theatrical
conception. It attacks the seducers of St. Yves in a further way by
focussing on the hero's slow realization of the act and of the self-
reproach that are killing his beloved. At the moment of illumination,
he forgives her so-called crime and thus makes the death "ironic"
in the banal, circumstantial sense of the word, for St. Yves' suffering
is then seen to be unnecessary. In fact two events are dramatized,
the gradual disappearance of the heroine and the gradual discovery
of her crime by the hero. The widest distance between the Ingénu's
information and that possessed by the young woman and by the
reader exists at the end of Chapter Eighteen when the heroine
delivers the Huron philosopher from prison. The ironic trajectory
thus goes from this moment of his innocent surprise to the moment
of coincidence, the public confession in the fourth paragraph of the
last chapter. This misunderstanding begins when the Ingénu exclaims, "Il est donc dans la beauté et dans la vertu un charme in-
vincible qui fait tomber les portes de fer, et qui amollit les cœurs
de bronze! " The ironic distance is further emphasized by the heroine's reaction to this statement; and a third voice, the narrator's,
adds itself and reverses entirely St. Yves' opinion of herself: "A
ce mot de *vertu,* des sanglots échappèrent à la belle St. Yves. Elle
ne savait pas combien elle était vertueuse dans le crime qu'elle se
reprochait." This kind of irony appears regularly. The prior says
she has changed; we know how, and her friends do not. The group
is amazed that she mixes sadness with joy; the reader understands.
Gordon condemns the governmental practice of imprisoning people
for their beliefs, and this launches redoubled praise of St. Yves. The

hero tells his hopes for the future with his liberator; everyone is
in ecstasy and praises her again.

The confession she makes to the group around her erases the
distance between their information and hers. She receives double
absolution, one from the Ingénu and, *mirabile visu,* one from Gordon
himself:

> "Qui? vous coupable! lui dit son amant; non, vous ne
> l'êtes pas; le crime ne peut être que dans le cœur, le vôtre
> est à la vertu et à moi." … Le vieux Gordon l'aurait con-
> damnée dans le temps qu'il n'était que janséniste; mais,
> étant devenu sage, il l'estimait, et il pleurait.

This redoubled pardon throws the entire crime onto the intrigue
and corruption of the court, yet another way in which governmental
and ecclesiastical collusion is condemned.

We saw that the other tales are neither character-centered nor
plot-centered but are instead thesis-centered and thus anecdotal and
apsychological. In this regard also *L'Ingénu* is different. The first
third is largely anecdotal, but then it becomes plot-centered and
psychological; that is, compared to the other stories, this one bears
a large amount of psychological observation. Certain characters'
feelings are described. Even the anecdotal section includes some
such comment:

> … comme elle était bien élevée et fort modeste, elle n'osait
> convenir tout à fait avec elle-même de ses tendres senti-
> ments; mais, s'il lui échappait un regard, un mot, un geste,
> une pensée, elle enveloppait tout cela d'un voile de pudeur
> infiniment aimable. Elle était tendre, vive et sage. (Ch. 5)

The hero's inner meditations are recounted in the first paragraph
of Chapter Seven.[20] "Plongé dans une sombre et profonde mélancolie," he wanders in a natural setting. His first thoughts of suicide
are recounted here as well as his plan to free St. Yves from her
prison. This serious view of his dilemma and the fact that he is
depicted as engaged in a conscious analysis of it contrast with the
return to comedy and the mock epic that follow when he defends

---

[20] Starobinski, "La doppietta"; the whole article treats this subject.

the coast against the English and then runs towards the convent with his little army. The tone of the meditative paragraph perhaps attenuates in some minds the comic potential of the battle, and it is certain that events and criticism darken considerably in the subsequent episodes.

Such lengthy notation of feeling does not recur until the beginning of Chapter Eighteen where the narrator paints a psychological portrait of the heroine. He begins the portrait by saying why it is difficult to paint it. In this overt mention of his producing the text the authority and skill of the narrator fail before the chaos of St. Yves' emotions:

> Il est difficile de peindre ce qui se passait dans son cœur pendant ce voyage. Qu'on imagine une âme vertueuse et noble, humiliée de son opprobre, enivrée de tendresse, déchirée des remords d'avoir trahi son amant, pénétrée du plaisir de délivrer ce qu'elle adore! Ses amertumes, ses combats, son succès, partageaient toutes ses réflexions.

The reporter abandons accounting in complex syntax for the turmoil of her heart. Instead, he throws down a series of adjectives — *vertueuse, noble,* etc. — and then a short list of nouns, so many brushstrokes transmitting confusion by a contiguous series of highly charged words. At the end of the chapter, he tells two of her opinions; and they of course continue to accuse the state that persecutes her: "Elle sentait qu'elle devait faire tout ce que son amant exigeait: elle voulut écrire [asking St. Pouange to release Gordon also], sa main ne pouvait obéir." The narrator prepares the second revelation of her feeling: "... ainsi, à chaque action honnête et généreuse qu'elle faisait, son déshonneur en était le prix. Elle regardait avec exécration cet usage de vendre le malheur et le bonheur des hommes." In the nineteenth chapter the feelings of the whole company are reported by going from their general astonishment to the mention of the sentiments of each; for the action of the chapter is in part the passage from joy to sadness and fear on the part of the company. St. Yves' feeling are the stable element as her health changes, "éperdue de l'altération qu'elle apercevait sur le visage de son amant" or "oppressée, éprouvant dans son corps une révolution qui la suffoquait."

Although the second paragraph of Chapter Twenty has been criticized as being poorly integrated, one might see Gordon's analysis of the relation between mind and body as perfectly pertinent to a fourteen-page drama in which the heroine's "âme tuait son corps." The four questions asked — "... quelle mécanique incompréhensible a soumis les organes au sentiment et à la pensée?" etc. — precede the statement that they are his ideas. The delayed attribution might be considered awkward, but the violence of the series of interrogations follows well upon the announcement that the illness has become fatal. Once again the narrator declares his impotence in translating feelings, for the strongest ones he must tell are unsayable. He wishes to show us the hero: "Mais qui pourrait peindre l'état de son amant? Nulle langue n'a des expressions qui répondent à ce comble des douleurs; les langues sont trop imparfaites" (Ch. 20). The monstrosity of the causes of these events is presumably proportionate to its unspeakableness. [21]

The broadest use of ironic mode invites comparison with *Candide* and *Zadig* and defines another aspect of the tale's didactic potential. One view of the world generated by *Candide* has been expressed as a tension between the pessimism of its facts and the optimism of the way in which they are presented. [22] Jean Starobinski describes it more finely as pathos in the narrative, the destiny of the hero, contrasted with irony in the style, the cleverness of the author. [23] The double view stimulates a double — manifest and immanent — opposition at all moments of its phrasing, the binarity of pathos and irony does not arise from it simultaneously but occurs sequentially or successively in the course of its unfolding. In addition to the incidental uses of antiphrasis, the situational irony of reunion and separation, and the dramatic irony of the last long scene, the wider circumstantial ironic vision is gathered into the epiphoneme of the last line, whereas that kind of expliciter of an ironic view punctuates *Candide* and *Zadig* regularly in the voice of each hero.

---

[21] Haydn Mason believes the tale provides a fable for the times about persecution in France, that the theme "is essentially persecution whether the target be Protestant or Jansenists or *parlementaires* ..." *Voltaire* (New York: St. Martin's, 1975), pp. 73, 79.

[22] Brumfitt and Davis, p. L.

[23] "Sur le style," p. 197.

This occurs because in them each episode generates the entire lesson. All of *L'Ingénu* could be gathered and concentrated to form one incident of *Candide*.[24] Its entirety offers just one more cause for pessimism in human affairs.

As I have already noted, the final didactic measure taken is the epiphoneme — "Combien d'honnêtes gens dans le monde ont pu dire *malheur n'est bon à rien!*" — making of the story a whole that is condemned, its history or societal backdrop as well as individual actors playing on the stage. If in *Micromégas* the incident of the blank book is a fable inserted as a story in the episodic plot but one that encompasses its lesson, one might say that *L'Ingénu* is in its entirety a single fable. The first and last paragraphs detach themselves from it, and they point to it but do not constitute *mises-en-abyme*. They send forward and back to the fable itself without replicating it in any way: the legend of St. Dunstan points to the tale to follow as a legend, and the last exclamation is a judgment of the intervening events. *L'Ingénu* is not parabolic in the manner of *Micromégas,* of *Zadig,* or of *Candide.* They can be seen as a series of parables for a number of propositions, and they seem to be launched on a potentially infinitely open trajectory. This difference is one of the ways in which *L'Ingénu* fulfills its generic definition as history and distances itself from myth.

IV.5. METAHISTORY, METAMYTH

When the narrator says that Clio has to be equipped with Melpomene's dagger, he acknowledges that history must have style to have effect. In other words, it needs to be art:

> Il lut des histoires, elles l'attristèrent. Le monde lui parut trop méchant et trop misérable. En effet, l'histoire n'est que le tableau des crimes et des malheurs. La foule des hommes innocents et paisibles disparaît toujours sur ces vastes théâtres. Les personnages ne sont que des ambitieux pervers. Il semble que l'histoire ne plaise que comme la

---

[24] Haydn Mason (1975) makes a similar point by noting the difference between St. Yves' death, the breaking of a human spirit, and the many deaths in *Candide,* that are due to an "accidental shrug of the universe," p. 76.

tragédie qui languit si elle n'est animée par les passions, les forfaits et les grandes infortunes. Il faut armer Clio du poignard comme Melpomène. (Ch. 10)

Although art does not equal truth, Voltaire nonetheless calls his artistic story a true one. Lionel Gossman has tied this view of history to Voltaire's feeling that the barbaric and irrational in history must be rejected and that it must instead be infused with order.[25] In the passage quoted the *philosophe* recognizes a principle of selection that operates even before the historian begins to write — only crimes and misfortunes come to his attention — and he seems to regret that the subsequent revelation of fact obeys artistic rules, further selecting and arranging the already partial materials. His recognition of the methods of tragedy in the telling of events is surprising neither in an age that sees itself as bringing light to darkness and order to chaos, nor in the context of its view of both history and *contes* as related to spectacle and drama and of the *conte* and *nouvelle* as related, by their exemplary or newsworthy qualities, to history.[26] The historians of the eighteenth century are thus first philosophical artists, and it seems that Voltaire tried to create a sense of tragic history in his tale.

History, tragedy, and myth: *L'Ingénu* appeals to our experience of all three. As we have seen, it pretends to be a true story, refers to persons and to actions of French history, and displays the elements of a chronicle, announcing beginnings, dates, and hours. At the same time it bears the signs of the survival of a mythic element, and it joins the features of the mythical heroic cycle to biography,

---

[25] "Voltaire's *Charles XII*: History into Art," *Studies on Voltaire and the Eighteenth Century* 25 (1963), 691-720.

[26] Gossman, pp. 709-710; Angus Martin cites Marmontel's remarks on the parallelism between theater and story: "Introduction" to his *Anthologie,* pp. 32, 35-36. Georges Mailhos reports that some have seen in *Charles XII* the architecture of a tragedy in five acts: "Introduction" to *Histoire de Charles XII* (Paris: Garnier-Flammarion, 1968). *Charles XII* has also been called a "picaresque mock epic," a phrase that combines the history with yet another literary genre (Gossman, p. 691). Observers of eighteenth-century histories clearly anticipated the fundamental intuition of Hayden White's *Metahistory,* cited in Section 1 of this chapter. Karlheinz Stierle notes in passing the presence in Voltaire of history both in the syntagmatic framework of universal history and its insertion into the paradigm of a collective example: "L'Histoire comme Exemple, l'Exemple comme Histoire," *Poétique,* 10 (1972), 176-98.

a form of history that Voltaire also practiced. The historical and the mythical are two seemingly antithetical explanations of events. The nature of historical truth and the logic of its reasonings, its search for causes, seem to have little to do with the function and the value of mythical readings of human and natural events. Different concepts of time and of order and thus different relations with eternity inspire the two genres; the simplest "objective" history claims to be chronicle and is both linear and secular whereas myth's formulations are cyclical and divine. Their union is often attempted, however, in theater, in tragedy most precisely. Events dramatized there usually concern real kings and queens, their loves and their wars; but they often take on the prestige of myth, and spectators grant to them a meaning that transcends the simple news-worthy aspects of the conflicts portrayed. One could also say that their authors read events and shape them already into a form dictated to them by their participation in the myths of their culture. Whatever the site of the phenomenon — in genesis, in reception, or in both — classical tragedy, like painting, draws on both history and myth and tries to inspire strong emotions in response.

Reviewing in these perspectives some aspects of the story at hand, we discern the traces of both the mythical and historical models of narration in a relation of coexistence and of contradiction. In the sections above, I have often mentioned the points of isomorphism in the adventures of the two heroes; their common object, initiative, travel, seduction, imprisonment, thoughts of suicide, their recapitulations and transformations. The Huron changes twice in ways that resemble the mythological type: in the first, his baptism, a ritual designed in any case to alter the status of its object, his name is changed as he becomes a Christian; and the second, his entry into prison, a presumably closed and dark place, is a symbolic death. Both these transformations take place in the course of the story and not at its end, thus further conforming to heroic myth. The heroine is also locked up, and she emerges with resolve and energy; but she dies. The obvious loss of isomorphism when one lives and the other does not makes St. Yves' death "news" of a disappearance that forces an ending without cyclical recovery other than her lover's telling and retelling of her story. In the two trajectories which are parallel and then reversed, she undergoes destruction while he is regenerated. This kind of bifurcation is often a feature of myth, and the simultaneity of her degradation and his ascension activates another response to myth, the sacred resonance of a martyr's death. Masculine and feminine destinies differ as each responds to the same enemies. Woman's body is offered in secret; man's is sold on the battlefield with honor. The woman is portrayed as losing the meaning of her life in this bargain for she does not surrender herself in love. It is *for* love, however, that she accepts seduction, just as it is for love of her that he accepts baptism. This juxtaposition manifests once again the similarity — seduction and conversion — and illustrative difference in the outcome of each. That the simultaneity of her fall and his rise is interpreted as cause and effect in the events — she liberates him from prison — is a trait characteristic of history. The opposite fates are related to myth by their morphology — destruction and regeneration — and semantically, through the explicited relation between the two events, they rejoin the intertext of history.

Although both heroes are persecuted by the same forces in the *histoire,* the mythical status of the male protagonist is augmented by the fact that a positive thesis is incorporated into his story. His transformation, his synthesis of natural law and of civilization, have the prestige of a primordial scheme. It proposes a structural model of man's best formation. St. Yves' adventure does not offer a model of the world. Another way of saying this, by following Lotman's theories of plot, is that the whole text correlates the two schemes, myth and news, dialogically, that the hero's trajectory resembles a one-sentence — initial ideal state, lack, reparation — imposition of order onto chaos, and that the heroine's pathway depicts the triumph of disorder.[27] The story is thus a polyphonic one, myth and history combined. In it, a regulated trajectory equipped with high meaning coexists with another line fraught with excess and anomaly. The negative pole concerns tragic events and the violation of order while the positive one manifests itself as miracle, the resolution of conflict by the hero's liberation. The liberation of the Huron is not a miracle in the story, the unrolling of cause and

---

[27] Lotman, pp. 173-74. In this part of his essay he draws on Bakhtin's study of Dostoyevsky.

effect being only too clear. It is, however, taken as miraculous by him and the family until their doubts increase and St. Yves disabuses them. Their initial marveling and their joy remind the reader of the sacrifice depicted as extreme and thus as a sort of miracle of love.[28] Furthermore, even though crude cause and effect — copulation and documents — account for the hero's freedom, other results of St. Yves' sacrifice echo the awesome consequences frequently attached to a martyr's death: the Ingénu is not only freed but is promoted to an important position; and the heroine's body, like a saint's relic, causes a return to goodness on the part of her aggressor. In "*malheur n'est bon à rien!*" the text finally re-creates scandal and articulates its own deconstruction by the epiphoneme become epitaph. It is, however, scandal that both produces the miracle and results from it as a saint gives herself up in sacrifice and earns only the fragile eternities of memory and literature.

---

[28] Richardson's *Clarissa* offers an earlier example, there forcible, of rape that causes the heroine's death from shame.

CONCLUSIONS

... n'oublie jamais qu'une œuvre est chose finie,
arrêtée et matérielle. L'arbitraire vivant du lecteur
s'attaque à l'arbitraire mort de l'ouvrage.

Mais ce lecteur énergique est le seul qui im-
porte — étant le seul qui puisse tirer de nous ce
que nous ne savions pas que nous possédons.

Paul Valéry, "Tel Quel,"
Œuvres complètes, II, 626.

By regarding the *conte philosophique* as a producer of meaning
instead of as a reflector or container, its student concentrates on the
text as a sign and engages in an exercise that renews critical discourse applied to it. I have constantly distinguished between two
types of reading, the cooperative and the deconstructive. In analyzing
the first I endeavored to isolate the principal mechanisms of the
tales' capacity to function as didactic sign. This treatment describes
the process by which the works appear to be largely univocal, highly
constraining of the cooperative reader. In pointing to the second
type of reading in the fifth section of each chapter above, I showed
the work's and reader's potential for discerning traces of cultural
assumptions and patterns that combine to undo or to predict the
undoing of the text's claims to truth and to unity. It is thus seen
in its synchrony as *fragmented,* bearing the trace of several often
contradictory texts in dispersion (Derrida's *dissémination*), and as
a fragment, torn from infinite diachrony, the successive reformula-
tion of prior texts. The meta-reader, one conscious of reading and
of herself as a similar site of loosely gathered patterns, realizes in
both senses of the verb the various aspects of the text that de-

construct the others or some other. That the tale thus fragmented undermines its own premises is perhaps the result least expected in any examination of authoritative texts.

The clarity that each tale offers to a cooperative reading has as its resources structural anaphora and various other paradigmatic effects that are reinforced by the repeated guidance of the narrator's interventions and his modal communications. According to the contract made with the reader willing to receive the tale and a lesson, those factors effectively check the play of meaning. To what extent does my analysis make explicit the various operations that actualize the philosophical tale? What typology of Voltaire's *conte* can be drawn from it? In summarizing the typology, I shall abbreviate as *M, Z, C,* and *I* the four stories treated in the chapters above.

All four titles prepare the reader for the fusion of a fiction and of the philosophical reflection that is to persuade her. This happens for various reasons. Three of the proper names are metonyms: *Micromégas, Candide,* and *L'Ingénu* all name one of the characteristics of their heroes. *Zadig* and *Candide* are completed by "ou La Destinée" and "ou l'optimisme," which announce philosophical meanings to come. *M, Z,* and *I* name themselves further in their respective subtitles, "histoire philosophique," "histoire orientale," and "histoire véritable." There is a certain redundancy already present in the addition of *histoire philosophique* to a name deciphered as *Big-Little,* and in *orientale* describing something called *Zadig.* *True story* complements the name of the fourth hero, who will always be known as *the* something, the Huron or the Ingenuous one. This kind of pointing augments the truth-claims of the subtitle, for the definite article refers to something supposedly known and is thus a form of deictic in the story: *le Huron* and *l'Ingénu* can be seen as implying that the reader knows him once he has been presented by the indefinite "un jeune homme" and "un Huron." At the same time, the designation tends to universalize its object, thus generalizing the statements made about it. In a similar, though sequential way, the title *Candide ou l'optimisme* includes an extremely precise designation, the proper name, and the definite article before *optimisme* marks the passage to the universal. The other preparations for multiple reading — metonyms, mention of the philosophical problems of destiny and of optimism, redundant descriptive subtitles, and the presuppositive definite article — invite the reader's apprenticeship in a particular form of sense-making. The subtitle of the fourth offers it as true, but the name of the hero nonetheless concretizes an abstraction and thus also invites the expectation of some form of instruction or generalization of the supposedly isolated case.

The claim to truth gives I a status different from the others in the second step of the reader's training. M, Z, and C all utter the words *il y avait* (M: "... il y avait un jeune homme de beaucoup d'esprit," Z: "... il y avait à Babylone un jeune homme nommé Zadig," C: "Il y avait en Vestphalie ... un jeune garçon") and after exposition of time, place, and circumstances, they present the first discriminated occasion ("un jour," C) that begins the series of episodes composing the tale. I begins instead with two discriminated occasions, "Un jour," the first words, marking St. Dunstan's visit, and "En l'année 1689, le 15 juillet au soir," presenting the initial event of the principal story. These two sets of precise details serve to attach the story to the genre of chronicle, the truth-claims of which are absolute. I is also an exception to the preliminary and concentrated exposition of the other three; for an important part of the hero's past, his parentage, is revealed only in the second chapter and is related by dramatization in the scene where with the help of the portraits he is recognized by his uncle and aunt. This presentation of the relation between characters and its consequences — special tenderness, interest in establishing him in society, calming of the aunt's lust — is coherent with the transmission of motivation and of psychology that also differentiates the I from the other more mechanically episodic tales. They are little interested in character. Their exposition is compact, and it scarcely intervenes once the multiplication of examples has begun.

The patterned order of the episodes in all cases conforms to a folkloric paradigm generated by each. The distribution of events is already significant: M's big-to-little order of planetary travel; Z's two sequences of rise and fall; C's universalization, by geographical completeness, of the problem posed; and the passage from country to city by each of the heroes and their imprisonment in I. These kinds of movement in space lay out the novelistic paradigm of each tale, that is, the feeling they give of adventure and of progress. At the same time the individual episodes in *M, Z,* and *C* and in the first portion of *I* give a strongly static impression of the structures presented, and this is one of the important sources of the redundancy that serves the actualization of the lesson in each case. A largely analogical relation predominates between and among the episodes. The presence of oppositional structures within them is a constant and is the clearest source of the principal theme or topic upon which the tale focuses. *M* reiterates the idea of disproportion — of man and the universe, of man's abilities and his pretensions, of the uses for science and for metaphysics — by constructing episodes that express and show proportions, dramatizing such discrepancies as well as shifting their value; the disproportion between man and universe is nuanced by the dramatization of man's power to understand the immensity that dwarfs him. *Z* poses the question of knowing why the good suffer and constantly shows them doing so while evil is rewarded. The reader is encouraged to modify this vision by noting the persecuted one's influence on the destiny of others, and she thus arrives at a composite view of chance and its reign. *C* interrogates theodicy by dramatizing the juxtaposition of that doctrine and catastrophe. It also permits the reader to witness repeated examples of the instinct for survival that assimilates horror even as it desires to go on. *I* is not focussed in the same way on a philosophical question of knowing how and why things are. It knows the reasons for the problem it dramatizes and so repeatedly stages French society's oppression of two innocent heroes and demonstrates the kinds of formation available to them as a result. Each of its episodes contrasts the powers of a certain knowledge with the weakness of ignorance's representatives, but the reader is led to see the opposition more broadly as experience against innocence and to give the victory to the latter since a certain kind of experience is the entire cause of the evil depicted. The oppositional structures of the *contes* thus do not come into play in a simple manner. The manifest opposition is transmitted directly by the fable, that is, by its sense; but it refers implicitly to another opposition, actualized as meaning, and contradicting it. One goes from an opposition in which one of the terms is valorized and the other devalued to a reversal of values that modifies the opposition and gives each term a new meaning and a new value. This is the constant mechanism of the fusion of story and lesson, and I think this technique of double encoding and of correction of one code by the other is a characteristic proper of Voltaire's *contes*.

Another kind of opposition revealed in the episodic course is that between active and reflective events. In *M* this appears in the fable as the alternation between astral movement and static conversation, but both contents transmit the same structures named above. In *Z* and *C* it is particularly evident in the hero's frequent laments and recapitulations, which are pauses in the propulsive action, but which are not extraneous either to the lessons conveyed. The static moments in the fable of *I* are the conversations between the hero and the Bretons, his talks with Gordon in prison, and the scenes of gradual revelation that take place within the long scene showing the heroine's decline into death. There is in this tale a reversal of the proportion found in the other three between mobility and its opposite. This too corresponds to the increased interest in revelation of character, of the effect of ideas and of events on the formation of two young persons. These pauses in the physical trajectories are not just commentary on the rest; they advance the part of the action that is interior to the characters. The thematic oppositions also structure these scenes of introspection. Another kind of reflective event occurs in *Z* and *C* where tales are told by a character of the principal story. The events thus condensed and revealed are violent; but their entirety is offered as one more document, a demonstration of the thesis, that is, of the good being punished in one case and of catastrophe accompanying providential explanations in the other.

Part of the folkloric paradigm to which the episodic events correspond is the spheres of action. Various characters perform the acts that are seen as the domain of the mandator, hero, object, aggressor, helper, magic aid, and false hero. In all except *Z* the nominal hero at some moments shares his sphere with others moving toward the same goal. In *M,* the dwarf, after playing the role of aggressor in the first encounter with the hero, enters the latter's sphere and quests after the same kind of knowledge in a similar way (travel), although with less talent for observation and for induction. Other aggressors, men in philosophical combat (16^3 in Fig-

ure I.A) defeat the hero when they win the battle (18³neg.) by their
mathematical skill, but they enter the sphere of false hero when
they claim to answer metaphysical questions (24) and are defeated
by the hero's approval of Locke's disciple (28). Even Micromégas
finally detaches himself from the hero's sphere and can be seen as
attaining the status of narrator and of reader when he plays the
trick of the blank book, a *mise-en-abyme* of his own adventure.
Candide is joined in his sphere by all his friends when they perform
one visitation in the final quest for a cure to boredom. The presence
of this microcosmic population amplifies the question and the answer
to suggest their applicability to all humanity, and it is thus an
abstractive procedure and a generalizing device. In *I*, observation
of the cross-overs in spheres creates significance beyond sense and
meaning. St. Yves and the Huron are at the same time heroes and
the object of each other's quest. This split into hero and false hero
as defined by their functions underscores a truth about the societal
role and possibilities for the two sexes, and the sense of injustice
it creates by denouncing (killing) the false hero intensifies the criticisms of societal structures that are more insidious and far-reaching
than its religious and political institutions alone.

Another doubling and reinforcing of part of the folkloric paradigm gives a further example of abstractive procedures. Each hero
pursues two quests, one material and the other philosophical. Each
is also a victim, and the questor-victim coupling corresponds to the
way the *philosophes* saw themselves as well. In *M* the material
search is negative — exile — and undeveloped; the philosophical
one — forming his mind and heart — motivates the movement
through the universe and the pauses for discussion. In *Z, C,* and *I*
the material quest is that for a lover from whom the hero has been
separated, and the philosophical one, voluntary in *Z* and *C* and
forced in *I*, motivates in the first cases repeated interrogations of
experience and in the second changes in the hero's and heroine's
material condition and a transformation of their understanding of
the world. The last tale studied also possesses the particularity of
depicting two heroes each having a material goal, the other, and
undergoing her or his individual formation. The double meaning
of the quest is one of the mythic structures of the *contes*. A paradigm marks each tale; it includes adversity in pursuit of a material

goal and instruction that comes from the effort. The figure of death and transfiguration also marks all four. In this too *M* conforms minimally to the structure; the exile of the story is related after concentrated description of the events leading up to it, and it mimes the going out from an enclosure and the changes that are characteristic of that mythic figure. In *Z* and *C,* the going into a dark place and the emergence are treated more elaborately: Zadig spends a night in a tent, his armor is stolen, he goes out in humiliating dress and returns in disguise, and then recovers his original clothes; and Candide take a terrifying and noisy twenty-four hour trip on rapid waters going through the rock tunnel ("une voûte de rochers") of the river that carries him to Eldorado and he returns from that place, the signs of his transformation being wealth borne by red sheep. Both are burlesque by the low content joined to the elevated pattern of mythic renewal. In *I* the hero and heroine undergo separate imprisonments, and they change upon their release: the political prison is the site of the Ingénu's acculturation; St. Yves goes out of her religious prison with resolve and courage for action. These events resemble one feature of heroic adventure, and coupled with the tension between the linear succession and vertical structuration of each episode, they lift items of news ("once upon a time" and "one day") to the generality of myth.

Counterbalancing the double kinship of myth in *I* is the motivated ending which attaches it to the category of news and which thus leaves what is perhaps its most lasting impression with the reader. The other three remain closer to the mythic paradigm which does not end with the death of the hero but contains it only in the middle, projecting the possibility of eternal renewal of anecdotes or adventures. In *M, Z,* and *C* the closing event is not rendered necessary by the fable. In those three tales mythic pattern is replaced instead of being altered. One scheme, closure, is substituted for the repeated and infinitely repeatable situation.

The reiterated structures are one form of redundancy. The *mise-en-abyme* is another of which there are two types. In *Z* and *C* the reflexive events mentioned above, that is, the tales told by secondary characters, as well as the recapitulations of events by the heroes, are both concentrated reflections that intensify the lines of the principal action by repeating them. Interrupting the linear plot and pausing, they call attention to the ideological aspect — the perplexity before misfortune. In *M, Z,* and *C* the other sort of *mise-en-abyme* points to the entire process of interpretation of each. The episode of the blank book as metaphor of the *tabula rasa* on which experience shall be written re-writes mankind's quest for absolute knowledge and declares it useless. The blank book is a model, a didactic image, a paradoxical invitation to experience. By refusing to accord the promised revelation, Micromégas shares the lesson-giving function of the author-narrator, and leaving his own role as questing hero, points to the vanity both of a certain ideological quest and of a certain esthetic, the desire for metaphysical ending to narration, that is, for closure, "le bout des choses." The angel Jesrad also promises to interpret all things, and that incident thus stands out in *Z* as a concentrated replica of the hero's repeated efforts to make sense of events. Instead of explaining, the revelation takes the form of a book that is not blank but that is as unreadable as the whole tale that contains it.

In *C* the structures of two of the three gardens combine to replicate the third; the last one is the *mise-en-abyme* of the two idyllic ones, the chateau and Eldorado, in relieving the protagonist from harm; but it continues to contain the reminiscence of catastrophe that fills all the other episodes. Instances of global redundancy abound in *C*; for teaching, learning, interrogation, and consultation are the actions constituting many episodes. At the minimum, efforts at interpretation follow each catastrophe; and the investigation of Eldorado and the visit with Pococuranté are extended examples of this kind of quest for universal understanding. The sum of results is again negative, however, and thus replicates the lack of ideological resolution to the adventure as a whole. The positive component of the solution finally adopted — *cultivons notre jardin* — is the imitation of single example, the *bonhomme*'s actions (preparation of *sorbets, cédrat confit, oranges, pistaches*) and the negative portion — *sans raisonner* — invalidates the entirety of the reactions to events represented in the tale. Redundancy in *I* differs from the others, and it differs in a way coherent with its final predominantly sequential nature. Each protagonist performs only one recapitulation, but each hero's trajectory is the *abyme* of the other and spreads out across the entire story instead of concentrating itself into one kind of incident. Mirror images of each other, like the right and left hand, male (right) and female (sinister) end by diverging and by re-informing the shorter reiterated accusation made against the society that offers opposite conclusions to each. In these terms life is a mirror-image of death; the commonplace according to which each implies the other finds incarnation in this special, horizontal *mise-en-abyme.*

All of these forms of didactic repetition characterize Voltaire's *contes.* Oppositional structures constituting most episodes, recapitulations, inserted tales, and reflections, these forms of reiteration are compensation for what the reader necessarily receives as the story's drastic reduction of the contingency of the world.

The narrator's relation with his *récit* and with the reader is another area of constancy in the tales. The kinds of instructions for reading have been described above; the alert to double decoding, to the combination of sense and didactic meaning; use of nudges and nods in the form of invective, deictics, reference, and invitations to reversal that plot a zone of experience shared by narrator and reader, and the self-consciousness portrayed by the teller's affection for his narrative. These factors determine his authority, omniscience, reliability; and they constitute a perpetual seduction of the reader's sympathy. They attain unprecedented density, however, in the scenes depicting St. Yves' agony, at which time some readers rebel at the constraints they find suffocating. All these aspects of the narrator's control give much of the generic tone.

The narrator has also a particular relation to his heroes. In all four stories, he tells us that they are good and beautiful, so they are sympathetic; he shows us that they are also eirons. Candide and Zadig often reason and act with ignorance and simplicity; Micromégas is ignorant of life on earth, although he reasons well once in contact with it; the Ingénu is naïve and ignorant of everything he encounters, thereby throwing it all — religion, literature, and politics — into question. Because of the initial credit accorded the hero, the distance between the narrator and the eiron never widens to the point of endangering the reader's adherence to his enterprise; and his constant presence on the page and the moments in which the narrating voice echoes the hero's own statements of his dilemmas, validating the eiron's descriptions of situations even though it does not always follow him to his conclusions, also contribute to assuring our fidelity to him. The splitting of the didactic hero and thus balancing the comic nature and serious purpose of heroes who are constantly being surprised and expressing amazement is one of the appealing features of the stories, one that allows a certain amount of identification — perplexity and error are not unknown to us — and at the same time encourage reflections satisfyingly superior to that of the nonetheless likeable protagonists.

The presence of the eironic hero is just one of a series of factors requiring certain reversing operations in reading. The eiron's simple questions can be seen as in fact profound, and our first judgment of them is reversed. The sense of many statements can be understood as meaning their opposite. The simplest case of replacement of one word by another of opposite value to antiphrasis at the level of the sentence; dramatic irony; parody, which reverses the prestige of an entire generic intertext; echoes of parody; ironic mention; and the general irony of events — all exercise the reader's capacity for actualizing meaning not said, and they put her in the special state of awareness to the vast *writable* portions of otherwise simply *readable* texts. The instability in this area, the potential shifting of each moment's resolution, joins the fragile character of endings that resolve events in the story but that do not solve the ideological problem posed. The ironic operation is thus the ever-renewed emblem of the joining of philosophy to a sequence of events. This observation should be underlined: stated another way, it constantly transmits the perception that the relation *between philosophy and events is fundamentally ironic*. The resolution of the one — sequence — seems to be the solution of the other — the question posed; but the grammar of resolution, of finding a status quo or returning to it, is eternally subverted by the answer's absence, grammar emptied of substance. In this the tales subvert their archetypal fictions. The ideal of truth dictates a certain chaos in events represented, in the multiplication of episodes that are the tale's schematicized offering of experience. This formalized swarming and expanding is nonetheless controlled by an impulse to coherence, to order, and event to causality. It is shown in the efforts to make sense of events, efforts depicted as taking place in the *histoire;* and it is seen in each ending's implied assertion that it finally makes sense of the tale *(récit).*

A still broader source of irony exists in the intertextuality of each *conte*. Although reversal is only one of the possible relations the text can have with its antecedents, the relation that stands out most clearly is indeed the one that opposes another text in order to deny its validity. In *C*, Voltaire's version of Leibniz's theodicy is the clearest example of this and its actualization requires little skill since almost every episode puts it on stage with a spokesman and ridicules it and him. The intertexts of *M* enjoy subtler treatment: Locke's insistence upon observation through the senses is entirely approved long before he is named, and Pascal's disproportion is reflected while its consequences are denied. In *Z* the classic "Why do the good suffer?" is proposed approvingly, but after a pretend-answer — "Because everything is meaningful" — is given to it, it just goes away. *Z* also plays in ironic fashion with comic and tragic convention, sliding from one to the other, making each the reversal of the other and thus representing most thoroughly the structure of general irony in the universe.

Finally the diverse cuttings that I have made of the text lead to an undeniable convergence. My goal was to make explicit the nature of what one could call a strategic conspiracy in the text. In this way also, literary criticism escapes the well-known dilemma between the hermeneutic project and the formalist one. By restricting the movement toward a text seen as transparency or as reflection, we respect its materiality, giving back its original opacity, the "chose finie, arrêtée, matérielle" of the epigraph to these conclusions.

Respect for its opacity also requires a degree-zero approach to the problem of genre. What makes a text literary in the first place is not its evident concrete features but rather the way it is read. Once a reader has agreed to traverse a given stretch of discourse by granting to it the status of literariness, other choices come into play as she is guided in her consent to the codes in force.[1] The

---

[1] A corollary of this would be the idea that differing interpretations of the same text are in fact the result of differing generic assumptions, such as Douglas A. Bonneville's seeing Voltaire's tales essentially as novels in his *Voltaire and the Form of the Novel* (Banbury: *Studies on Voltaire and the Eighteenth Century*, 158 [1976]) or Philip Stewart's seeing them as parodies of novels, that is, I add, as themselves readers and reversers of the novel: "Holding up the Mirror to Fiction: Generic Parody in *Candide*," *French Studies*, 33 (1979), 411-19.

disposition to read the text as a certain genre is also arbitrary; it is determined by features as obvious as titles and sub-titles, which are reinforced by the particular discourse-relation established within the situation of cooperation and consent. The *conte philosophique* advertizes itself as needing interpretation, that is, as offering the possibility of meaning immanent to the text. While any utterance restricts the number of its decodings, the *conte* does so in definable ways by reiterating in all areas of the text the structures of its message. In this context its parts are so many *exempla* of its assertion or theme. By this kind of insistence, it is eminently *readable,* for it marks the pathways to its own best reading. Indeed critics and creative writers alike have noted the essential conservatism of the literary tale in general, which is another way of saying that the form is closed and that its tenor is socially reactionary. Iser observes that didacticism does not threaten order; it simply re-arranges it. Didactic literature is not there to produce an esthetic object that will rival the real world, but it offers instead a compensation for certain deficiencies in specific systems of thought. Jean François Lyotard remarks that, "Le récit est la forme par excellence de ce savoir [traditionnel] ..." and that "Les récits définissent ainsi ce qui a le droit de se dire et de se faire dans la culture." [2]

I think that we can object, however, that this kind of assessment works in application to the philosophical tale only when it supposes a willing, participating, and docile reader. The genre is restrictive and conservative if one is obedient to the codes the text announces and incorporates and if one follows the instruction for the kind of cooperation sought. The critic, one who watches herself reading, that is, who assesses the text as sign in all its aspects, escapes this enclosure. What is clear when the text is allowed to make itself clear is not absolute and is undone by the fragmented and fragmenting subject who observes the text's potential for absence of clarity, that is, for tracing other discourse. By an act of differentiation that replaces adherence, she mediates the act of reception.

In differing ways, the *contes* examined undermine the concepts and processes conveyed in sense and meaning. Postulating the ac-

---

[2] *La Condition postmoderne* (Paris: Editions de Minuit, 1979), pp. 38, 43.

tualizing subject's fragmentation means rejecting the sign as closed upon its sense or on any one of its meanings and perceiving instead its deconstruction, that is, its essentially open nature. Viewed like this, signifier and signified do not form a seamless whole; they are not two sides of Saussure's *feuille*. Some of the signifieds contradict the premises of others, and they and their processes attack the idea of text itself. *M* simultaneously represents proportions, reasons by means of them, and incriminates the conclusions thus obtained. It thereby pursues its century's critique of analogical thought, and it traces the demolition of the value of comparison as proof that a creator exists in proportion to his creation in the same way that *homo faber* exists in proportion to his. It escapes the tradition it reflects. *Z* stages multiple attempts at interpretation and presents a scene that claims by its forms to deliver the Answer. It is about interpretation and against it. The promised lesson is fragmented and its mimetic claims denied. It advances and mocks the idea of hero and by giving rise to tragico-mythic and comico-ironic response to him. It thus destroys itself as lesson and as representation. *C* represents a lot of lesson-learning, but the methods are given as questionable. The busiest teacher and the most earnest student are ridiculed by the meanings generated when they apply themselves to drawing lessons from events; and the act of lesson-drawing is finally explicitly abandoned.

The other ostensible function of the philosophical tale, recounting a story, is also frequently represented, and all the stories strive to make a point as they amuse or at least divert their audience. They resist the linear movement of the main action and weaken its pretension to change and to final resolution. The links between events and lesson are denied, and the ascension or progress of ideal narrative is thwarted. Neither philosophy nor literature has the plenitude it claims; yet *Candide* by its renown both contradicts its own deconstruction and preserves it at the same time. In the act of denying itself it generates a lesson in immanence and so constitutes itself anew each time it reiterates its own destruction. *L'Ingénu* makes a conventional claim to be history and then does indeed follow the traditional heroic paradigm of many histories written before it. The *faits-et-gestes* suscitate, however, a complex actualization that denies its denial and elevates it to a special and even more venerable model, that of death and the maiden, agent of transfiguration. Thus supposed truth finds only a pre-existing arrangement for its vehicle; it is deconstructed by its representation. Cast ineluctably in the heroic mold, even this deformation escapes into another and annihilates the idealist pretension of historical truth. Even truth-claims that arise from convention and that rely on shared pretense deviate from any kind of purity, and their pretend-ontology expires. By tracing a history that is paradigmatic, already modeled and thus removed from "true" history, and by tracing a mythical model as well, the text points to the vanity of mimetic privilege and insists on its own quality as sign.

Perception of its deconstructive processes works a certain revenge on the closed and authoritative text. Instead of allowing polyphony, the greater liberty of interpretation that would result by the greater effacement of creating intelligence — the tale recounts things, interpreting itself as it goes and telling us what to do about it. Our retaliation is to be conscious of our own status as text that loosely circumscribes many codes, past and present, and to see their traces in the encounter with the literary discourse's pretension to univocity, that is, to truth. Absolute adherence, our first step in the heuristic process, gives way under this hyper-conscious scrutiny and leaves instead difference between the intention projected and receivable. We are consequently able to see the work in a continuum of harmonious receptions and in a synchronous aggregate of conflicting structures.

Familiarity with the continuum and with the various codes gathered by text and by reader leads one to ask to what extent the *conte philosophique* belongs in its actualization to the category of literary fragment. The experiences recorded and the structures generated are isomorphs and thus susceptible of infinite repetition; yet they are arrested arbitrarily and are left resembling a page torn out of universal experience. Seen in this way, in its quality as fragment, the text both surpasses itself and in the *dépassement* becomes conscious of its insufficiency.

WORKS CITED

Ariès, Philippe. *L'Homme devant la mort*. Paris: Le Seuil, 1977.

Ascoli, George, ed. *Zadig*. Paris: Didier, 1962.

Bakhtin, Mikhail. *Esthétique et théorie du roman*. Trans. Daria Olivier. Paris: Gallimard, 1978.

——. *Rabelais and His World*. Cambridge, Mass.: MIT Press, 1968.

Barchilon, Jacques. "Uses of the Fairy Tale in the Eighteenth Century." *Studies in Voltaire and the Eighteenth Century*, 24 (1965), 111-38.

Barguillet, Françoise. *Le Roman au XVIIIe siècle*. Paris: Presses Universitaires de France, 1981.

Barthes, Roland. "Introduction à l'analyse structurale du récit." *Communications*, 8 (1966), 8-11.

——. *S/Z*. Paris: Le Seuil, 1970.

Benveniste, Emile. *Problèmes de linguistique générale*, I. Paris: Gallimard, 1966.

Bettleheim, Bruno. *The Uses of Enchantment: the Meaning and Importance of Fairytales*. New York: Random House, 1977.

Blanchot, Maurice. *Le Livre à venir*. Paris: Gallimard, 1971.

Bonneville, Douglas A. *Voltaire and the Form of the Novel*. *Studies on Voltaire and the Eighteenth Century*, 158 (1976).

Brumfitt, J. H. and M. I. Gerard Davis, eds. *L'Ingénu*. Oxford: Blackwell, 1970.

Cox, Thomas. "The Inchoative Aspect in French," *French Review*, 56 (1982), 228-40.

Chatman, Seymour. *Story and Discourse: Narrative Structure in Fiction and Film*. Ithaca: Cornell University Press, 1978.

Coulet, Henri. "La Distanciation dans le roman et le conte philosophiques." In *Roman et lumières an 18e siècle*. Paris: Editions Sociales, 1970, pp. 438-47.

Daly, Mary. *Gyn/Ecology: The Metaethics of Radical Feminism*. Boston: Beacon Press, 1978.

Derrida, Jacques. *De la grammatologie*. Paris: Editions de Minuit, 1967.

Duisit, Lionel. *Satire, Parodie, Calembour: Esquisse d'une théorie des modes dévalués*. Stanford: Anma Libri, 1978.

Eco, Umberto. *The Role of the Reader*. Bloomington: Indiana University Press, 1979.

L'Encyclopédie, ou Dictionnaire raisonné des sciences, des arts, et des métiers. Ed. Denis Diderot and Jean LeRond d'Alembert. 17 vols. Paris: Briasson, David, Le Breton, Durand, 1751-1766.

Fish, Stanley. *Is There a Text in This Class?* Cambridge: Harvard University Press, 1980.

Fontanier, Pierre. *Les Figures du discours.* Paris: Flammarion, 1968.

Fowler, Roger. *Linguistics and the Novel.* London: Methuen, 1977.

Gaillard, Pol. *Candide.* Paris: Hatier, 1972.

Genette, Gérard. *Figures III.* Paris: Le Seuil, 1972.

Ginsberg, Allen. *Reality Sandwiches.* San Francisco: City Lights, 1963.

Gossman, Lionel. "Voltaire's *Charles XII*: History into Art." *Studies on Voltaire and the Eighteenth Century,* 25 (1963), 691-720.

Greimas, A. J. *Du sens.* Paris: Le Seuil, 1970.

———. "Eléments pour une théorie de l'interprétation du récit mythique," *Communications,* 8 (1966), 28-59.

———. *Sémantique structurale.* Paris: Larousse, 1966.

Greimas, A. J. and J. Courtès. *Sémiotique: dictionnaire raisonné de la théorie du langage.* Paris: Hachette, 1979.

Groupe μ. "Ironique et iconique," *Poétique,* 36 (1978).

Henein, Eglal. "Hercule ou le pessimisme. Analyse de *L'Ingénu.*" *Romanic Review,* 72 (1981), 149-65.

Heuvel, Jacques van den. *Voltaire dans les contes.* Paris: A. Colin, 1967.

Highman, David E. "*L'Ingénu:* Flawed Masterpiece or Masterful Innovation?" *Studies on Voltaire and the Eighteenth Century,* 143 (1975), 71-83.

Iser, Wolfgang. *The Act of Reading.* Baltimore: Johns Hopkins University Press, 1978.

Jameson, Fredric. *The Prison-House of Language: A Critical Account of Structuralism and Russian Formalism.* Princeton: Princeton University Press, 1972.

Jones, S. Paul. *A List of French Prose Fiction from 1700 to 1750.* New York: H. W. Wilson, 1939.

Jones, William R., ed. *L'Ingénu.* Geneva: Droz, 1957.

Kayser, Wolfgang. *Das Groteske, seine Gestaltung in Malerei und Dichtung.* Oldenburg: G. Stalling, 1957.

Kermode, Frank. *The Sense of an Ending.* New York: Oxford University Press, 1967.

Kra, Pauline. "Note on the Derivation of Names in Voltaire's *Zadig,*" *Romance Notes,* 16 (1975), 342-44.

Kristeva, Julia. "Le Mot, le dialogue, et le roman." In *Séméiotikè.* Paris: Le Seuil, 1969.

Lotman, Jurij. "The Origins of Plot in the Light of Typology," *Poetics Today,* 1 (Autumn, 1979), 161-184.

Lyotard, Jean François. *La Condition postmoderne.* Paris: Editions de Minuit, 1979.

McGhee, Dorothy. *Voltairian Narrative Devices.* Menasha, Wisc.: Banta, 1933.

MacQueen, John. *Allegory.* London: Methuen, 1970.

Mailhos, Georges, ed. *Histoire de Charles XII.* Paris: Garnier-Flammarion, 1968.

Martin, Angus. *Anthologie du conte en France 1750-1759.* Paris: Union Générale d'Editions, 1981.

Mason, Haydn. "The Unity of Voltaire's *L'Ingénu*." In *The Age of Enlightenment: Studies Presented to Theodore Besterman*. Edinburgh and London: Oliver and Boyd, 1967, pp. 93-106.

———. *Voltaire*. New York: St. Martin's, 1975.

———. *Voltaire: A Biography*. Baltimore: The Johns Hopkins University Press, 1981.

———. "Voltaire's 'Contes': an 'Etat présent,'" *Modern Language Review*, 65 (1970), 19-35.

May, Georges. "Diderot et l'allégorie." *Studies on Voltaire and the Eighteenth Century*, 89 (1972), 1049-1076.

Meletinskii, E. "L'Etude structurale et typologique du conte." Trans. Claude Kahn. In V. Propp, *Morphologie*, pp. 201-254.

Monter, E. William. *European Witchcraft*. New York: Wiley, 1969.

Morier, Henri. *Dictionnaire de poétique et de rhétorique*. Paris: Presses Universitaires de France, 1975.

Morot-Sir, Edouard. "La Dynamique du théâtre et Molière," *Romance Notes*, 15, Supp. No. 1 (1973), 15-49.

———. "Texte, référence, et déictique," *Text*, 1 (1982), 113-42.

Moureaux, J.-M. "Voltaire, l'écrivain." In *Résumé des communications*. Paris: CNRS, 1978.

Muecke, D. C. *Irony*. London: Methuen, 1970.

Mylne, Vivienne. "Literary Techniques and Methods in Voltaire's *contes philosophiques*." *Studies on Voltaire and the Eighteenth Century*, 57 (1967), 1055-1080.

Nivat, J. "*L'Ingénu* de Voltaire, les Jésuites et l'affaire La Chalotais." *Revue des Sciences Humaines*, 66 (1952), 97-108.

Pandolfo, Maria. *Zadig: Análisè da narrativa*. Rio de Janeiro: Vozes, 1978.

Pascal, Blaise. *Œuvres complètes*. Ed. Louis Lafuma. Paris: Delmas, 1947.

Peirce, C. S. and Victoria, Lady Welby. *Semiotic and Significs: The Correspondence between Charles S. Peirce and Victoria, Lady Welby*. Bloomington: Indiana University Press, 1977.

Pratt, Mary Louise. *Toward a Speech-Act Theory of Literary Discourse*. Bloomington: Indiana University Press, 1977.

Prince, Gerald. *A Grammar of Stories*. The Hague: Mouton, 1976.

Propp, Vladimir. *Morphologie du conte*. Trans. Marguerite Derrida and Tzvetan Todorov. Paris: Le Seuil, 1965.

Pruner, Francis. *Recherches sur la création romanesque dans "L'Ingénu" de Voltaire*. Paris: Archives des Lettres Modernes, 1960.

Richter, David H. *Fable's End: Completeness and Closure in Rhetorical Fiction*. Chicago: University of Chicago Press, 1974.

Ridgway, R. S. *Voltaire and Sensibility*. Montréal: McGill-Queens University Press, 1973.

Sareil, Jean. "L'Exagération comique dans les contes de Voltaire." *French Literature Studies*, 2 (1975), 50-63.

———. "Le Vocabulaire de la relativité dans *Micromégas* de Voltaire." *Romanic Review*, 64 (1973), 273-85.

Segre, Cesare. *Structures and Time*. Trans. John Meddeman. Chicago: University of Chicago Press, 1979.

Sherman, Carol. *Diderot and the Art of Dialogue*. Geneva: Droz, 1976.

———. "Diderot's Speech-Acts: Essay, Letter, and Dialogue," *French Literature Series*, 9 (1982), 18-29.

Sherman, Carol, Katherine Stephenson, and Keith Davis. "Folkloric Intertexts in Voltaire's *L'Ingénu.*" *Romance Notes,* 2 (1980), 193-99.

———. "Response Criticism: 'Do Readers Make Meaning?" *Romance Notes,* 18 (1977), 288-92.

Starobinski, Jean. "La doppietta di Voltaire," *Strumenti Critici,* 1 (1966-7), 13-32.

———. "Sur le style philosophique de *Candide,*" *Comparative Literature,* Summer 1976, 193-200.

Sternberg, Meir. *Expositional Modes and Temporal Ordering in Fiction.* Baltimore: The Johns Hopkins University Press, 1978.

Stewart, Philip. "Holding Up the Mirror to Fiction: Generic Parody in *Candide.*" *French Studies,* 33 (1979), 411-19.

Stierle, Karlheinz. "L'Histoire comme Exemple, l'Exemple comme Histoire." *Poétique,* 10 (1972), 176-98.

Suleiman, Susan. "Le Récit exemplaire." *Poétique,* 32 (1977), 468-89.

Suleiman, Susan R. and Inge Crosman, eds. *The Reader in the Text.* Princeton: Princeton University Press, 1980.

Tompkins, Jane, ed. *Reader-Response Criticism: From Formalism to Post-Structuralism.* Baltimore: The Johns Hopkins University Press, 1980.

Valéry, Paul. "Tel Quel." In *Œuvres.* Vol. II. Paris: NRF, 1957.

Verrier, Jean. "Notes de lecture." *Le Français aujourd'hui,* 43 (Sept. 1978), 97-99.

Vovelle, Michel. *Mourir autrefois: attitudes collectives devant la mort aux XVIIᵉ et XVIIIᵉ siècles.* Paris: Gallimard, 1974.

Wade, Ira. *Voltaire's "Micromégas": A Study in the Fusion of Science, Myth and Art.* Princeton: Princeton University Press, 1950.

White, Hayden. *Metahistory: The Historical Imagination in Nineteenth-Century Europe.* Baltimore: The Johns Hopkins University Press, 1973.

Wilson, W. Daniel. "Readers in Texts," *PMLA,* 96 (1981), 848-63.

NORTH CAROLINA STUDIES IN THE ROMANCE LANGUAGES AND LITERATURES

I.S.B.N. Prefix 0-8078-

Recent Titles

DELIE. CONCORDANCE, by Jerry Nash. 1976. 2 Volumes. (No. 174).

FIGURES OF REPETITION IN THE OLD PROVENÇAL LYRIC: A STUDY IN THE STYLE OF THE TROUBADOURS, by Nathaniel B. Smith. 1976. (No. 176). -9176-2.

A CRITICAL EDITION OF "LE REGIME TRESUTILE ET TRESPROUFITABLE POUR CONSERVER ET GARDER LA SANTE DU CORPS HUMAIN", by Patricia Willett Cummins. 1977. (No. 177).

THE DRAMA OF SELF IN GUILLAUME APOLLINAIRE'S "ALCOOLS", by Richard Howard Stamelman. 1976. (No. 178). -9178-9.

A CRITICAL EDITION OF "LA PASSION NOSTRE SEIGNEUR" FROM MANUSCRIPT 1131 FROM THE BIBLIOTHEQUE SAINTE-GENEVIEVE, PARIS, by Edward J. Gallagher. 1976. (No. 179). -9179-7.

A QUANTITATIVE AND COMPARATIVE STUDY OF THE VOCALISM OF THE LATIN INSCRIPTIONS OF NORTH AFRICA, BRITAIN, DALMATIA, AND THE BALKANS, by Stephen William Omeltchenko. 1977. (No. 180). -9180-0.

OCTAVIEN DE SAINT-GELAIS "LE SEJOUR D'HONNEUR", edited by Joseph A. James. 1977. (No. 181). -9181-9.

A STUDY OF NOMINAL INFLECTION IN LATIN INSCRIPTIONS, by Paul A. Gaeng. 1977. (No. 182). -9182-7.

THE LIFE AND WORKS OF LUIS CARLOS LÓPEZ, by Martha S. Bazik. 1977. (No. 183). -9183-5.

"THE CORT D'AMOR". A THIRTEENTH-CENTURY ALLEGORICAL ART OF LOVE, by Lowanne E. Jones. 1977. (No. 185). -9185-1.

PHYTONYMIC DERIVATIONAL SYSTEMS IN THE ROMANCE LANGUAGES: STUDIES IN THEIR ORIGIN AND DEVELOPMENT, by Walter E. Geiger. 1978. (No. 187). -9187-8.

LANGUAGE IN GIOVANNI VERGA'S EARLY NOVELS, by Nicholas Patruno. 1977. (No. 188). -9188-6.

BLAS DE OTERO EN SU POESÍA, by Moraima de Semprún Donahue. 1977. (No. 189). -9189-4.

LA ANATOMÍA DE "EL DIABLO COJUELO": DESLINDES DEL GÉNERO ANATOMÍSTICO, por C. George Peale. 1977. (No. 191). -9191-6.

RICHARD SANS PEUR, EDITED FROM "LE ROMANT DE RICHART" AND FROM GILLES CORROZET'S "RICHART SANS PAOUR", by Denis Joseph Conlon. 1977. (No. 192). -9192-4.

MARCEL PROUST'S GRASSET PROOFS. *Commentary and Variants,* by Douglas Alden. 1978. (No. 193). -9193-2.

MONTAIGNE AND FEMINISM, by Cecile Insdorf. 1977. (No. 194). -9194-0.

SANTIAGO F. PUGLIA, AN EARLY PHILADELPHIA PROPAGANDIST FOR SPANISH AMERICAN INDEPENDENCE, by Merle S. Simmons. 1977. (No. 195). -9195-9.

BAROQUE FICTION-MAKING. A STUDY OF GOMBERVILLE'S "POLEXANDRE", by Edward Baron Turk. 1978. (No. 196). -9196-7.

THE TRAGIC FALL: DON ÁLVARO DE LUNA AND OTHER FAVORITES IN SPANISH GOLDEN AGE DRAMA, by Raymond R. MacCurdy. 1978. (No. 197). -9197-5.

A BAHIAN HERITAGE. An Ethnolinguistic Study of African Influences on Bahian Portuguese, by William W. Megenney. 1978. (No. 198). -9198-3.

"LA QUERELLE DE LA ROSE": Letters and Documents, by Joseph L. Baird and John R. Kane. 1978. (No. 199). -9199-1.

TWO AGAINST TIME. *A Study of the Very Present Worlds of Paul Claudel and Charles Péguy,* by Joy Nachod Humes. 1978. (No. 200). -9200-9.

When ordering please cite the *ISBN Prefix* plus the last four digits for each title.

Send orders to: University of North Carolina Press
                 Chapel Hill
                 North Carolina 27514
                 U. S. A.

NORTH CAROLINA STUDIES IN THE
ROMANCE LANGUAGES AND LITERATURES

I.S.B.N. Prefix 0-88438

Recent Titles

TECHNIQUES OF IRONY IN ANATOLE FRANCE. Essay on *Les Sept Femmes de la Barbe-Bleue,* by Diane Wolfe Levy. 1978. (No. 201). *-9201-7.*

THE PERIPHRASTIC FUTURES FORMED BY THE ROMANCE REFLEXES OF "VADO (AD)" PLUS INFINITIVE, by James Joseph Champion. 1978. (No. 202). *-9202-5.*

THE EVOLUTION OF THE LATIN /b/-/ɥ/ MERGER: A Quantitative and Comparative Analysis of the *B-V* Alternation in Latin Inscriptions, by Joseph Louis Barbarino. 1978. (No. 203). *-9203-3.*

METAPHORIC NARRATION: THE STRUCTURE AND FUNCTION OF METAPHORS IN "A LA RECHERCHE DU TEMPS PERDU", by Inge Karalus Crosman. 1978. (No. 204). *-9204-1.*

LE VAIN SIECLE GUERPIR. A Literary Approach to Sainthood through Old French Hagiography of the Twelfth Century, by Phyllis Johnson and Brigitte Cazelles. 1979. (No. 205). *-9205-X.*

THE POETRY OF CHANGE: A STUDY OF THE SURREALIST WORKS OF BENJAMIN PÉRET, by Julia Field Costich. 1979. (No. 206). *-9206-8.*

NARRATIVE PERSPECTIVE IN THE POST-CIVIL WAR NOVELS OF FRANCISCO AYALA "MUERTES DE PERRO" AND "EL FONDO DEL VASO", by Maryellen Bieder. 1979. (No. 207). *-9207-6.*

RABELAIS: HOMO LOGOS, by Alice Fiola Berry. 1979. (No. 208). *-9208-4.*

"DUEÑAS" AND "DONCELLAS": A STUDY OF THE "DOÑA RODRÍGUEZ" EPISODE IN "DON QUIJOTE", by Conchita Herdman Marianella. 1979. (No. 209). *-9209-2.*

PIERRE BOAISTUAU'S "HISTOIRES TRAGIQUES": A STUDY OF NARRATIVE FORM AND TRAGIC VISION, by Richard A. Carr. 1979. (No. 210). *-9210-6.*

REALITY AND EXPRESSION IN THE POETRY OF CARLOS PELLICER, by George Melnykovich. 1979. (No. 211). *-9211-4.*

MEDIEVAL MAN, HIS UNDERSTANDING OF HIMSELF, HIS SOCIETY, AND THE WORLD, by Urban T. Holmes, Jr. 1980. (No. 212). *-9212-2.*

MÉMOIRES SUR LA LIBRAIRIE ET SUR LA LIBERTÉ DE LA PRESSE, introduction and notes by Graham E. Rodmell. 1979. (No. 213). *-9213-0.*

THE FICTIONS OF THE SELF. THE EARLY WORKS OF MAURICE BARRES, by Gordon Shenton. 1979. (No. 214). *-9214-9.*

CECCO ANGIOLIERI. A STUDY, by Gifford P. Orwen. 1979. (No. 215). *-9215-7.*

THE INSTRUCTIONS OF SAINT LOUIS: A CRITICAL TEXT, by David O'Connell. 1979. (No. 216). *-9216-5.*

ARTFUL ELOQUENCE, JEAN LEMAIRE DE BELGES AND THE RHETORICAL TRADITION, by Michael F. O. Jenkins. 1980. (No. 217). *-9217-3.*

A CONCORDANCE TO MARIVAUX'S COMEDIES IN PROSE, edited by Donald C. Spinelli. 1979. (No. 218). 4 volumes, *-9218-1* (set); *-9219-X* (v. 1); *-9220-3* (v. 2); *-9221-1* (v. 3); *-9222-X* (v. 4.)

ABYSMAL GAMES IN THE NOVELS OF SAMUEL BECKETT, by Angela B. Moorjani. 1982. (No. 219). *-9223-8.*

GERMAIN NOUVEAU DIT HUMILIS: ÉTUDE BIOGRAPHIQUE, par Alexandre L. Amprimoz. 1983. (No. 220). *-9224-6.*

THE "VIE DE SAINT ALEXIS" IN THE TWELFTH AND THIRTEENTH CENTURIES: AN EDITION AND COMMENTARY, by Alison Goddard Elliot. 1983. (No. 221). *-9225-4.*

When ordering please cite the *ISBN Prefix* plus the last four digits for each title.

Send orders to: University of North Carolina Press
Chapel Hill
North Carolina 27514
U. S. A.